Legal Origins and the Efficiency Dilemma

Economists advise that the law should seek efficiency. More recently, it has been suggested that common law systems are more conducive of economic growth than code-based civil law systems. This book argues that there is no theory to support such statements and provides evidence that rejects a 'one-size-fits-all' approach. Both common law and civil law systems are reviewed to debunk the relationship between the efficiency of the common law hypothesis and the alleged inferiority of codified law systems.

Legal Origins and the Efficiency Dilemma has six aims: explaining the efficiency hypothesis of the common law since Posner's 1973 book; summarizing the legal origins theory in the context of economic growth; debunking their relationship; discussing the meaning of 'common law' and the problems with the efficiency hypothesis by comparing laws across English speaking jurisdictions; illustrating the shortcomings of the legal origins theory with a comparative law and economics analysis; and concluding there is no theory and evidence to support the economic superiority of common law systems. Based on previous pieces by the authors, this book expands their work by including new areas of analysis (such as trusts), detailing previous analysis (such as French law versus common law in the areas of contract, property and torts), and updating for recent developments in the academic discourse.

This volume is of interest to academics and students who study microeconomics, comparative law and foundations of law, as well as legal policy analysts.

Nuno Garoupa is Professor of Law at Texas A&M University, School of Law, and holds the Chair in Research Innovation at Católica Global School of Law, Lisbon, Portugal.

Carlos Gómez Ligüerre is Professor of Private Law at the Pompeu Fabra University (Universitat Pompeu Fabra), Barcelona, Spain.

Lela Mélon is Adjunct Professor of Law at the Pompeu Fabra University (Universitat Pompeu Fabra), Barcelona, Spain.

The economics of legal relationships

Sponsored by Michigan State University College of Law

Series Editors:

Nicholas Mercuro
Michigan State University College of Law

Michael D. Kaplowitz
Michigan State University

A full list of titles in this series is available from www.routledge.com/economics/series/ELR.

12 The Legal-Economic Nexus
Warren J. Samuels

13 Economics, Law and Individual Rights
Edited by Hugo M. Mialon and Paul H. Rubin

14 Alternative Institutional Structures
Evolution and impact
Edited by Sandra S. Batie and Nicholas Mercuro

15 Patent Policy
Effects in a national and international framework
Pia Weiss

16 The Applied Law and Economics of Public Procurement
Edited by Gustavo Piga and Steen Treumer

17 Economics and Regulation in China
Edited by Michael Faure and Guangdong Xu

18 Law, Bubbles and Financial Regulation
Erik F. Gerding

19 Empirical Legal Analysis
Assessing the performance of legal institutions
Edited by Yun-chien Chang

20 Predatory Pricing in Antitrust Law and Economics
Nicola Giocoli

21 The Role of Law in Sustaining Financial Markets
Edited by Niels Philipsen and Guangdong Xu

22 Law and Economics
Philosophical issues and fundamental questions
Edited by Aristides N. Hatzis and Nicholas Mercuro

23 Public Procurement Policy
Edited by Gustavo Piga and Tünde Tatrai

24 Legal Origins and the Efficiency Dilemma
Nuno Garoupa, Carlos Gómez Ligüerre and Lela Mélon

Legal Origins and the Efficiency Dilemma

Nuno Garoupa, Carlos Gómez Ligüerre
and Lela Mélon

Routledge
Taylor & Francis Group

LONDON AND NEW YORK

First published 2017 by Routledge

2 Park Square, Milton Park, Abingdon, Oxfordshire OX14 4RN

52 Vanderbilt Avenue, New York, NY 10017

Routledge is an imprint of the Taylor & Francis Group, an informa business

First issued in paperback 2019

British Library Cataloguing in Publication Data
A catalogue record for this book is available from the British Library

Library of Congress Cataloging in Publication Data
Names: Garoupa, Nuno, author. | Gómez Ligüerre, Carlos, author. | Mélon,
Lela, author.
Title: Legal origins and the efficiency dilemma / Nuno Garoupa, Carlos
Gómez Ligüerre and Lela Mélon.
Description: New York, NY : Routledge, 2017. | Includes index.
Identifiers: LCCN 2016031097| ISBN 9781138232877 (hardback) | ISBN
9781315311210 (ebook)
Subjects: LCSH: Law--Economic aspects. | Law and economic
development.
Classification: LCC K487.E3 G37 2017 | DDC 340/.1--dc23
LC record available at https://lccn.loc.gov/2016031097

ISBN: 978-1-138-23287-7 (hbk)
ISBN: 978-0-367-25101-7 (pbk)

Typeset in Times New Roman
by Saxon Graphics Ltd, Derby

To my daughters, Beatriz and Anna
NG

To my family
CG

To my family, my strength: Kevyn, Nermin, Slavi, Alen, Chantal, Michel and Audrey
LM

Contents

List of illustrations   *xi*
Acknowledgments   *xiii*

PART I
**Legal origins in a nutshell – inherent dangers of its blind
acceptance**   **1**

1 **Introduction**   **3**

2 **The danger of a globally accepted theory containing major
   flaws**   **11**

3 **The efficiency of the common law hypothesis**   **14**

4 **Legal origins: the comparative perspective**   **22**

5 **The evolution of the common law and efficiency: what is the
   meaning of common law?**   **30**
   Why efficient common law 34
   Tort law 39
   Defamation law 41
   Professional responsibility 42
   Cost rules in civil litigation 42
   Civil juries 43
   Brief examples to guide to more detailed overviews 45

viii   Contents

PART II
Piercing the veil – application of legal origins to specific legal institutes   57

6   **Contrasting common and civil law: private law**   59
   Bona fide purchase 61
   Titling of property 63
   Principle of non-cumul *in torts and contracts 64*
   The Good Samaritan Rule 67

7   **Contrasting common and civil law: legal governance and the specialization of courts**   77
   The model 77
   Administrative courts 80
   Commercial courts 82
   Constitutional courts 83

8   **The puzzle of mixed law jurisdictions**   90
   Contrasting common and civil law: the role of trusts and mixed legal jurisdictions 99

PART III
Modern dilemmas in US and EU law as representatives of the two distinct legal families   113

9   **Contrasting civil and common law: the area of intellectual property**   115
   Why intellectual property law? 115
   On intellectual property 116
   How are the US and the EU approaching the field? 117
   Efficiency of trademark protection in common and civil law systems 117
   Geographic indications 120
   Patent protection in the US and EU 124
   The efficiency of the 'fair use' doctrine under the conditions of two distinct copyright law systems 132

10   **Contrasting common and civil law: corporate law in the US and EU**   144
   Inherent flaws of the legal origins in researching the field of corporate law: the taxonomy of countries 144

*Inherent flaws of the legal origins in researching the field of
  corporate law: coding errors 147*
*The inherent dangers of the persisting influence of legal origins
  theory on the international level 150*
*The US and EU: legal origins and individual institutes in US and
  EU corporate laws 151*

Bibliography   170
Index   192

Illustrations

Figures

1.1 Comparison between the yearly GDP growth rates of USA and
France in the period 1998–2013   4
4.1 World map of legal origins   23

Tables

1.1 Examples of legal systems   5
4.1 Government regulation and legal origin   24
7.1 Costs and benefits of specialized courts   78
8.1 Mixed legal systems   92

Acknowledgments

The authors are grateful to one anonymous referee, Jesús Alfaro, Benito Arruñada, Amitai Aviram, Daniel Berkowitz, Justin Borg Barthet, Donald J. Boudreaux, Henry Butler, Francisco Cabrillo, Peter Cane, Tony Duggan, Anna Ginès Fabrellas, Michael Faure, Fernando Gómez Pomar, Jean-Louis Halperin, Pierre Larouche, Bob Lawless, Álvaro Lobato, Ejan Mackaay, Bertrand du Marais, Nicholas Mercuro, Andrew Morriss, Anthony Ogus, Ken Oliphant, Eric Posner, Mark Ramseyer, Mathias Reimann, Leonor Rossi, Paul Rubin, Mathias Siems, Greg Taylor, Andrew Torrance, Catherine Valcke, Stephen Waddams, the Searle-Kauffman (2009–2010) fellows at the Orange County meeting, and the participants at the Spanish Association of Law and Economics meeting (Madrid, 2010) for helpful comments and suggestions. We have also benefited from comments by seminar participants at Harvard law school (program for Spanish legal scholars), University of Illinois law school, University of Toulouse economic department, Fundación Rafael del Pino (Madrid), and ENS (Paris). Caroline Belloff, Dana Noya-Damasco, Roya H. Samarghandi and Tatiana Triveri have provided superb research assistance. The usual disclaimers apply.

Carlos Gómez Ligüerre acknowledges the financial support granted by the Spanish Department of Economy (DER2013-47560-R).

Chapters 2 to 4, 6 and 7 are inspired by Nuno Garoupa and Carlos Gómez Ligüerre, 2011, *The Syndrome of the Efficiency of the Common Law*, Boston University International Law Journal, vol. 29 (2), pp. 288–335. Chapter 5 is based on Nuno Garoupa and Carlos Gómez Ligüerre, 2012, *The Evolution of the Common Law and Efficiency*, Georgia Journal of International and Comparative Law, vol. 40 (2), pp. 307–340. Chapter 8 follows closely Nuno Garoupa and Carlos Gómez Ligüerre, 2012, *The Efficiency of the Common Law: The Puzzle of Mixed Legal Families*, Wisconsin International Law Journal, vol. 29 (4), pp. 671–693.

Part I

Legal origins in a nutshell – inherent dangers of its blind acceptance

1   Introduction

Discussion on the efficiency of legal rules implies a connection of two distinct scientific fields: law and economics. In economic analysis of law, the term 'efficient' legal rule does not carry a unified meaning; its meaning depends on the context in which discussion takes place. Still, in this book, we will use 'efficiency' in the most canonical understanding within the economic analysis of law, that is, in the sense of the maximization of the social willingness to pay.[1] Even with a clear definition, there is an immediate question, how can we assess which rule that governs the exact same issue in different legal systems is more efficient? Looking at the rules on the basis of which the so-called legal origins theory has been established[2] (more to be detailed later, but at the moment it suffices to say that the legal origins theory suggests that common law is more conducive of economic growth than civil law[3]), can we claim that US rules on shareholder protection (US being a union of states ruled by common law) are more efficient than French rules on shareholder protection? Economists think an efficient outcome of those rules would in its broadest terms predict prosperous and growing financial markets, which in turn should induce a constantly higher economic growth of a country with common law system.

When comparing the economic growth of France[4] and USA in the last eighteen years, a different picture occurs, as shown also by other academics.[5]

In the last decades, France has not been always lagging behind the US, even if we neglect at this point the fact that the US and France are not the only common and civil law countries in the world (obviously, other countries perform better or worse). Economists have also shown that the level of shareholder protection in different countries is not invariant but it changes over time, with France having highest shareholder protection and the US the lowest in their last examined periods.[7] While this simple empirical observation does not negate the claim that the common law rules are more efficient, it does counter the claim that higher levels of shareholder protection automatically bring about stronger financial markets and higher economic growth. The efficient rule here, according to the legal origins theory, would be the one offering the most protection, and at the same time the 'model' common law country, the US, seems to be changing its rules and lowering their levels of shareholder protection, while the civil law countries are systematically making such protection higher.

Economic growth: the rate of change of real GDP

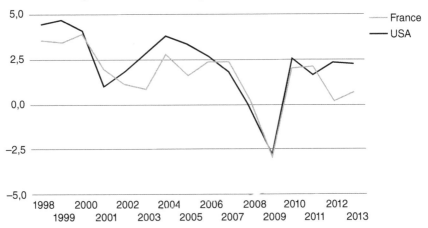

Figure 1.1   Comparison between the yearly GDP growth rates of USA and France in the period 1998–2013[6]

Source: TheGlobalEconomy.com, World Bank.

With only this extremely simplified example one might guess that by broadening the scope of the legal origins literature to other fields, such as the procedural rules, the question of judicial independence, the regulation of entry, labour laws, bankruptcy law etc., the problems with supporting the theory become even more obvious.[8]

We already stated that France and the US are not the only civil and common law countries respectively. A larger list of countries, as we can see in Table 1.1, introduces more variation and more localized explanations. Each country has a particular legal origin and there are many explanations for why the law in Spain or the law in South Korea today looks the way it looks. Moreover, we can find many explanations for how the law in Malaysia or the law in Norway affects current economic performance. The legal origins theory looks for a more general framework that provides a reasoning independent of local contexts.

The possible efficiency of the common law has generated discussion among legal economists quite early in the law and economics literature. The controversial thesis was introduced by Judge Posner in the first edition of his seminal book in 1973.[9] His main argument was that there is an implicit economic logic to the common law. In his view, the doctrines in common law provide a coherent and consistent system of incentives, which induce efficient behaviour, not merely in explicit markets but in all social contexts (the so-called implicit markets). For example, common law reduces transaction costs to favour market transactions when that is appropriate. Quite naturally, Judge Posner recognized that not all doctrines in common law are economically justifiable or even easy to understand from an economic perspective. Economics does not offer a complete and exhaustive theory of the common law, but his view is that it offers a balanced and significant explanation.

Table 1.1 Examples of legal systems[10]

Common Law	French Civil Law	German Civil Law	Scandinavian Civil Law
England and Wales	France	Germany	Sweden
USA	Italy	Austria	Norway
Canada	Spain	Switzerland	Denmark
Australia	Portugal	Japan	Iceland
New Zealand	Belgium	South Korea	Finland
India	Netherlands	Taiwan	
Nigeria	Romania	Slovenia	
Malaysia	Brazil		
Singapore	Argentina		
Ireland	Mexico		
Burma	Chile		
Jamaica	Angola		
Barbados	Egypt		
Zimbabwe	Lebanon		
Pakistan	Turkey		

More recently, legal economists have emphasized the superiority of the common law system over French civil law (while absolving German and Scandinavian civil law from a similar fate).[11] It is this perspective that has become popular in legal scholarship as well as in legal policy making (in particular under the auspices of some programmes associated with the World Bank)[12] under the label of the legal origins theory.

We argue that the legal origins literature cannot be easily based on the efficiency hypothesis of the common law, which has its own problems. But even if the efficiency hypothesis is true, it is insufficient to provide a theoretical framework to support the alleged superiority of the common law over French civil law. By debunking the relationship between the efficiency hypothesis and the legal origins literature, we are left with no consistent theory to support the latter. At that stage, it is clear that the legal origins literature is based on a particular, biased selection of 'cherry-picked' legal doctrines.

Our research shows that a diverse selection of 'cherry-picked' legal doctrines produces a completely different assessment. The selection of particular legal doctrines is important when we analyse the 'policy version' of the legal origins literature (the *Doing Business* reports). There are no theoretical reasons to select particular bundles of legal doctrines in order to measure the efficiency of a particular legal system since, in order to do that, we first need a theory. Our thesis states that no such theory exists; therefore, we are left with no explanation as for why one particular set of doctrines is better than another. Even excluding tort law, there are enough variations in property and contract law, substantively and procedurally, to foster a serious debate.[13]

We do not propose that our 'cherry-picked' legal doctrines are better than those favoured by the legal origins literature. Our point is simple: a different set of legal doctrines produces a different conclusion. Since there are no good theoretical or empirical grounds to support one set or another, this methodology does not advance the discussion. It is also the wrong methodology with which to select policy variables, as legal reforms based on it are likely to ignore relevant dimensions such as legal education, judicial human capital or legal culture.

Our project does not suggest that French law is more conducive to efficiency than common law. Rather, our criticism is essentially methodological. The relative efficiency merits of the common law and of French civil law cannot deter a deeper analysis of legal institutions worldwide. Mere generalities without a careful examination of rules and legal institutions invalidate the inefficiency hypothesis of French law. A sophisticated theory has to be developed. We are sceptical that such a theory can ever be sustained. Our argument is that the current prevalent methodology embraced by many legal economists is incapable of producing such a theory.

The efficiency of the common law hypothesis is discussed extensively in chapter 3, following the debate in chapter 2 on the importance of the need for reassessment of the legal origins theory, while the legal origins theory is explained and assessed in chapter 4. We argue that there are significant unanswered questions with both of these approaches. At the same time, we debunk the relationship between the efficiency of the common law hypothesis, the superiority of judge-made law over statutory law and the comparative analysis suggested by the legal origins literature.

In this book, we also consider the evolution of the common law in chapter 5. By making use of the mathematical models developed by legal economists to explain the efficiency hypothesis of the common law, we analysed two different problems. First, there is not a single efficient rule or doctrine, but a multiplicity of possible equilibria depending on selective litigation. Second, for each specific set of selective litigation, there is no guarantee that there will be convergence to efficiency, depending on judicial attributes and the preponderance of precedent.

The identification of the efficiency of the common law is much more intricate and multifaceted than anticipated by the literature. A mere comparison of how a specific predicament is addressed in each jurisdiction, as inspired by the legal origins literature, is not only insufficient, but likely to produce gross mistakes. The observation that each jurisdiction provides a different legal outcome says very little about efficiency. First, there are multiple efficient legal solutions. Second, the variables that determine efficient outcomes vary significantly across the common law jurisdictions (England and Wales, US, Canada, Australia, New Zealand and Ireland). A proper analysis requires a clear understanding of local determinants, including judicial preferences, before we can jump to the conclusion that the common law is undoubtedly efficient (or, more precisely, which common law is undoubtedly efficient).

In chapter 6. we look at examples in substantive law and procedure in the core areas of property, contracts and torts. These are areas documented as being crucial for economic growth (albeit the controversy over torts). For each core area considered, we 'cherry-pick' a doctrine that seems more efficient, more market-oriented or more conducive to economic growth under French law rather than under common law.

Our book is not a treaty in private comparative law. We do not discuss the complex details of each legal doctrine. Our examples have been previously noted in the English-speaking law and economics literature, in some cases extensively.[14] Our goal is to present and discuss these examples in light of the legal origins literature. Our level of detailing is the same level that legal scholars have used to praise the Anglo-American option for contractual damages and to criticize the French preference for specific performance in the context of contractual breach.[15]

We consider the organization and governance of the legal system in chapter 7. Their correlation with economic growth is debatable, but recognized in the literature. They have been part of the argument against the efficiency of French civil law.[16] We argue that under an economic model of specialization and capture, the French archetype is more appropriate under certain conditions. In particular, we discuss the existence of separate administrative law jurisdictions in French law. Legal economists have criticized this institutional arrangement as not providing an effective control over discretion by executive power and therefore facilitating state expropriation. Given the French preference for big government and significant state intervention in the economy, our argument is that the current institutional arrangements in France concerning administrative law could be more appropriate for the French case. Similarly, the current institutional arrangements in common law jurisdictions could be more appropriate for the Anglo-American countries. In fact, in this book, we are agnostic concerning the relationship between significant state intervention in the economy and economic growth. Our point is that if two legal systems have different institutional arrangements in administrative law, it does not necessarily imply that one must be more conducive of economic growth than the other. Depending on local determinants, either institutional arrangement may be appropriate.

We address mixed jurisdictions in chapter 8. Under the efficiency of the common law hypothesis and the more recent legal origins theory, we should expect mixed jurisdictions to disappear. If common law is universally conducive to economic growth, the existence of jurisdictions that keep a hybrid legal system where private law (that is, the area of the law that more directly deals with business and investment) is of civil law tradition is puzzling.

The combination of civil and common law has two historical reasons: intercolonial transfer (most examples) and merger of sovereignties (few cases). There are a couple of variations, but generally private law tends to be codified and entrenched while public law follows common law. Legal institutions are usually transplanted from the common law colonial power. Such a broad description makes the existence of mixed jurisdictions more puzzling. They keep an allegedly inefficient legal system for private law (precisely the area of law supposedly more relevant for economic growth) embedded in institutional arrangements and public law transplanted from a common law jurisdiction.

In chapter 9 we turn our focus on the area of intellectual property law, an important field of law that has been in need for change in the world of fast technological change. We show through examples in trademark regulation, regulation of geographical indications, regulation of patents and the Fair Use doctrine that even in these fields, crucial in modern international trade, the common law institutes do not necessarily have the upper hand. In fact, we assess the extent to which there is a pattern of convergence across intellectual property law and argue that current differences hardly support the view that common law is globally more efficient.

Chapter 10 introduces corporate law in detail. The initial appeal of the legal origins theory was precisely its development within the economics of corporate law. We review the flaws of the legal origins theory of corporate law and document several areas for which the common law solutions are challenged in their efficiency hypothesis.

Our book is about economics and comparative law. We do not reject efficiency as paramount principle to assess different legal institutions across the world. In fact, we use an efficiency approach quite extensively in the book although recognizing that efficiency does not exclude other possible normative principles to evaluate law. We also do not pursue the argument that common law and civil law are irrelevant and fundamentally obsolete concepts (although they have different relevance today than 200 years ago). Our main message is fundamentally different.

This book aims to accomplish two goals. On one hand, we provide a methodological criticism of the current literature on legal origins. We argue that a theoretical baseline for the efficiency of the common law vis-à-vis French law must necessarily be micro-oriented, and we provide important examples (for market efficiency and for economic growth) where French law seems to be plausibly better or more adequate. It must be reemphasized that the purpose of our thesis is not to propose the opposite of the efficiency of the common law literature – that is, French law as the benchmark for market efficiency. Our thesis is that without a detailed analysis of common law and French law institutions, it is not possible to theorize the legal origins literature. However, when such detailed analysis is performed, it is not obvious which legal system has more pro-market or pro-economic growth legal institutions. The persistence of the alleged superiority of the common law requires a proper theorization that must be complex and intrinsically difficult.

Our second goal is to explain why the syndrome of the efficiency of the common law is based on the implicit assumption that one size fits all. In our view, different designs do not indicate that one is correct and the other is incorrect. It might simply indicate that the balance of costs and benefits is structurally different. This conclusion is very important from the viewpoint of legal reform and legal transplanting, particular in the context of the *Doing Business* project. The identification of legal and institutional impediments to economic growth cannot be exclusively based on a benchmark exercise where common law legal institutions serve as a role model. We emphasize once more that such exercise is relevant and provides useful information that should be an important input in the design of legal reforms. However, legal institutions are more complex, and mere analogies with legal institutions elsewhere cannot be the rigorous basis for reform. In fact, policies based on such methodology can be counter-productive and may replace current institutions with more problematic and less pro-economic growth transplanted institutions. The design of a legal system must conform to local conditions and determinants that have first to be identified. Only such careful analyses can accurately assess the advantages and disadvantages of replacing certain institutional arrangements with others.

It is clear to us that successful legal reforms need to address local problems under local restrictions and specific determinants. Legal reforms based on misperceptions and generalizations are harmful.[17] In this light, our research is an alert. We argue that there is currently no robust economic model to generate the prediction that French law is less conducive to economic growth than common law. If indeed French law is less friendly to economic growth than common law, then legal economists have to propose a sophisticated theory to substantiate that contention, not a theory based on a 'cherry-picking' of legal doctrines and short-sighted comparisons. We do not believe that a sophisticated theory is possible. Still, the burden of proof lies with those legal economists who firmly believe that French law is problematic in terms of economic growth when compared with common law. The standard of proof has to be high. Mere simple correlations clearly do not satisfy the necessary standard of proof. Legal reforms affect millions of lives. They cannot be based on poor theories and empirical conjectures. Yet, very unfortunately, a few legal reforms around the world in the last decade have been based on the alleged inferiority of French law. We are not surprised that the results have been very disappointing.

Notes

1 Lewis Kornhauser, 'The Economic Analysis of Law' in *The Stanford Encyclopedia of Philosophy* (Summer 2015), http://plato.stanford.edu/archives/sum2015/entries/legal-econanalysis/ (accessed 28 September 2015).
2 It started with the field of shareholder protection and then later on spread on other fields. For more detail, see Ralf Michaels, 'Comparative Law by Numbers? Legal Origins Thesis, *Doing Business* Reports and the Silence of Traditional Comparative Law' (2009) 57 *American Journal of Comparative Law* 765.
3 In the late 1990s, Rafael La Porta, Florencio Lopez-de-Silanes, Andrei Shleifer and Robert W. Vishny ('LLSV') launched a research project examining connections between legal rules governing investor protection and economic development. Working on the assumption that legal rules could be measured and quantified, LLSV purported to demonstrate that common law countries were more protective of outside investors – and, thus, more hospitable to economic development – than civil law countries. In the ensuing years, LLSV and other economists have expanded and refined their work, constructing the grandly named Legal Origins Theory, which holds that legal systems are important determinants of economic development. the influence of legal origins theory is not confined to economics journals, but may be seen in policy reforms through the World Bank's *Doing Business* reports. See more in Andrei Shleifer and Robert Vishny, 'A Survey of Corporate Governance' (1997) 52 *Journal of Finance* 737–783 and Andrei Shleifer and Daniel Wolfenzon, 'Investor Protection and Equity Markets' (2000) NBER Working Paper 7974.
4 As France is being defined as the least performant legal family of all by the legal origins theory, see Rafael La Porta et al., 'The Economic Consequences of Legal Origins' (2008) 46 *Journal of Economic Literature* 285.

5 Sonja Fagernäs, Prabirjit Sarkar and Ajit Singh Fagernäs, 'Legal Origin, Shareholder Protection and the Stock Market: New Challenges from Time Series Analysis' (2007) Centre for Business Research, University of Cambridge Working Paper 343, 25.
6 Found at www.theglobaleconomy.com/compare-countries/ (accessed 9 July 2015).
7 Fagernäs et al. (n5) 25.
8 Michaels (n2).
9 Richard A. Posner, *Economic Analysis of Law* 8th ed. (New York: Aspen 2011).
10 As they appear in the legal origins theory; the doubts that we share with several comparativists concerning this classification will be expressed in the third part of the book, when the taxonomy of countries will be taken under scrutiny.
11 Rafael La Porta et al., 'Law and Finance' (1998) 46 *Journal of Political Economy* 1113.
12 Vivian Grosswald Curran, 'Symposium on Legal Origins Thesis: "[N]on scholae sed vitae discimus"' (2009) 57 *American Journal of Comparative Law* 863.
13 Yoram Barzel, 'Dispute and its Resolution: Delineating the Economic Role of the Common Law' (2000) 2 *American Law and Economics Review* 238 (arguing the efficiency of common law in contracts and property, but not in torts).
14 Paul Mahoney, 'The Common Law and Economic Growth: Hayek Might Be Right' (2001) 30(2) *Journal of Legal Studies* 503; La Porta et al. (n4); Gani Aldashev, 'Legal Institutions, Political Economy, and Development' (2009) 25 *Oxford Review of Economic Policy* 257.
15 Henrik Lando and Caspar Rose, 'On the Enforcement of Specific Performance in Civil Law Countries' (2004) 24 *International Review of Law and Economics* 473.
16 Mahoney (n14).
17 Benito Arruñada, 'Pitfalls to Avoid When Measuring the Institutional Environment: Is *Doing Business* Damaging Business?' (2007) 35 *Journal of Comparative Economics* 729.

2 The danger of a globally accepted theory containing major flaws

Under the legal origins theory, legal systems are not measured or assessed by the kinds of principles they put forward, but by how efficiently they facilitate market interactions and prevent unnecessary and burdensome state regulation.[1] These mechanisms in turn are related and should be conducive of strong economic growth.

More consistently, the legal origins literature claims that common law model is superior to the civil law alternative in that it generally provides more efficient solutions because the right regulatory response is often 'simply less government' so we should expect all systems to gravitate to the basic features of the model over time, as barriers to convergence are removed as a result of the expansion of global trade and the removal of formal restriction on cross-border capital flows.[2] Although this theory has been criticized from a theoretical as well as empirical level, under different approaches, by economists and non-economists, it has found its (remarkably quick) way to the international level of policymaking, where its importance furthermore and inevitably gained weight. Empirical studies have generally failed to find evidence of a direct link between legal origin and the rate of growth of national GDP, depending on samples, periods, methods.[3] Moreover, the claim that countries whose legal systems derive from the common law place greater emphasis on freedom of contract and protection of private property than those with civil law roots gained influence over policy reforms in many countries over the past decade through the *Doing Business* reports of the World Bank, which is in this way is effectively promoting convergence to common law systems.[4]

It is not only the developing countries who are influenced by the claims of the legal origins theory; a number of countries followed the example of Poland in promoting judicial independence as can be seen in common law[5] while at the same time Chile experimented with common law by changing its inquisition procedure in its criminal law with an adversarial one.[6] Moreover, the case of Zambia shows how World Bank's focus on reducing cost to business only carries with it potential negative consequences of failing to consider the social impact of investment climate reforms. The risk of perpetuating and entrenching the imbalances in the country has been realized since due to its constant regulatory reforms by recommendations of the World Bank made it climb up the *Doing Business* ranking, but Zambia nonetheless remained one of the poorest and most unequal countries in the world.[7] In fact, quite astonishingly, there is no systematic empirical evidence relating improvements in the *Doing Business* ranking and GDP growth rates.

International actors have played a big role endorsing the legal origins theory. Particularly in the context of the World Bank, this whole new field of comparative economics appeared with new central thesis that a country's legal institutions and its underlying legal system can determine its prospects for development, with the critiques of civil law playing a large role in shaping a wide range of judicial reform initiatives.[8] Loans are granted to countries, as well as technical expertise, that cause pressure to demonstrate that the money given is achieving result under the dominance of the legal origins paradigm. Therefore such countries shape their institutions to the rankings of the *Doing Business* reports, allegedly adopting instruments of common law origins with the minimum regulation possible, since the civil law (in the words of the World Bank) is linked with heavy regulation, corruption and inefficiency.[9]

The first *Doing Business* report has been issued in 2004, titled 'Understanding Regulation', suggesting that the civil legal tradition is a handicap for developing countries when compared to the common law tradition and arguing that a country's choice of legal system influences its regulatory scheme.[10] Excessive regulation is deemed bad for economic growth and it drives businesses into the informal market, resulting in poor economic outcomes. Moreover, the principal factor associated with the level of regulation in a country was determined to be country's legal tradition: countries with a French civil law tradition appeared to be more interventionist than common law countries.[11] As an example, in 2004 *Doing Business* report, France has been rated forty-fourth (behind Jamaica, Botswana and Tonga), in 2009 as the thirty-first (behind Israel, Latvia and Lithuania), while by contrast in 2009 Annual Report of the World Economic Forum, France has been rated sixteenth.[12] The whole *Doing Business* project from its beginning aims at motivating reforms through country benchmarking and its reports enjoy a huge success worldwide, being used as models for other reports, legislative reforms and investment decisions.[13] Although in some aspects even this first 2004 report was ambiguous,[14] the only message that seemed to catch the attention of the public is that the civil law is bad for business and that common law regularly guarantees better results. Although this 'one-size-fits-all' approach has been deleted from subsequent reports, this widespread propaganda of the legal origins theory is undoubtedly harmful, as the theory lacks significant theoretical and empirical grounds to be accepted as such. In the last decade research has shown an absence of overall correlation between law systems and financial market developments, indicating that laws work best when they are embedded in particular configuration of institutions at national level as opposed to being transplanted from outside.[15]

The importance given to the topic in the international community was the reason why we took the path of uncovering the misunderstandings and misconceptions behind the legal origins theory and portraying its insufficiency in this particular book.

Notes

1 Emma Phillips, 'The War on Civil Law? The Common Law as a Proxy for the Global Ambition of Law and Economics' (2010) 24 *Wisconsin International Law Journal* 915, 920.
2 Simon Deakin et al., 'An End to Consensus? The Selective Impact of Corporate Law Reform on Financial Development' (2011) ECGI – Law Working Paper 182/2011, 6.
3 Phillips (n1) 919.
4 Ibid. 916.
5 Also Russia, Bulgaria, Moldova, a number of Eastern European and Latin American countries. See more in Phillips (n1) 926.
6 Ibid. 916.
7 Sarah Montgomery, 'What is the Social Impact of the World Bank's Support to Regulatory Reform? Don't Ask the Bank' (2014). Online at www.brettonwoodsproject. org/2014/11/social-impact-banks-support-regulatory-reform-dont-ask-bank/ (accessed 28 September 2015).
8 Phillips (n1) 921.
9 Ibid. 927.
10 Ibid. 942.
11 Phillips (n1) 944.
12 Anne-Julie Kerhuel and Bénédicte Cosson-Fauvarque, 'Is Law an Economic Contest? French Reactions to the *Doing Business* World Bank Reports and Economic Analysis of the Law' (2009) 57 *American Journal of Comparative Law* 811, 812.
13 For example, only from June 2013 until June 2014 the report documented 230 business reforms, 145 of those aimed at reducing the complexity and cost of complying with business regulation and 85 aimed at strengthening legal institutions. See more in Kerhuel and Cosson-Fauvarque (n12).
14 It stated that the creation of specialized commercial courts can help resolve commercial disputes faster and more efficiently (on the basis of those existing in France and Spain) and that high costs if proceedings can significantly impede the effective functioning of courts (Netherlands given as an example of affordable fees). See more in Phillips (n1).
15 Deakin et al. (n2) 25.

3 The efficiency of the common law hypothesis

Judge Posner's hypothesis in its raw state demands all legal rules to be efficient and claims that virtually every common law legal rule follows this requirement.[1] He claims that judge-made rules are better than statutes because judges can be expected to make efficient law due to two reasons: efficiency is a widely held value and judges can figure out more or less what rules are efficient and, at the same time, there is no other widely held value that judges are in a position to achieve.[2] This idea itself was not in its entirety new. It can be traced back to the evolutionary theory of the common law suggested by Justice Holmes in the 1880s.[3] Justice Holmes's main argument is that the development of the common law was driven by judicial responses to public policy rather than by some internal logic. According to Holmes, the ability of the common law to adjust appropriately to external needs relied on the recruitment of the judiciary as representatives of the community. Notably, the theory strongly opposed the then-prevalent codification movement in the US[4] Justice Holmes never used an efficiency argument for the common law (and against codification). Nevertheless, it is clear that Judge Posner's understanding of the common law is very close to the theory developed by Justice Holmes, since according to both lines of reasoning judges are the ones observing law in reality and are the ones pushing and guiding force in the development of law.

It is important to stress that the common law considered by Justice Holmes and Judge Posner traces back to the Blackstonian definition. According to Sir William Blackstone, writing in 1796, the common law consists of general customs by which the judges and the courts are guided and directed.[5] Alternatively, the common law includes all legal doctrines that do not require a written form to be valid, but rather rely on the usage by courts.[6] Therefore, under the common law, statutes have a secondary and subordinate role. They are essentially declaratory (to restate the common law) or remedial (to correct the flaws of the common law).

However, in American legal history, the Blackstonian understanding of the common law has not been without controversy. For example, Justice Cardozo saw clear advantages in the codification process and recognized some advantages of the French legal method in shaping judgments.[7] The American codification debate in the nineteenth century clearly shows that there are multiple understandings of the role of the common law.[8] By proposing the efficiency hypothesis of the common law, Judge Posner seems to take one side of the discussion. Unfortunately, most legal economists have not realized that the Posnerian hypothesis has to be understood in the context of a richer debate. Looking at the debates in the past, the traditional arguments for the Blackstonian common law included flexibility, stability and the ability to develop better rules without the need for statutes.[9] The conventional arguments against the Blackstonian understanding of the common law mentioned uncertainty (because of conflicting precedents), difficulty of non-lawyers to understand the law (due to higher transaction costs in modern economic language), and the error of allowing judges to legislate.

In this context, consider the analytical models developed by legal economists. The models discuss under which conditions respect for precedent generates evolution to efficiency (hence supporting the Posnerian hypothesis). The models never consider the limitations imposed by multiple and conflicting precedents. Inadvertently or not, legal economists have disregarded the different arguments for and against the Blackstonian common law. They have entered the discussion without paying enough attention to its numerous existing viewpoints that are both in favour of, and against, the common law.

In fact, Judge Posner's hypothesis of the efficiency of the common law begs for a more detailed explanation from the start. In particular, the hypothesis lacks a more explicit mechanism for why the common law should be efficient. Due to the fact that Judge Posner's hypothesis cannot fully offer a complete model of evolution to efficiency, a remarkable literature emerged as a consequence. Legal economists proposed different explanations that have been evolutionary models identifying the forces that have shaped the common law to generate efficient rules.[10]

One explanation is that judges have a preference for efficiency.[11] Another explanation is that efficiency is promoted by the prevalence of precedent (more efficient rules more likely to survive through a mechanism of precedent).[12] A third explanation relies on the incentives to bring cases and the role of court litigation (since inefficient rules are not welfare maximizing).[13] Nevertheless, the precise nature of the mechanism that justifies the efficiency hypothesis is problematic even taking these early explanations into account.[14]

The search for a more convincing setup for the efficiency of the common law hypothesis has sparked important academic work. This literature essentially looks at how litigation improves the law, or some specific legal doctrine, taking into consideration that only a self-selected number of cases are actually litigated.[15] In particular, the efficiency of the common law is unequivocally related to the observation that litigation follows private interests.[16] Presumably, bad rules are challenged more often than good rules; thus, court intervention will naturally improve the overall quality of the law.[17] However, this line of reasoning has problematic shortcomings. It is possible that the subset of cases actually litigated is inadequate to trigger the necessary improvements, hence biasing the evolution of legal rules against efficiency.[18] Furthermore, the emergence of efficiency in common law depends on a number of factors in the evolutionary mechanism, namely initial conditions, path dependence, and random shocks.[19] Finally, if the common law is evolutionarily efficient, we are left with no explanation for the important doctrinal differences across common law jurisdictions (in particular, taking into account that presumably they have the same *de jure* initial condition, namely English law).[20]

The literature on the efficiency of the common law that followed Posner's hypothesis is not comparative in nature, but effectively looks at judge-made law. Therefore, the alleged efficiency should hold in any jurisdiction with respect to either judge-made law or general principles of law developed by courts (as it is better known in civil law jurisdictions). In fact, from the perspective of civil law countries, the argument could be rephrased as court interventions improving the overall efficiency of the legal system because of the common biases of litigation (i.e., more inefficient laws will be subject to more court intervention than less efficient laws). It is well known that tort law is an area of French law that has been systematically developed by case law given the absence of specific codification in the 1804 civil code (all French tort law is based on article 1382 of the civil code).[21] As a consequence, we should treat torts from the perspective of the efficiency of the common law similarly in both the United States and France. The only relevant question, then, is the extent to which the litigation biases in the area of torts increase or decrease efficiency of the law.[22]

Let us suppose that there are more occasions for court intervention and judgment in a common law legal system than under code law. It could therefore be argued that the appropriate mutation towards efficiency will be faster in common law than in civil law. However, such a conclusion relies on the inability of statute creation and modification to supplement any 'delays' in the evolutionary process. In that spirit, some scholars also argued that the procedural formalism (more often present in the civil law than common law systems) undermines economic efficiency by fostering rent-seeking and corruption. Since such reasoning fails to show that rent-seeking and corruption seem to be higher in civil law than common law systems, opposing research looked closely into the issue and shown that there exist complementarities between judicial independence (presumed more typical in common law systems) and judicial accountability (ensured by the mentioned judicial formalism).[23] When researched in more depth, it has been found that timeliness, written procedures and the right to counsel have a robust positive effect on growth, whereas the number of independent procedural actions and the presumption of innocence have negative effects on economic growth,[24] while legal origins did not have a significant influence on the average growth rate in the sample chosen.[25] The argument was therefore put forward that some procedural devies (formalisms) are likely to improve the state's capacity to credibly commit to the promises contained in its laws, which will be reflected in higher rates of economic growth.[26] And last but not least, the importance of de facto and de jure judicial independence has been elaborated upon, which has not been taken into account by Posner and will not be further elaborated by us at this point but rather put forward as one of the most elementary ideas that undermine the value of Posnerian hypothesis as a whole.

At the end of the day, the Posnerian hypothesis does not place common law in a better position than civil law in the evolution towards efficient rules. It does not provide a convincing framework to argue that judicial precedent is a superior way to promote an efficient solution than a statutory rule precisely because the focus is on judge-made law.[27] Under the common law reasoning, bad decisions are overruled in the same way that under civil law bad statutes can be effectively corrected by the judiciary.[28] There is no theoretical or empirical basis to assert that courts and juries are in a better position in common law, rather than in civil law, jurisdictions to calculate the consequences of their decisions more appropriately than the government.[29] That judge-made law can be better understood as a set of rules designed to maximize economic efficiency, as Judge Posner proposed, is not an exclusive feature of common law jurisdictions.[30] Furthermore, Judge Posner finds important functional differences between the United States and Britain, and recognizes important similarities between the current institutional arrangements in Britain and in continental Europe.[31]

If the Posnerian hypothesis is true, at least in the long run, rules that do not promote efficient results should be repealed regardless of the legal system. Therefore, the central question is not whether one legal family or another promotes an economic efficiency solution, but which of these two main legal families reaches the adequate result (always from the economic perspective) at a lower cost in terms of delays and opportunity costs.[32] From a solely cost perspective, it is not clear that the type of cost attached to general axiomatic legal solutions, characteristic of civil law approaches, is necessarily higher than litigation costs incurred in the approach developed by common law.[33]

Our argument is that the next step of arguing that judge-made law is more efficient than statute law requires further reasoning. The mere Posnerian efficiency hypothesis of the common law cannot support the conclusion that lawmaking by legislation is necessarily less efficient than court intervention. One of the main arguments for the superiority of judge-made law is that private interests are more likely to capture the legislature than the courts, although such argument is debatable at the theoretical, as well as empirical, level.[34] In fact, there is no systematic evidence that rent-seeking is more persistent with the legislature than with the courts, since demand and supply conditions are fundamentally different.[35] Moreover, courts and legislators have their own goals in terms of enhancing their influence, which complicates the potential effect of private interests in law-making.[36]

The more adversarial nature of litigation in common law rather than in civil law could generate more rent-seeking and more rent dissipation in the process of rulemaking.[37] Furthermore, given the growing predominance of statute law in common law jurisdictions, the inevitable conclusion is that the overall efficiency has been reduced.[38] This conclusion is reinforced by the argument that the efficiency of the common law is not really demand-side-induced (i.e., through the incentives provided by litigation) but rather supply-side-induced. The historical competition between common law and equity courts was the driving force; once these courts were merged and monopoly had been achieved, the efficiency forces lost stimulus.[39] Nevertheless, a similar historical competition between royal, guild and ecclesiastical courts existed in civil law jurisdictions.[40]

Notice that the relative efficiency of judge-made versus statue law, by itself, does not provide a good framework to justify the superiority of the common law system as compared to the civil law system. First, statute law is important in common law jurisdictions; many important areas of private law, such as torts or even commercial law, are essentially common law even in civil law jurisdictions. Second, the biases of legislation and litigation are not qualitatively and quantitatively similar in both legal systems due to procedural and substantive differences. Once again, the efficiency hypothesis of the common law coupled with the alleged bias of legislation for private capture are insufficient to support the argument that French civil law is necessarily inferior to the common law.

In fact, the traditional Posnerian analysis could be transposed to French civil law in multiple forms. The general law (or code) is arguably more efficient than specific statutory interventions that are potentially prone to more capture. It could also be said that bottom-up law (for example, case law piling up under general code provisions such as tort law under article 1382 of the French civil code) is more appropriate than top-down law (including very detailed code provisions as well as specific statutes). Nothing in the discussion makes the argument unique to common law systems. It also does not provide a rigorous framework from which to derive any implications for comparative law.

Notes

1 Lewis Kornhauser, 'The Economic Analysis of Law' in *The Stanford Encyclopedia of Philosophy* (Summer 2015), http://plato.stanford.edu/archives/sum2015/entries/legal-econanalysis/. access date
2 David D. Friedman, *Law's Order: What Economics Has To Do With Law and Why it Matters* (Princeton, NJ: Princeton University Press 2000), ch. 19.
3 Oliver Wendell Holmes, *The Common Law* 1945ᵉ édition (Little, Brown & Co. 1881).
4 Sheldon M. Novick, 'Introduction' in Oliver Wendall Holmes, *The Common Law* (New York: Dover 1991).
5 William Blackstone, *The Commentaries on the Laws and Constitution of* England (1796).
6 Ibid.
7 Benjamin N. Cardozo, *The Nature of the Judicial Process* (New York: Feather Trail Press 2009).
8 Andrew P. Morriss, 'Codification and Right Answers' (1999) 74(2) *Chicago-Kent Law Review* 355.
9 Ibid. 376–379.
10 Paul H. Rubin, 'Micro and Macro Legal Efficiency: Supply and Demand' (2005) 13 *Supreme Court Economic Review* 19.
11 Richard A. Posner, 'Utilitarianism, Economics, and Legal Theory' (1979) 8 *Journal of Legal Studies* 103.
12 Paul H. Rubin, 'Why is the Common Law Efficient?' (1977) 6 *Journal of Legal Studies* 51, 53–57.
13 George L. Priest, 'The Common Law Process and the Selection of Efficient Rules' (1977) 6 *Journal of Legal Studies* 65.
14 Nicola Gennaioli and Andrei Shleifer, 'The Evolution of Common Law' (2007) 115 *Journal of Political Economy* 43; Nicola Gennaioli and Andrei Shleifer, 'Overruling and the Instability of Law' (2007) 35 *Journal of Comparative Economics* 309; Thomas J. Miceli, 'Legal Change: Selective Litigation, Judicial Bias, and Precedent' (2009) 38

Journal of Legal Studies 157. Posner's original hypothesis posits that judges seek efficiency, whereas the later works by Rubin and Priest propose an invisible hand. Gennaioli and Shleifer show that even if judges are efficiency seeking, precedent and overruling must be balanced in an appropriate way. A judicial bias might distort the law in the short run, but also provides the mechanism to improve the law in the long run. Miceli introduces the possibility of selective litigation to show that convergence to efficiency is still possible as long as the biases do not overwhelm the likelihood that inefficient laws will be more often litigated. Strong precedent is socially valuable if judges are significantly biased.

15 See generally Paul H. Rubin, *Business Firms and the Common Law: The Evolution of Efficient Rules* (New York: Praeger 1983), 14; Francesco Parisi and Vincy Fon, *The Economics of Lawmaking* (Oxford: Oxford University Press 2009), 85–88; Maxwell L. Stearns and Todd J. Zywicki, *Public Choice Concepts and Applications in Law* (St Paul, MN: West 2009), 464–467; John C. Goodman, 'An Economic Theory of the Evolution of the Common Law' (1978) 7 *Journal of Legal Studies* 393; Robert Cooter and Lewis Kornhauser, 'Can Litigation Improve the Law Without the Help of Judges?' (1980) 9 *Journal of Legal Studies* 139; Peter R. Terrebonne, 'A Strictly Evolutionary Model of Common Law' (1981) 10 *Journal of Legal Studies* 397; Georg von Wangenheim, 'The Evolution of Judge-Made Law' (1993) 13 *International Review of Law and Economics* 381; Vincy Fon and Francesco Parisi, 'Litigation and the Evolution of Legal Remedies: A Dynamic Model' (2003) 116 *Public Choice* 419; Vincy Fon, Francesco Parisi and Ben Depoorter, 'Litigation, Judicial Path-Dependence, and Legal Change' (2005) 20 *European Journal of Law and Economics* 43; Vincy Fon and Francesco Parisi, 'Judicial Precedents in Civil Law Systems: A Dynamic Analysis' (2006) 26 *International Review of Law and Economics* 519; Anthony Niblett, Richard A. Posner and Andrei Shleifer, 'The Evolution of a Legal Rule' (2010) 39 *Journal of Legal Studies* 325 (discussing application of empirical testing of common law in commercial areas converging to efficiency). A critical view of this literature is provided by Frederick Schauer, *Thinking Like a Lawyer: A New Introduction to Legal Reasoning* (Cambridge, MA: Harvard University Press 2009), 103–108.

16 William M. Landes and Richard A. Posner, 'Adjudication as a Private Good' (1979) 8 *Journal of Legal Studies* 235 (noting that judicial opinions are a public good that arbitration fails to provide).

17 Rubin (n15); Priest (n13).

18 Gillian K. Hadfield, 'Bias in the Evolution of Legal Rules' (1992) 80 *Georgetown Law Journal* 583, 584–585.

19 Mark J. Roe, 'Chaos and Evolution in Law and Economics' (1996) 109 *Harvard Law Journal* 641, 642–643.

20 That is, unless we consider adaptation to distinct local circumstances across the Anglo-American world, but such explanation is exogenous to the original model. See chapter 5.

21 Eva Steiner, *French Legal Method* (Oxford: Oxford University Press 2002), 90.

22 Yoram Barzel, 'Dispute and its Resolution: Delineating the Economic Role of the Common Law' (2000) 2 *American Law and Economics Review*..

23 Bernd Hayo and Stefan Voigt, 'The Relevance of Judicial Procedure for Economic Growth' (2008) CESifo Working Paper 2514, p.3.

24 Ibid.

25 Sample period of fifteen years for the judicial indicators, using standard explanatory variables against the control variables and two sets of variables proposed in pro-efficiency researchers before (Matrix D referring to Djankov and Matrix L to La Porta), see more in Hayo and Voigt (n23) pp.9–13.

26 Ibid, p.23.

27 For a technical model, see Giacomo A. M. Ponzetto and Patricio A. Fernandez, 'Case Law Versus Statute Law: An Evolutionary Comparison' (2008) 37 *Journal of Legal*

Studies 379 (predicting the progressive convergence of common and civil law toward a mixed system). See also Giuseppe Dari-Mattiacci, Bruno Deffains and Bruno Lovat, 'The Dynamics of the Legal System' (2001) 79 *Journal of Economic Behavior and Organization* 95 (explaining the relationship between high litigation rates and the balance between case law and legislation); Carmine Guerriero, 'Democracy, Judicial Attitudes, and Heterogeneity: The Civil Versus Common Law Tradition' (2009) University of Cambridge Working Paper 0917 (arguing that case law outperforms statute law when political institutions are weak).

28 See, e.g., Fon and Parisi (2003) (n15) discussing jurisprudence constant.

29 Although we recognize, for example, the role of Brandeis brief in American litigation. The Brandeis brief is certainly a mechanism to improve knowledge concerning factual consequences. As to the more general discussion about the relative merits of courts and juries versus the legislative and executive branches, see Raoul C. Van Caenegem, *Judges, Legislators and Professors: Chapters in European Legal History* (New York: Cambridge University Press 1987) 127–168. In his view, legislation has the advantage of being binding and authoritative, even if less flexible. On the other hand, he accepts that case law is more certain if *stare decisis* prevails, which is hardly the case in most common law jurisdictions nowadays, since precisely good legal arguments can undermine precedent and hence provide more flexibility. However, according to Caenegem, common law lacks generalization and a conceptual framework.

30 Posner (n11).

31 Richard Posner, *Law and Legal Theory in England and America* (Oxford University Press 1996) 69–114; Jonathan E. Levitsky, 'The Europeanization of the British Legal Style' (1994) 42 *American Journal of Comparative Law* 347.

32 See the critique of Posner's argument in David D. Friedman, *Law's Order: What Economics Has to Do With Law and Why it Matters* (Princeton, NJ: Princeton University Press 2000) 15–17.

33 A different perspective is defended by John P. Dawson, *The Oracles of the Law* (Ann Arbor: University of Michigan 1968). In his view, common law is a by-product of litigation confirmed by creative adjudication. Initially, a small group of judges with a decentralized court system administered and controlled the remedies of common law. However, because the common law was captured and monopolized by a dominant group, it became narrower, insular and unable to respond to the emerging needs of the late eighteenth and nineteenth centuries. On the contrary, in France, there was a reaction to an over-powerful judiciary under customary law. The *Parlement* of Paris emerged as a central court after 1250. Customs were developed by a combination of central and local courts. The *Parlement* was the highest judicial body and lawmaker. The codification was a reaction to excessive judicial interference. The basic idea of codification was not to eliminate case law, but to introduce the need for explaining and defending decisions when supplying new rules. Hence, the birth of reasoned opinion was a response to perceived excessive judicial interference in law-making.

34 The most devastating criticisms are Gordon Tullock, *The Case Against the Common Law* (Durham: Carolina University Press 1997) and Gordon Tullock, 'Rent-Seeking and the Law'. In *The Selected Works of Gordon Tullock: The Organization of Inquiry, Volume 3*, Charles K. Rowley ed. (Liberty Fund 2005). See also Michael A. Crew and Charlotte Twight, 'On the Efficiency of Law: A Public Choice Perspective' (1990) 66 *Public Choice* 15 (arguing that common law is less subject to rent-seeking than statute law); Paul H. Rubin, 'Common Law and Statute Law' (1982) 11 *Journal of Legal Studies* 205, 211–216 (arguing that both are influenced by private interests to advance their goals); Barbara Luppi and Francesco Parisi, 'Litigation and Legal Evolution: Does Procedure Matter?' (2012) 152 *Public Choice* 181.

35 See generally William M. Landes and Richard A. Posner, 'The Independent Judiciary in an Interest-Group Perspective' (1975) 18 *Journal of Law and Economics* 875; W. Mark Crain and Robert D. Tollison, 'Constitutional Change in an Interest-Group

Perspective' (1979) 8 *Journal of Legal Studies* 165; W. Mark Crain and Robert D. Tollison, 'The Executive Branch in the Interest-Group Theory of Government' (1979) 8 *Journal of Legal Studies* 555; Thomas W. Merrill, 'Does Public Choice Theory Justify Judicial Activism After All?' (1997) 21 *Harvard Journal of Law and Public Policy* 219; Thomas W. Merrill, 'Institutional Choice and Political Faith' (1997) 22 *Law and Social Inquiry* 959; Fred S. McChesney, 'Rent Extraction and Rent Creation in the Economic Theory of Regulation' (1987) 16 *Journal of Legal Studies* 101 (discussing several theories of capture in rulemaking).

36 See generally A. C. Pritchard and Todd J. Zywicki, 'Finding the Constitution: An Economic Analysis of Tradition's Role in Constitutional Interpretation' (1999) 77 *North Carolina Law Review* 409, 496–497. For an interesting comparison of lawmakers' influences under English and French systems, see J. W. F. Allison, *A Continental Distinction in the Common Law: A Historical and Comparative Perspective on English Public Law* (Oxford University Press 1996) 114–127.

37 Todd J. Zywicki, 'Spontaneous Order and the Common Law: Gordon Tullock's Critique' (2008) 135 *Public Choice* 35, 44–46.

38 Rubin (n12) noting that the common law might have been more efficient in the past when the organization of interests was more costly, but not now. Also, these arguments face a serious challenge in areas such as antitrust law, which are statute law precisely because the traditional principle of fair trade in common law did not protect market competition and courts were excessively deferential to monopolies.

39 Todd J. Zywicki, 'The Rise and Fall of Efficiency in the Common Law: A Supply-Side Analysis' (2003) 97 *Northwestern University Law Review* 1551 (arguing for supply-side explanations based on the competition between several court systems, particularly common law and equity). A more comprehensive discussion is provided by Daniel Klerman, 'Jurisdictional Competition and the Evolution of the Common Law' (2007) 74 *University of Chicago Law Review* 1179 (arguing that institutional structures that were able to produce more innovative legal rules tended to prevail in English law). However, he challenges the efficiency of the supply-side competition between these courts. He notes that there was a pro-plaintiff bias that generated certain (hardly efficient) rules given the way judges were paid. Important changes to judicial compensation and salaries corrected the pro-plaintiff bias in the nineteenth century.

40 Harold J. Berman, *Law and Revolution: The Formation of the Western Legal Culture* (Cambridge, MA: Harvard University Press 1983); Harold J. Berman, *Law and Revolution II: The Impact of the Protestant Reformations on the Western Legal Tradition* (Cambridge, MA and London: Belknap 2003). More recently, unlike the common law jurisdictions, the civil law jurisdictions have seen serious competition between supreme courts and constitutional courts to maximize their jurisdiction. See Nuno Garoupa and Tom Ginsburg, 'Building Reputation in Constitutional Courts: Party and Judicial Politics' (2012) 28 *Arizona Journal of International and Comparative Law* 539.

4 Legal origins
The comparative perspective

More recently the debate has been essentially empirical.[1] The so-called legal origins theory sees law as exogenous to the analysis, since historically most countries received their law through colonial transplantation. Its proponents divided countries on group adhering to common law or to three distinct families of civil law, French, German and Scandinavian, and tried to find correlations between such groups and economic indicators. This new literature defends the premise that legal systems with origins in the English common law have superior institutions for economic growth and development than those of French civil law for two reasons.[2] First, common law provides more adequate institutions for financial markets and business transactions, which in turn fuels more economic growth.[3] Second, French civil law presupposition of a greater role for state intervention is detrimental for economic freedom and market efficiency.[4] For a clearer view of the world division based on legal families see the image hereunder.

The relationship between growth or economic performance and the type of legal system carries an implicit assumption: law and legal institutions matter for economic growth.[5] This assumption, as critical and debatable as it can be, is unrelated to the two previous questions concerning the efficiency hypothesis of the common law and the inferiority of legislation. Nevertheless, these questions loosely inspired the two mentioned explanations for the alleged empirical evidence.

The legal origins approach goes a step further by basing its findings on some questionable premises, namely that law and legal outcomes are measureable, that legal systems themselves can be ascribed to legal origins that are markedly different and that these origins have a deep impact on the laws and legal institutions of countries which produce important effects in economic outcomes. It suggests that, not only law matters for economic growth, but common law systems are better equipped than civil law systems (in particular, French legal origin). Nevertheless, the observed correlations beg for an explanation in order to suggest persuasive causality mechanisms. Without these possible mechanisms, the correlations have little explanatory power and cannot make sense from a legal policymaking point of view.

The main conclusion of the legal origins approach so is that law varies across the world, that these variations can be measured quantitatively by indicators and these indicators support that those variations are best understood by legal tradition

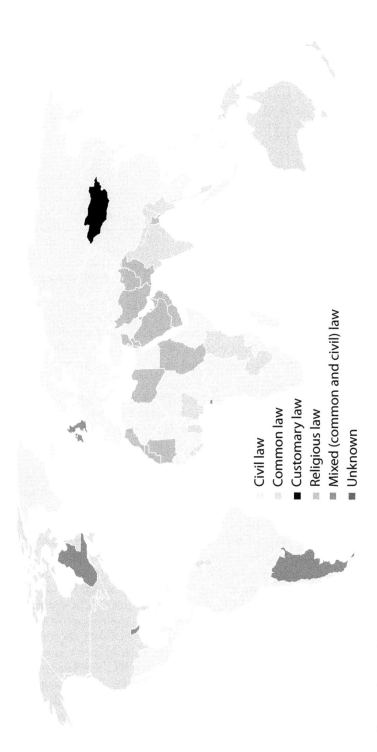

Civil law

Common law

Customary law

Religious law

Mixed (common and civil) law

Unknown

Figure 4.1   World map of legal origins[6]

Table 4.1 Government regulation and legal origin[7]

	Regulation of entry (1999)	Regulation of labour (1997)	Press government ownership (1999)	Conscription (2000)
French legal origin	0.6927[a] (0.0929)	0.2654[a] (0.0362)	0.2095[a] (0.0834)	0.5468[a] (0.0772)
German legal origin	0.5224[a] (0.1206)	0.2337[a] (0.0473)	0.1100 (0.0926)	0.8281[a] (0.0794)
Scandinavian legal origin	−0.1922 (0.1352)	0.3978a (0.0443)	0.1308[b] (0.0555)	0.7219[a] (0.2015)
Ln (GDP per capita)	−0.1963[a] (0.0367)	−0.0083 (0.0164)	−0.1753[a] (0.0307)	−0.0382 (0.0331)
Constant	3.4367[a] (0.3037)	0.3703[b] (0.1520)	1.6565[a] (0.3024)	0.4702[c] (0.2802)
Observations	85	84	95	146
R-squared	61%	42%	37%	34%

[a] Significant at the 1% level.
[b] Significant at the 5% level.
[c] Significant at the 10% level.

(the fundamental difference in terms of policy building and state intervention of civil law versus market enhancing strengths of common law). Finally, since these variations explain patterns of economic and social development, legal origins are a significant determinant.

In connection with the basic efficiency hypothesis of common law, the legal origins theory does not only confirm it, but it adds to it an empirical note on micro and macro level, showing for all variables a significant positive effect of having a common law legal origin and significant negative effect of having a civil law origin, especially French origin.

These logical steps demand two different developments. First, as we have insisted, an empirical analysis that establishes that law matters for economic growth and that those aspects that matter are directly correlated with legal origins. Second, a conceptual framework that explains why legal origins determines economic growth (or financial markets in the case of those who claim the main channel is through these markets). Some authors have put their findings in distinct tables, one of them being presented here to illustrate the theory.[8] The opposing theories rose in the decade after the legal origin's original work; not only has it been proven that France and the UK had seen the largest rises in aggregate index of shareholder protection,[9] but also that in the US the developments in shareholder protection have oscillated between rise and fall,[10] which does not correspond to the findings of the legal origins. Since legal origins based their research only on six variables in their static view, a new approach was mandated. This 2007 research based its findings on sixty variables and found that the US and the UK as the common law countries do not have a higher level of shareholder protection than France and Germany, the civil law countries.[11] Moreover, this research, albeit conducted in the 1970–2005 period, also comprised a cross-section view of five-year periods, and in all of these seven periods the predictions of the legal origins were rejected by the data: if the UK and US were considered together and compared with the combined France and Germany, at each of the five-year intervals the civil law countries had higher shareholder protection that the common law countries.[12] The same study found no long run relationship between stock market capitalization and different legal indexes governing the share market,[13] and has at the same time rejected the hypothesis on the existence of significant direct link between the level of economic activities (as indicated by GDP) and stock market development (as indicated by the turnover ratio).[14] No positive link has been found between better shareholder protection and higher stock market activities in the so-called legal origin 'mother' countries,[15] and this has held true also in the case of less developed countries.[16]

At this point it is useful to once again reiterate that our goal is not to claim that the correlations and numbers of legal origins are wrongly determined, but to show that there is no theory underlying those numbers, therefore they are not useful in proving the contents of the claims of the proponents of the legal origins theory.

The initial version of the legal origins approach had no clear mechanism to relate legal family and economic growth.[17] Later work has conceptualized two potential mechanisms.[18] The so-called 'adaptability channel' proposes that the common law is more effective in promoting economic growth since due to its foundations in the development of case law it is more adaptive to economic needs. At the same time, civil law judges are more severely constrained by codified principles. Comprehensive statutory codification undermines judicial ability to make law in new circumstances and where economic needs are pervasive. The 'adaptability channel' evidently echoes the efficiency of the common law hypothesis.

The second suggested mechanism has been known as the 'political channel'. Here the argument is that common law emphasizes private property rights and contractual approaches while the civil law gives a greater play to social or collective rights and mandatory rules. As consequence, common law courts are more independent and more effective in restraining state expropriation while civil law courts are weak in controlling the executive branch power. In this reasoning, the efficiency of the common law hypothesis is implicit; it only makes sense if courts are better than legislators at promoting law more conducive of economic growth.

As others have recognized, these two mechanisms are actually the same. The 'adaptability channel' only works if the 'political channel' exists.[19] As a consequence, the legal origins approach is simply based on the idea that common law courts promote economic growth while civil law courts do not. Moreover, these two potential channels are introduces as exogenous mechanisms while in fact they are endogenous to the political process. In this light, these channels are themselves shaped by economic and social outcomes. If so, we have now an argument for reverse causality which inevitably undermines the alleged theoretical argument.

In fact, these explanations are more problematic when we recognize that France has experienced more economic growth than the United States in most of the period of the nineteenth and twentieth centuries.[20] It would have to be the case that the 'adaptability channel' and the 'political channel' operated only in the last decades while for most of the last two hundred years they were largely unimportant. In our view, no clear explanation has emerged to fill the gap between the development of legal origins two hundred and more years ago and its impact on economic growth only two centuries later.

Our work is not the first to criticize the methodology employed by the legal origins literature. However, it appears that the current criticism is different from ours. Many authors have focused on the particular econometrics, which is very important to the legal origins literature given the empirical bias of the whole project.[21] Our book complements the econometric critique by arguing that the whole project has no theory. Without a theory, it is doubtful that the empirical results can support consistent growth policies.

Other authors have attacked the legal origins literature as a bad exercise in comparative law due to its shortage of details.[22] They argument that the economists started taking interest in the dichotomy of legal families at the same time as comparative lawyers were actually abandoning this rough division.[23] As the economists were claiming that the legal families persist through history, the comparative lawyers showed that they are in decline. Moreover, the said dichotomy of civil versus common law family can be traced only to the early twentieth century and not before.[24] And for as much as the duality of legal families can still be seen today, it seems that the categories were following a parabolic and not linear path.[25] The problem with this line of inquiry is that it inevitably concludes that legal systems are not comparable and that efficiency and economic growth are not useful to understanding legal systems.[26] We disagree with such criticism. Our book avoids the details of a traditional comparative law approach precisely because such an approach does not help with understanding the limitations of the legal origin literature and self-defeats any meaningful and tractable efficiency analysis. Moreover, when transposed to other fundamental legal areas such as constitutional law (as the basis of civil or common law system in question), the legal origins do not fit easily into the reality of legal developments; constitutional reviews around the world have been proven to be seen as a political 'insurance' contract, not connected to the legal origins and not developing through the international dissemination of ideas or with the consideration for the economic efficiency, but rather as a consequence of domestic electoral politics.[27] And if constitutional law cannot be explained on the efficiency basis, neither can it be argued to take into account any efficiency considerations, how can we claim that the rest of the legal system deriving its content from the highest legal norms has efficiency consequences per se, as a whole?

Finally, there is growing literature produced by French scholars rejecting efficiency as a measure of performance. The literature is very critical of law and economics and any kind of economics-oriented argument.[28] The novelty of our approach is to make arguments favourable to French civil law without abandoning the efficiency framework.

Many legal scholars have opposed the legal origins theory while recognizing the novelty of the approach and the power of empirical analysis. Other parameters are identified and associated with legal systems that are more conducive of economic growth; they can be satisfied by either common or civil law systems.[29] Organization of courts and judiciary, information mechanisms about the law, procedures, enforcement of judicial decisions and the production of legal services play important roles in this light. An approach based on economic incentives and organizational aspects seems more promising; it could simultaneously explain the persistence of the common law as well as statutory codification as two ways to promote economic growth rather than necessary opposing legal approaches.[30] However, it should be noted that these later developments in the literature undermine the narrowest meaning of legal origins since they suggest that certain relevant parameters shape economic growth, and not the common versus civil origin of the law.

Notes

1 Gani Aldashev, 'Legal Institutions, Political Economy, and Development' (2009) 25 *Oxford Review of Economic Policy*, Paul Mahoney, 'The Common Law and Economic Growth: Hayek Might Be Right' (2001) 30(2) *Journal of Legal Studies*, Rafael La Porta et al., 'The Economic Consequences of Legal Origins' (2008) 46 *Journal of Economic Literature*. A recent survey summarizes forty-nine scholarly articles on this matter (with around two-thirds proposing empirical evidence to support the legal origins claim; see Guangdong Xu, 'The Role of Law in Economic Growth: A Literature Review' (2011) 25 *Journal of Economic Surveys* 833. The most critical claim is against French law, since other civil law systems (German and Scandinavian) perform at least as well as common law. La Porta et al. (above). For a more recent article finding the opposite result when focusing on the quality of the court system, see Frank B. Cross and Dain C. Donelson 'Creating Quality Courts' (2010) 7 *Journal of Empirical Legal Studies* 490 (concluding common law is negatively correlated to the quality of courts in Europe).
2 Kenneth W. Dam, *The Law-Growth Nexus: The Rule of Law and Economic Development* (Washington: Brookings Institution Press 2006); Mark J. Roe and Jordan I. Siegel, 'Finance and Politics: A Review Essay Based on Kenneth Dam's Analysis of Legal Traditions in the Law-Growth Nexus' (2009) 47 *Journal of Economic Literature* 781. With respect to the taxonomy problem posed by common versus civil law see Ugo Mattei, 'Three Patterns of Law: Taxonomy and Change in the World's Legal Systems' (1997) 45 *American Journal of Comparative Law* 5.
3 La Porta et al. (n1).
4 Mahoney (n1).
5 Frank B. Cross, 'Law and Economic Growth' (2002) 80 *Texas Law Review* 1737.
6 www.andrewcusack.com/2006/the-world-of-law/ (accessed 30 September 2015).
7 La Porta et al. (n1) 285–322.
8 La Porta et al. (n4) 19, Table II Appendix.
9 Sonja Fagernas, Prabirjit Sarkar and Ajit Singh, 'Legal Origin, Shareholder Protection and the Stock Market: New Challenges from Time Series Analysis' (2007) WEF Working Papers 0023, ESRC World Economy and Finance Research Programme, Birkbeck, University of London, p.9.
10 Ibid.
11 Ibid. p.11.
12 Ibid.
13 Ibid. 13.
14 Ibid. 15.
15 Ibid. 15 (UK, US, France and Germany).

16 Shown for India in Prabirjit Sarkar, 'Stock Market Development and Capital Accumulation: Does Law Matter? A Case Study of India', paper presented at Queens Seminar (University of Cambridge, 6 February 2007), available online at http://ssrn.com/abstract=963171 (accessed on 23 May 2016).

17 La Porta et al. (n1).

18 Thorsten Beck, Asli Demirguc-Kunt and Ross Levine, 'Law and Finance: Why Does Legal Origin Matter?' (2003) 31 *Journal of Comparative Economics* 653.

19 John Reitz, 'Toward a Study of the Ecology of Judicial Activism' (2009) 59 *Toronto University Law Review* 185.

20 Dam (n2).

21 Beth Ahlering and Simon Deakin, 'Labor Regulation, Corporate Governance and Legal Origin: A Case of Institutional Complementarity?' (2007) 41 *Law and Society Review* 865; John Armour et al., 'How Do Legal Rules Evolve? Evidence from Cross-Country Comparison of Shareholder, Creditor and Worker Protection' (2009) 57 *American Journal of Comparative Law* 579; John Armour et al., 'Shareholder Protection and Stock Market Development: An Empirical Test of the Legal Origins Hypothesis' (2009) 6 *Journal of Empirical Legal Studies* 343; John Armour et al., 'Law and Financial Development: What We are Learning from Time-Series Evidence' (2009) *Brigham Young University Law Review* 1435; Holger Spamann, 'Contemporary Legal Transplants: Legal Families and the Diffusion of (Corporate) Law' (2009) *Brigham Young University Law Review* 1813; Holger Spamann, 'The 'Antidirector Rights Index' Revisited' (2010) 23 *Review of Financial Studies* 467; Holger Spamann, 'Legal Origin, Civil Procedure, and the Quality of Contract Enforcement' (2010) 166 *Journal of Institutional and Theoretical Economy* 146; Mathias Siems and Simon Deakin, 'Comparative Law and Finance: Past, Present, and Future Research' (2010) 166 *Journal of Institutional and Theoretical Economics* 120; Daniel Klerman et al., 'Legal Origin and Colonial History' (2011) 3 *Journal of Legal Analysis* 379.

22 Antonina Bakardjieva Engelbrekt, *Toward an Institutional Approach to Comparative Economic Law?* in Antonina Bakardijeva and Joakim Nergelius eds *New Directions in Comparative Law* (Cheltenham: Edward Elgar 2010) pointing out the following problems: fallacies in classifying or measuring legal families, legal dynamics and transplants (difficulty of attributing law to legal families), ideal types.

23 Mariana Pargendler, 'The Rise and Decline of Legal Families' (2012) 60(4) *American Journal of Comparative Law* 1043, 1045 and Nuno Garoupa and Mariana Pargendler, 'A Law and Economics Perspective on Legal Families' (2014) 7(2) *European Journal of Legal Studies* 33.

24 Pargendler (n23), 1046.

25 Ibid. 1073.

26 H. Patrick Glenn, 'Are Legal Traditions Incommensurable?' (2001) 49 *American Journal of Comparative Law* 133; Mathias M. Siems, 'Numerical Comparative Law: Do We Need Statistical Evidence in Law in Order to Reduce Complexity?' (2005) 13 *Cardozo Journal of International and Comparative Law* 521; Mathias M. Siems, 'Legal Originality' (2008) 28 *Oxford Journal of Legal Studies* 147; Holger Spamann, 'Large-Sample, Quantitative Research Designs for Comparative Law?' (2009) 57 *American Journal of Comparative Law* 797.

27 See more in Tom Ginsburg, 'Why Do Countries Adopt Constitutional Review?' (2014) 30 *Journal of Law, Economics and Organization* 587; Davide Ticchi and Andrea Vindigni, 'Endogenous Constitutions' (March 2010). Available from https://works.bepress.com/davideticchi/. Bernd Hayo and Stefan Voigt, 'Endogenous Constitutions: Politics and Politicians Matter, Economic Outcomes Don't' (2013) 88 *Journal of Economic Behavior and Organization* 47.

28 For an English overview, see Claude Ménard and Bertrand du Marais, 'Can We Rank Legal Systems According to Their Economic Efficiency?'(2008) 26 *Washington University Journal of Law and Policy* 55. Other critiques in the same vein include Ruth

V. Aguilera and Cynthia A. Williams, '"Law and Finance": Inaccurate, Incomplete, and Important' (2009) 6 *Brigham Young University Law Review* 1413 (proposing economic sociology as a better methodology) and Pierre Legrand, 'Econocentrism' (2009) 59 *University of Toronto Law Journal* 215 (criticizing the excessive economic focus of the legal origins literature). For a response to these critiques, see Gillian Hadfield, 'The Strategy of Methodology: The Virtues of Being Reductionist for Comparative Law' (2009) 59 *University of Toronto Law Journal* 223.

29 Gillian K. Hadfield, 'The Levers of Legal Design: Institutional Determinants of the Quality of Law' (2008) 36 *Journal of Comparative Economics* 43.

30 Nuno Garoupa and Andrew P. Morriss, 'The Fable of the Codes: The Efficiency of the Common Law, Legal Origins and Codification Movements' (2012) *University of Illinois Law Review* 1443.

5 The evolution of the common law and efficiency

What is the meaning of common law?

Besides the obvious lack of detailed explanation of the theory, its bases and outcomes as discussed in chapters 1 and 2, other issues arise with the content of the legal origins theory. Let us imagine that all the above-mentioned issues would not exist. Does the theory carry with it some other foundation flaws?

One of such problems with the economic literature on this topic is the confusing use of 'common law' to describe different legal features. In 1856 the common law has been simply described as '[t]hat which derives its force and authority from the universal consent and immemorial practice of the people'.[1] A simple modern definition from *Black's Law Dictionary* 2014 simply describes it as '[t]he body of law derived from judicial decisions, rather than from statutes or constitutions'.[2]

Our definition is following this simplistic form as the standard one: 'a body of general rules prescribing social conduct', originally enforced by the ordinary royal courts in England (as opposed to equity, local, or ecclesiastical courts), and characterized by the development of its own principles in actual legal controversies (through the use of judicial precedents), by the procedure of trial by jury, and by the doctrine of the supremacy of law (all agencies of government are subject to court review and compelled to follow legal procedure such as due process).[3] The common law developed and so did the definitions, trying to capture its essence. As an example, let us take a look at the following:

> The ancient law of England based upon societal customs and recognized and enforced by the judgments and decrees of the courts. The general body of statutes and case law that governed England and the American colonies prior to the American Revolution. The principles and rules of action, embodied in case law rather than legislative enactments, applicable to the government and protection of persons and property that derive their authority from the community customs and traditions that evolved over the centuries as interpreted by judicial tribunals.[4]

This definition shows that the development of the common law changed its nature. In the thirteen colonies the development of the common law followed different paths that were not only distinct from the original English common law, but also between the colonies themselves.[5] Unlike in the English tradition, colonial law tended to be codified with the exception of Maryland.[6] Some of these colonial law codes departed significantly from the English common law, in particular in New England (Massachusetts most importantly) and Pennsylvania.[7] In other cases, such as Virginia and the Carolinas, English law was influential in adjudication, for example, but subsidiary to colonial law.[8] In a show of the general respect for self-rule, appeals from colonial courts to the English Privy Council were generally not allowed and drastically discouraged.[9] Thus, it was not English common law, but these local departures that shaped the general reasoning and principles of American common law.[10] Therefore even when talking about American common law, there is no unitary concept of the phenomena that could carry the weight of the one-size-fits-all concept.

All the same, it is unquestionable that the English common law influenced and formed the American common law.[11] No doubt there were political and economic factors helping the convergence with English law.[12] But the very different realities faced by the colonies and the metropolis led to significant departures from the English common law in many fields of law, notably property (including inheritance, alienability and trespass), contracts (including remedies and restitution), torts (from negligence rules to proximate causation), slavery laws and family (marriage and divorce rules).[13]

In fact, we could describe the early stages of American common law more accurately by recognizing the existence of thirteen different legal systems with different degrees of codification (quite significant in Massachusetts due to the Puritan distrust of lawyers).[14] English law was important more in the sense of providing a background and legal method than the elements of substantive law.[15] The situation changed in the eighteenth century, when colonial courts became more English in nature.[16] The British developed more interventionist methods of governing the colonies, which resulted in a strengthening of the executive power.[17] Although the British did not opt for a model of giving the courts in London jurisdiction over colonial courts, the role of the Privy Council was enhanced.[18] Colonial statute law was subject to review by the Privy Council.[19] A process of convergence in substance and style was imposed by the Privy Council.[20] Yet frequent delays and the permissive attitude of the Council (more political than truly judicial) undermined the possibility of full conformity of the colonial courts by the time of independence.[21]

Today, the common law in the US states differs in composition from one state to another. The most important observation is that it is not composed only of judicial decisions, but that statutes today also have an important role. As an illustration, let us take a look at three US states: New York, Louisiana and California. New York was originally a Dutch colony and began the codification of its law in the nineteenth century, leaving behind the codification of a law of general obligations that shows how civil law tradition continued in New York. The state of California has codified its common law (California codes in the nineteenth century), replacing the pre-existing system based on Spanish civil law, but retained the concept of community property derived from civil law. Should this imply that this concept is more efficient than the solutions of the common law? Posnerian approaches did not answer that question. Finishing this brief illustrative overview with Louisiana (otherwise excluded due to its specialty from our analysis), one can notice that it actually has its Louisiana Civil Code. Once again, this does not go in line with the theory on legal origins. This code is based on principles of law from continental Europe with some common law influences and as such persists in the Louisiana law system.

Similar trends of development are found in other common law jurisdictions, such as Australia, Canada, New Zealand and Ireland.[22] Their common law systems have been formed and shaped by the English common law. Yet local determinants and different historical events have affected important departures from the original law in significant areas.[23]

If local determinants shape the common law differently, the literature needs to address these particularities that have been largely ignored. The consequence is that there might be no single efficient outcome, thus undermining the 'one-size-fits-all' theory of the legal origins literature. Alternatively, it could be the case that the common law only converges to efficiency under some conditions that could be undermined by specific local determinants.

It seems clear that the common law adjusts to local determinants that vary across the world, therefore producing different doctrines and legal outcomes. This argument contributes by further casting doubt on the selected 'cherry-picking' methodology of the legal origins literature and the corresponding macro-generalizations. If the common law of a certain field, such as property or contracts, produces significantly different doctrines depending on local determinants, it is unclear which 'cherry-picked' doctrine is being used to distinguish the common law from other legal families. A light version of the 'one-size-fits-all' theory could suggest that not all rules across common law jurisdictions are actually efficient. Rather, the legal origins literature proposes that the model for creating rules (but not the substantive laws) is the same across common jurisdictions and more efficient than alternative methods (even if the substantive rules may turn out to be very different looking). The problem with this version is, as we show, the indeterminacy of the outcome. The empirical analysis employed by the 'one-size-fits-all' theory focuses on the rules and doctrines, not the mechanisms.

Quite importantly, we want to focus on asymmetric developments of the common law based on case law, rather than those imposed by statute law. For example, there are significant differences in the way common law jurisdictions treat class or group litigation. However, many of these differences are explained by statute law in the United States,[24] Australia,[25] England and Wales[26] and Canada,[27] notwithstanding the significant influence of judge-made law.[28] A similar remark can be made in the context of the common law presumption of individual rights, with Australia being the outstanding exception,[29] while the United Kingdom,[30] United States,[31] Canada[32] and New Zealand[33] have developed important statutory law.

Property law is a remarkable illustration in this context.[34] Created by courts, property rights are always conveyed as a result of an exchange among people. It is both important to determine who owns the right to control a certain resource or a specific good and to discover the ability of the owner to transmit or limit the use of the resource. The problem is common to movable as well as real estate property. In the latter case, given the costs and the use as collateral in modern economics, it is more relevant to identify the owner and to know the legal status of the property in order to protect purchasers. It is easy to understand that, in every legal system, a great part of the rules governing real estate property is intended to promote a reliable way to convey and exchange property. The main goal involves the protection of potential purchasers and their abilities to get loans. As it is well known, real estate security and stability play a role of the utmost importance in economic growth.

The Torrens system of land registration was developed in the nineteenth century in Australia.[35] It was later implemented in New Zealand, Western Canada and other British possessions.[36] However, in many areas of Britain (mainly Scotland and Ireland), Canada and the United States, a traditional system of land recording has persisted.[37] The main difference between these two title systems is that registration generates a provisional priority for claims, whereas recording does not.[38] As a consequence, in the case of a valid claim by a third party, the current owner keeps the land under registration (the rightful claimant gets compensated by the public system of registration), whereas under recording the current owner loses the land (but usually receives compensation if an insurance mechanism is in place).

Recording and registration have been shaped by judge-made law, but the Torrens system was not introduced by the courts.[39] A similar analysis can be developed for adverse possession. The traditional common law approach to adverse possession has been changed by important legislation in the United Kingdom,[40] where significant differences are now observable.[41]

One immediate explanation for observed differences across common law countries could be the asymmetric role of statute law.[42] Even if statutory law prevails over judge-made law in all common law jurisdictions today, such preponderance varies. In that case, the potential inefficiencies could be possibly unrelated to the common law itself, in particular, if we take the view suggested by legal economists that statute law is intrinsically less efficient than judge-made law.[43] In fact, one of the main arguments for the superiority of judge-made law is that private interests are more likely to capture the legislature than the courts, although we think that such argument is debatable at the theoretical as well as at the empirical level.[44] From our perspective there is no systematic evidence that rent-seeking is more persistent with the legislature than with the courts, since demand and supply conditions are fundamentally different.[45] Moreover, courts and legislators have their own goals in terms of enhancing their influence, which complicates the potential effect of private interests in law-making.[46] However, we recognize that using statute law as the main source to explain differences across common law jurisdictions would be self-defeating in the eyes of those who believe in the efficiency hypothesis of the common law.

Our approach does not mean we reject the view held by other legal scholars that the interaction of judge-made law and statute law might actually improve rather than hurt convergence for efficiency. Most likely an appropriate mix of judicial precedent and statute rule should be the efficient outcome.[47] Otherwise, given the growth of statute law in all common law jurisdictions, the obvious conclusion should be that the overall efficiency has been reduced considerably in recent times.[48] The argument that the efficiency of the common law is not really demand-side induced (i.e., through the incentives provided by litigation) but supply-side induced reinforces this drastic conclusion. According to this account, as observed before, the historical competition between common law and equity courts was the driving force; once these courts were merged and a monopoly had been achieved, the efficiency forces had lost stimulus.[49]

Still, for the purpose of clarifying our arguments, both in the theoretical discussion as well as in the examples we consider, we have intentionally excluded the role of statute law as far as we can. In other words, we focus primarily on doctrinal and rule diversity fostered by judge-made law.

Our discussion focuses on 'pure' common law jurisdictions such as the United States (neglecting Louisiana for the purpose of our discussion), Canada (excluding Quebec in our analysis), England and Wales, Ireland, Australia or New Zealand. The reason is to make sure the observed relevant differences are not induced by other elements of the legal system that prevail in 'mixed' jurisdictions such as Israel or South Africa (by no means do we underplay the potential influence of Quebecois civil law in Canadian common law).[50] At the same time, we prefer to frame our discussion in the context of those jurisdictions rather than the American states (as well as the Canadian provinces or the Australian states) because it seems more appropriate when having in mind the current mathematical models of the evolution of the common law. Clearly there are important variations in common law within the American states. At the same time, given that they belong to a political union and are subject to identical federal law as well as the jurisdiction of the US Supreme Court, there is an inevitable contamination effect that shapes convergence. It seems to us that jurisdictions that are not part of the same political and institutional unit provide for a better testing of our predictions.

Saying that, let us take a closer look to the arguments given for the efficiency of common law and forget for a second that not even the term itself has a clear definition. What are the causes of efficiency ascribed to the common law?

Why efficient common law

If the common law is to be efficient, certainly there must be strong reasons to support such an assertion. As noted before, one immediate explanation for the Posnerian hypothesis is that judges have a preference for efficiency.[51] If judges pursue efficiency as the goal of law, it is no surprise that the common law is efficient. However, this does not seem to be a persuasive argument. Why would judges care about efficiency rather than equality or other possible goals? Moreover, from an empirical perspective, we now have an extensive literature showing that ideology and other significant non-efficiency oriented variables play a major role in explaining judicial behaviour.[52] From a comparative perspective, the argument is also unpersuasive, since there seems to be no strong reason for why American judges would care more or less about efficiency than Canadian or Australian judges.

A second possible explanation is that efficiency is promoted by the prevalence of precedent (more efficient rules are more likely to survive through a mechanism of precedent).[53] Another explanation relies on the incentives to bring cases and the role of court litigation (since inefficient rules are not welfare-maximizing).[54] Nevertheless, these two explanations require a particular mix of case litigation in order to derive an efficient outcome. In particular, variations concerning the prevalence of precedent (that traditionally was stronger in England than in America) and the mix of case litigation could explain differences across the common law world. However, it is unclear if such variations or differences indicate that the common law only achieves efficiency under some specific conditions.

In fact, the search for a more convincing setup for the efficiency of the common law hypothesis has sparked important academic work. This literature essentially looks at how litigation improves the law, or some specific legal doctrine, taking into consideration that only a self-selected number of cases is actually litigated.[55]

The efficiency of the common law must be unequivocally related to the observation that litigation follows private interests.[56] Presumably it is true that bad rules are challenged more often than good rules, so naturally court intervention could improve the overall quality of the law. However, this line of reasoning is not without problematic shortcomings. It could be that the subset of cases that are actually litigated are not representative enough to trigger the necessary improvements, hence biasing evolution of legal rules against efficiency.[57] Furthermore, the emergence of efficiency in common law necessarily depends on a number of factors in the evolutionary mechanism, namely initial conditions, path dependence and random shocks.[58]

More recent work has provided a more comprehensive analytical framework to show under which precise mathematical conditions the evolution of the common law tends toward efficiency.[59] For example, even if judges are ultimately efficiency-seeking, precedent and overruling must be balanced in an appropriate way. A judicial bias might distort the law in the short run but at the same time provide the mechanism to improve the law in the long run, depending on critical elements of the evolution of the common law.[60] The possibility of selective litigation driven by private interests (likely to be misaligned with social interests) just makes the whole process more complex; convergence to efficiency is still possible as long as the biases are not overwhelming to the point of hurting the likelihood that inefficient laws will be more often litigated. Naturally strong precedent could be socially valuable if judges are significantly biased.[61]

If the Posnerian hypothesis is true, at least in the long run, rules that do not promote efficient results should be repealed in any common law jurisdiction.[62] Therefore, the central question is why common law jurisdictions have different doctrines in property, contracts and torts. When common law jurisdictions have a different doctrine in a particular relevant area of the law there could be two possible interpretations. The first interpretation is that the evolution of the common law to efficiency generates multiple equilibria. Therefore, each common law jurisdiction is potentially efficient and there are multiple efficient doctrines depending on local determinants. The second interpretation is that there is one and only one efficient equilibrium, and many common law jurisdictions simply fail to achieve it. We use the analytical models developed in the law and economics literature to identify the two possibilities and understand the implications.[63] Quite the contrary, these possibilities are not mutually exclusive. Hence, we conclude this Part by addressing the more realistic model that allows for the coexistence of both interpretations.

When the fundamentals of the model vary across jurisdictions, we could have multiple efficient equilibria. Each jurisdiction converges to an efficient doctrine and rule in the long run, but they are not the same because there are local conditions and aspects that vary significantly.[64]

The process of convergence to an efficient and stable equilibrium is based on selective litigation. The selective litigation could be different across the common law world in response to local conditions and asymmetric shocks caused by local historical events. The circumstances under which an original rule or doctrine in common law is applied in different jurisdictions varies dramatically, since different sets of cases are litigated. As a consequence, the conditional probability that a given inefficient rule is challenged is not the same.[65] Therefore, the evolution of the common law follows different paths. Of necessity, the pattern of path dependence will be consistently diverse leading to distinctive, but equally efficient, equilibria.[66]

Legal historians seem to perceive this effect in explaining the development of the English common law and the early American common law. Colonial law responded mainly to local problems and conditions faced by the European settlers, which were radically distinct from the realities of the English (and possibly the Irish) society.[67] However, relying on these differences that resulted in dissimilar selective litigation to explain significant variations across the American colonies, Canada, Australia and New Zealand seems less persuasive.

If there are multiple efficient equilibria due to distinctive selective litigation, the implications for the efficiency hypothesis of the common law are twofold. First, the 'one-size-fits-all' approach taken by the legal origins literature is undermined. There is no single or unique common law as assumed by that literature, but a multiplicity of common law systems. The focus on a particular doctrine or rule is not very informative concerning the efficiency of legal arrangements, since the appropriate response varies across the common law jurisdictions. Second, under the efficiency hypothesis of the common law, when a particular jurisdiction adopts the common law approach as suggested by the legal origins literature, the 'efficient' outcome is difficult to predict since particular local determinants might generate yet another completely new path.[68]

Multiple efficient equilibria signal that the world is more complex than the approach taken by the legal origins literature. A mistaken focus on legal outcomes hides the interaction of different local determinants with dissimilar path dependencies. Under the current analytical models, the assessment of legal outcomes concerning efficiency cannot be disentangled from the varying selective litigation in each jurisdiction; certainly that has not been the approach taken by the legal origins literature.

Another possibility is that there is a single efficient equilibrium. Immediately we recognize that some common law jurisdictions seem to develop the efficient doctrine or rule, whereas others do not. There are several possible explanations for why some common law jurisdictions fail to achieve efficiency.

One possible reason is that the distribution of relevant attributes of judicial preferences is not the same.[69] For example, the proportion of pro-plaintiff and pro-defendant judges varies, with the consequence that the number of pro-efficient rule judges is different, and in some cases insufficient to force convergence to efficiency.[70] Alternatively, the biases favouring certain types of rules vary across the population of judges. In particular, more polarized judiciaries are less likely to achieve efficient doctrines and rules.[71] Efficiency requires a more unbiased judiciary and therefore more judicial polarization leads to significant social welfare losses.[72] At the same time, a varying degree of influence of special-interest groups in judicial politics could contribute toward shaping behaviour in different ways that preclude some particular institutional arrangements from converging to efficiency.[73] Moreover, the concern about the future evolution of the law measured by a specific discount factor (for example, how forward looking judges are) plays an important role in explaining efficiency. A judiciary too focused on the short run and less so on the long run is less likely to generate an efficient legal outcome.[74]

There are good reasons to think that the distribution of relevant judicial attributes varies across common law jurisdictions, with the US judiciary probably being distinct from other common law judiciary.[75] From the perspective of the current available models, these differences could be a by-product of specific appointment mechanisms (that can polarize the judiciary or empower the influence of special-interest groups), judicial tenure (including mandatory retirement), promotion and retention policies, or recruitment strategies (a wider or narrower pool of potential candidates to the judiciary that breeds different degrees of heterogeneity in the bench). The most interesting implication of these considerations is that most probably the US is the jurisdiction with the least likely judiciary (within the common law jurisdictions) to promote efficient legal outcomes according to the mathematical models.

Another reason for why some common law jurisdictions fail to converge to efficiency is the role of precedent. If the cost of changing precedent is too low, judicial biases prevail and the legal outcome in the long run is unlikely to be efficient.[76] To put it differently, the judicial gains from getting closer to an efficient outcome are insufficient when it is easy to change precedent.[77] Consequently, the value of precedent plays an important role. Frequent defections from an established precedent undermine the process of converging to efficiency. In the context of the common law jurisdictions, there are important differences on how precedent is respected. US judges seem to be more willing to change precedent than the English judiciary as a general observation (with particular reference to horizontal precedent).[78] Again, if that is so, it seems likely that the American common law is less likely to achieve efficiency than the English common law, due to the relative ease of changing a precedent in American common law compared with English common law.

There are important implications from a model with a single efficient equilibrium. The most immediate is that if doctrines and rules vary across the common law jurisdictions, only one is efficient and the remaining failed to achieve it. Given that the initial condition was presumably the same (English law) we can conclude that some judicial intervention helps efficiency but, under different conditions, judicial intervention is detrimental.

Another inference from this model is that the common law is efficient only under certain conditions. Not all common law jurisdictions satisfy those conditions, both in terms of judicial attributes and cost of changing precedent. A comparison across common law jurisdictions demands a focus on the local judiciary and the stickiness of precedent.

The consequences for the legal origins literature are quite obvious. A single efficient equilibrium supports the idea of a 'one-size-fits-all' approach. However, the details are the conundrum in this context as what we have is the potential efficiency of a specific common law system. At the same time, there are clear prescriptions to improve the performance of each common law institutional arrangement, in terms of reforming the judiciary and the preponderance of precedent.

Combining the two possible models we have considered so far, we derive a more complex and realistic overview of the efficiency hypothesis of the common law. First, there is not a single efficient rule or doctrine, but a multiplicity of possible equilibria depending on selective litigation. Second, for each specific set of selective litigation, there is no guarantee that there will be convergence to efficiency, depending on judicial attributes and the preponderance of precedent.

To sum up, different authors have been building on the legal origins theory. As seen, the reasons as to why the American judges should have a natural preference for efficiency is unknown, as it is also unknown why other common law judges are lacking this preference. Also due to the biases of private incentives for litigation, it is not always the case that the efficient rule would prevail through the mechanism of precedent. Moreover, if the Posnerian hypothesis would hold, there would be prevalence of the same doctrines in same fields of law throughout the common law world, while in reality it seems that there exist multiple equilibria, not allowing a 'one-size-fits-all' approach. And last but not least, it has been shown that where the cost of changing a precedent is low, individual interests can bias the outcomes of litigation thus leading away from efficiency. Ironically, in the common law world, the precedent is comparatively easiest to change in the US.

That being said, the most important consequence is that the identification of the efficiency of the common law is much more intricate and multifaceted than anticipated by the literature. A mere comparison of how a specific predicament is addressed in each jurisdiction, as inspired by the legal origins literature, is not only insufficient but also likely to produce gross mistakes. The observation that each jurisdiction provides a different legal outcome says very little about efficiency due to the existence of multiple efficient solutions and because the variables that determine efficient outcomes vary. A proper analysis requires a clear understanding of local determinants, including judicial preferences, before we can jump to the conclusion that the common law is undoubtedly efficient.

Next we introduce relevant examples to illustrate the difficulties of the exercise. They show that once we depart from a general and undefined efficiency hypothesis of the common law into specific doctrines and rules, the analysis is complex, dense and less clear than the legal origins literature portrays. They also illustrate situations where multiple equilibria are more likely and where a single efficient equilibrium is probable.

We look at illustrative examples starting with tort law, generally speaking, then the particularities of defamation and professional responsibility, followed by cost rules in civil litigation (we argue this is a good candidate for multiple equilibria), and conclude with civil juries (the diversity in the use of civil juries seems to provide an excellent example of an inefficient equilibrium). These examples are not exhaustive or suggested to be representative. Our choice of tort and procedure is merely practical. The differences across common law jurisdictions on tort law and procedure are widely documented. At the same time, they easily relate to theoretical and empirical literature in law and economics that is helpful in assessing the plausibility of multiple efficient equilibria in the context of our discussion.

Tort law

Tort law is one of the fields of law in which differences among common law jurisdictions are more acute and significant. Even though they have an identical origin in the old English common law, general theories on recovery and judgments have evolved in a different way in each and every jurisdiction. Clearly, all of them have in common the same foundational legal authorities. For abnormally dangerous things or activities, all quote the doctrine stated in *Rylands v. Fletcher*,[79] an English decision rendered by the House of Lords in 1868. The case established law according to which a person who carries out an activity that substantially increases the probability of causing harm to others assumes a stricter standard of liability.[80] In the same vein, common law jurisdictions share the doctrine of *Davies v. Mann*.[81] This is another important English case that established the last clear chance doctrine, the most commonly accepted modification of the contributory negligence rule.[82] Likewise, it is needless to point out the great influence of the English admiralty law in the general evolution of the common law of torts.

Although the old common law has influenced all jurisdictions, it has also grandfathered different and variable trends, especially regarding the compensation of personal injuries.[83] While some jurisdictions still apply the general doctrines in a very similar way to their original conception, others have established new doctrines based on punitive damages or even damages calculated by caps.[84]

More specifically, while Canada, Ireland, Australia and – obviously – the United Kingdom have remained quite similar to the principles that inspired the function of tort law institutions in early English law; other jurisdictions, in particular New Zealand and the US, have experienced a deep transformation in the last decades.[85]

In the vast sectors of the US law culture, tort law has come under fire in the last couple of years.[86] The biases of the civil juries in tort cases, and the alleged excessive amounts established in the context of punitive damages, have promoted a general sense that a reform of the tort system is needed.[87] Some US jurisdictions have been named as 'judicial hellholes' by the American Tort Reform Association,[88] a movement that reports on spurious litigation in tort and promotes legal change in order to contain the increase of damages.

In New Zealand, almost all personal injury damages actions are now barred from reaching the courts. Since 1974, damages are decided by a government agency, the Accident Compensation Corporation, which promotes no-fault benefits for victims of accidents.[89] The tasks of the agency have been expanded to include more areas of the law in the last decades. Its origins are linked to the damages due from labour accidents. Like in the vast majority of jurisdictions (both common law and civil law), damages are calculated on an objective basis previous to the claim being filed. For example, New Zealand is establishing objective criteria for medical malpractice claims.[90] Damages are calculated by caps that standardize compensations and bar the discussion on damages and compensation in the courts of law.[91]

New Zealand has embraced a pure compensation system that completely replaced the common law remedies for tort, an approach pursued by other jurisdictions for workers' compensation only.[92] In fact, the Woodhouse Report, so called in honour of the president of the commission that launched the reform, began its discussion focused on the alternative ways to improve workers' and road accident victims' compensation schemes. At that point, the members of the commission realized that spreading the system for all personal injuries caused by accidents and criminal offences would reduce administrative costs.[93] The most profound reform of the common law of torts began as a political decision, but did not find antagonism among the judiciary, and it has been fairly consensual in New Zealand.[94]

The above-mentioned examples show how deep the differences are in tort law within the common law jurisdictions.[95] As we have mentioned before, it is debatable that tort law evolves to efficiency.[96] The different trends followed in the common law jurisdictions make it even harder to talk about a common law of torts (since they are remarkably different by now) and which of them is more appropriate from an economic perspective. The creative developments in New Zealand make this jurisdiction a clear outlier at the moment. Yet, from an economic perspective, there are significant advantages (legal certainty, reduction of litigation costs) and important disadvantages (inappropriate compensation, ossification of the law). It is unclear if the New Zealand reform is efficient inasmuch as the common law principles of tort law could be inefficient. In the following two subsections, we look at further examples in detail.

Defamation law

Defamation is a tort concerned with the publication of false defamatory statements about another person that tend to injure a person's reputation by degrading them in the opinion of their neighbours or to make them ridiculous.[97] Defamation can be divided into libel, in which publication is in a permanent form, and slander, which is oral publication.[98] To find an action for publication, the offending matter must be published with a third party.[99]

The common law provides for the establishment of a defamation claim in tort and the applicable defences.[100] However, judge-made law has significantly changed defamation law in common law jurisdictions. In the United States, libel law came under the influence of federal constitutional law after 1964. In that year, in the case of *New York Times v. Sullivan*,[101] the United States Supreme Court ruled that state laws making newspapers strictly liable for false defamatory statements were generally inconsistent with First Amendment rights of freedom of press.[102] The reasoning was as follows: if public officials are allowed to recover damages for any false and defamatory statement, regardless of the level of care taken, then newspapers will be discouraged, or chilled, from printing stories on matters of public interest. To moderate this chilling effect, the Supreme Court imposed a standard of proof in libel cases involving public official plaintiffs which was much higher than that used in most state courts at the time.[103]

The United Kingdom followed a different approach. The Defamation Act 1952 restated and clarified the common law principles of defamation.[104] A strict liability rule operates and damages are usually compensatory. In the particular case of libel, no damage to the plaintiff has to be proved. In slander, special damage must be proved except where the statement is an imputation of a criminal offence.[105] With the exception of the special damage, the Defamation Act of 1952 was repealed and replaced by the Defamation Act 1996 and the relevant parts of the Electronic Commerce Regulations 2002.[106] The new law was partially developed under the influence of previous controversial case law and intended to limit claims of a tort of defamation.[107]

Other common law jurisdictions have restated the common law principles of the tort of defamation in their legislation, such as the New Zealand Defamation Act 1992, the Irish Defamation Act 1961 and Defamation Act 2009, or the Australian model Defamation Act 2006.[108] These statutes were deeply influenced by controversial case law such as *Oceanic Sun Line Special Shipping Co. v. Fay* or *Gutnick v. Down Jones & Co.* in Australia.[109] In Canada, defamation law is regulated by provincial statutes that have been shaped by legal doctrines developed by the Supreme Court of Canada in salient cases such as *Hill v. Church of Scientology*.[110]

The significant difference between the United States and the remaining common law jurisdictions is the more generous treatment of defendants in the United States.[111] Libel law deals with a clash of two important values: freedom of speech and freedom from defamation. The proper balance between these goals has been debated in economics. It is unclear if the American model is closer to efficiency than the traditional common law approach.[112] Significant differences between the political system, the media industry, or the prevalence of corruption could suggest that the different approaches can be equally efficient depending on local needs.

Professional responsibility

Under the traditional principles of the common law, lawyers acting as advocates have professional immunity and could not be sued for professional responsibility. The immunity for misconduct tort litigation was established in the eighteenth century. Although the scope and justification for the immunity have evolved in case law due to public policy considerations, it was largely confirmed by the House of Lords in *Rondel v. Worsley*[113] and in *Saif Ali v. Sydney Smith Mitchell & Co.*[114] However, more recently, in *Arthur J. S. Hall & Co. v. Simons*, the House of Lords has significantly eroded the immunity to the point of effective abolishment by reinforcing the professional duty to the court.[115] Unlike the House of Lords, the Australian High Court has confirmed the professional immunity for lawyers, as seen in the important case of *D'Orta-Ekenaike v Victoria Legal Aid*.[116] The professional immunity was never recognized in Canada or in the United States. The main reasoning seems to be that there was no formal distinction between barrister and solicitor in these jurisdictions.

Although there are important differences in the structure of the legal profession in common law jurisdictions, they do not seem to be a persuasive argument to justify the different approaches from an efficiency perspective. It seems unlikely, from an economic perspective, that a no liability rule can be efficient. Therefore, not only does the traditional principle of immunity in common law seem unlikely to be efficient, but this also presents a case of inefficient persistence.

Cost rules in civil litigation

The allocation of costs is critically important for civil litigation. In the United Kingdom, the so-called English rule largely prevails.[117] The general rule is that the unsuccessful party will be ordered to pay the costs of the successful party. However, the award of costs at the conclusion of a case is at the discretion of the court. The discretion extends to whether the costs are payable by one party to another, the amount of those costs, and when they are to be paid. In deciding what order they need to make about costs, the court must give regard to all the circumstances including the conduct of the parties.[118]

In Canada, a rule of shifting of costs in litigation by which the loser in a civil lawsuit must compensate the winner for a portion of the latter's legal costs is also applied.[119] Generally speaking, costs do not amount to full compensation, and the proportion of the winner's legal bill covered by an award of costs typically decreases over time as legal fees continue to rise. Yet, since the nature of the rule remains informal and discretionary, litigants cannot fully rely upon its application when deciding whether or not to litigate. The decision to award costs is made at the conclusion of the action, which means a plaintiff still risks a substantial loss if the claim is ultimately unsuccessful.

'Both Australia and New Zealand follow the English civil rule … unless the successful party has in some way behaved improperly in the course of the litigation.'[120] The same applies in Ireland where, as a general rule, the loser pays the costs.[121] The right to an order in these circumstances is not absolute, however, and the court can exercise its discretion based upon the facts of the particular case.[122]

In contrast, in the United States each side generally bears its own costs, the so-called American rule.[123] Notice that the English rule prevailed in the US until the nineteenth century.[124] The American rule was developed as lawyers gained the power to negotiate their contracts in a fairly unregulated framework. It became dominant by the 1850s.[125] However, variants of a loser-pays-all rule still exist in federal civil procedure, namely Rule 68 of Federal Rules of Civil Procedure by which a party might have to reimburse the costs of the other party if the award is less than a rejected offer of settlement (a similar rule has been adopted in England and Wales after the Woolf reforms to civil procedure in 1996).[126] In many cases, the court is allowed to order the losing side to pay the legal costs of the winner; however, this is often subject to the discretion of the judge.[127]

There is an extensive literature on the American versus English rule in civil litigation. There is no consensus in the theoretical literature concerning the overall effect of shifting litigation costs.[128] The controversial topics include the extent to which shifting costs promote settlement,[129] enhance civil litigation,[130] favour more meritorious claims or decrease the number of nuisance lawsuits.[131] The results depend on asymmetric information,[132] risk aversion,[133] strategic positions[134] and other procedural rules.[135] The empirical and experimental literature does not seem to be conclusive.[136]

It is clear that the English rule tends to prevail in common law jurisdictions.[137] The United States deviated from the general trend in the nineteenth century.[138] The evolution of the rules concerning cost allocation could be a good example of multiple equilibria where the final outcome is determined by local determinants. The different structure of the legal markets, the practice of contingency fees (largely confined to the United States until recently),[139] and the needs posed by different rates of growing civil litigation could easily determine the appropriate use of different rules.[140]

Civil juries

Whereas the United States continues to use civil juries, their use has drastically declined over the past decades in the UK,[141] Australia,[142] New Zealand,[143] Canada[144] and Ireland.[145] 'Until the mid-nineteenth century, jury trial was the only form of trial in the common law courts, and until the early twentieth century, it continued to predominate for civil as well as criminal cases.'[146] The civil jury has largely disappeared in England and Wales, and the right to a jury in criminal cases has been significantly reduced as well.[147] In the UK '[t]oday, less than one percent of civil trials are jury trials'; such trials are limited to cases of libel and slander, fraud, malicious prosecution and false imprisonment as defined by the Supreme Court Act.[148] However, even in these limited cases, the trial judge has the discretion to deny the right to a jury if the case is particularly complex.[149] In *Ward v. James*, the Court of Appeal held that a single judge should hear all personal injury litigation unless there were special considerations.[150]

In England and Wales, civil juries are most frequently used in defamation cases. The frequent large awards decided by juries have been a matter of controversy. In 1995, the Court of Appeal in *John v. MGN Ltd.* ruled to curb excessive jury awards by altering jury instructions.[151] The Defamation Act of 1996 further curtailed the role of juries in libel cases, establishing a summary procedure whereby judges, not juries, can dispose of libel claims up to £10,000.[152] The Court of Appeal has also issued guidelines on the directions given to juries assessing damages in cases of wrongful arrest and malicious prosecution brought against the police.[153] Case law, reinforced by specific statute law, has essentially eliminated civil juries in the UK.[154]

In Australia, civil juries are still available in all of the states except South Australia, but are rarely used outside New South Wales and Victoria.[155] Furthermore, trial by jury in Australian civil matters has substantially declined in the last decades.[156] Today, Australian judges decide the large majority of civil cases.[157] It is rare, particularly following recent legislative reforms to tort law, for a jury to decide a civil case.[158] In Australian jurisdictions without legislative mandates abolishing juries in civil actions, legislation 'tends to allow the parties to opt for trial by jury … but maintains the court's discretion to control that choice'.[159] '[T]he courts have discretion to order jury trials for certain types of lawsuits, such as defamation, fraud, false imprisonment, malicious prosecution, and motor vehicle accidents.'[160] However, courts will rarely order a jury trial in strictly commercial disputes.[161] Australian jury trials are 'almost always reserved for more serious criminal matters'.[162] The profound difference in the way the US and Australia treat civil juries has been recognized by the literature.[163]

Civil juries are also rarely used in New Zealand.[164] The Supreme Court Act of 1841 established a right to jury trial in all civil cases.[165] In 1860, the Supreme Court ruled that parties could consent to having judges alone determine issues of fact.[166] From 1862 to 1977, 'minor jury sittings' (began with six jurors but shifted to four jurors prior to abolishment) were established for cases under £100 in value and were used at the discretion of the trial judge.[167] Currently, the High Court provides the right to civil jury trial in most cases at the request of either party.[168] Nevertheless, civil jury trials are so rare in practice that the Department for Courts no longer even keeps statistics on it. When implemented, civil juries are largely confined to defamation and personal injury cases, and are sometimes used in actions against governmental bodies.[169] However, 'New Zealand effectively abolished juries in personal injury cases in 1972 by adopting a no-fault compensation system that replaced litigation.'[170] In New Zealand, we could say that there is still a theoretical right to a jury trial in civil cases, but such right is rarely used in practice.[171]

As with other common law jurisdictions, civil juries exist on the periphery in Canada.[172] In some Canadian jurisdictions the use of civil juries has been highly curtailed while in other jurisdictions it has been outright abolished.[173] Canadian courts retain the right to interfere with the judgment of a jury once it has reached a verdict;[174] however, judges usually show great deference to the jury's verdict.[175] Juries are most often used in motor vehicle accident litigation and are frequently sought by institutional parties.[176] They are most prevalent in Ontario.[177] Courts most often strike civil juries if the factual issues of a case are unduly complex.[178] Additionally, the Supreme Court held in 1997 that judges have the discretion to determine whether to strike a civil jury if jurors can reasonably infer that a defendant was insured against a finding of liability.[179]

Civil jury trials have almost entirely disappeared in Ireland.[180] In the Republic of Ireland, civil juries are retained only for libel, slander, assault and false imprisonment cases; in Northern Ireland, civil juries are retained only for libel claims or if the judge accedes to a particular application.[181]

It is clear that the US has not followed the path of other common law jurisdictions in eliminating or drastically reducing the use of civil juries.[182] In fact, legal scholars have suggested the advantages of following the Australian or the English models in the United States.[183] The economic literature has considered the multiple implications of using civil juries, including legal certainty, the impact on awards, the development of procedural rules and the potential additional litigation costs.[184] Both at the theoretical and at the empirical level, it is unclear if the use of civil juries is economically efficient.[185]

More fundamentally, it is difficult to see how civil juries should be efficient in the United States but not in the other common law jurisdictions nowadays. It is clear that all common law jurisdictions initially had civil juries, and most have abandoned such institution because of legal costs and uncertainty. However, given the role of civil juries in the United States, it is unclear how the efficiency hypothesis could explain the different paths taken. It could be the case that the US is behind the other jurisdictions in the evolutionary process, and so it is just a matter of time that civil juries are abolished in the United States. Such would be the most reasonable prediction under the efficiency hypothesis of the common law.

Brief examples to guide to more detailed overviews

All of the brief examples given already clearly broke the logic behind the legal origins theory or have at least shown severe deficiency of its reasoning. In the continuance of the book, the approach taken is still going to be our own 'cherry-picking' of examples showing that maybe the American common law solution in a specific law field is not the most efficient one and that more efficient solutions can be found either in the rest of the common law world or in civil law world (mixed legal systems are deliberately excluded from this deeper overview to avoid additional lack of clarity). The following chapters are our own version of 'cherry-picking'.

Notes

1 John Bouvier, 'Common law' in *A Law Dictionary, Adapted to the Constitution and Laws of the United States* (1856). Online at www.republicsg.info/dictionaries/1856_ bouvier_6.pdf (accessed 1 October 2015).

2 Bryan A. Garner ed., 'Common law' in *Black's Law Dictionary* 10th ed (Eagan, MN: Thomson Reuters 2014).

3 Arthur R. Hogue, *Origins of the Common Law* (Bloomington: Indiana University Press 1966) 178–179.

4 Jeffrey Lehman and Shirelle Phelps, 'Common law' in *West's Encyclopedia of American Law* 2nd ed. (Detroit: Gale 2005).

5 Paul Samuel Reinsch, 'English Common Law in the Early American Colonies'. Bulletin of the University of Wisconsin 1899, 9.

6 Ibid. 53.

7 Nevertheless, there were standard provisions to ensure that colonial law would not be radically in conflict with English common law. Ibid.

8 Ibid. 54.

9 But see Mary Sarah Bilder, *The Translantic Constitution* (Cambridge, MA: Harvard University Press 2009) (describing Rhode Island's struggle to prevent the private appeal to the Privy Council).

10 Reinsch (n5) (noting that the circumstances of the colonies influenced them to depart from English common law); Lawrence M. Friedman, *A History of American Law* (New York: Simon & Schuster 2005).

11 John H. Langbein et al., *History of the Common Law* (Austin and New York: Wolters Kluwer Law & Business 2009) 874.

12 Ibid. 878.

13 Ibid. 873–921 (cataloguing the differences between the English and American common law by subject).

14 Friedman (n10). Many colonial statutes have not been studied by modern legal historians because they have disappeared. See, for example, the recent discovery of the Laws and Liberties of Massachusetts from 1648.

15 Ibid.

16 Ibid.

17 Ibid.

18 Ibid.

19 Ibid.

20 Ibid.

21 Ibid.

22 Hogue (n3) 235 (explaining that the common law is the root of the legal systems in all past British colonies).

23 Matthew Hale, *The History of the Common Law of England* 2nd ed. (London 1716) 114–121 (detailing the specific divergence of the Irish common law from that of the English).

24 Federal Rules of Civil Procedure, r.23.

25 Federal Court of Australia Act 1976 (Cth) pt IV(a). This part came into force by the passage of the Federal Court of Australia Amendment Act 1991 (Cth) s3.

26 Civil Procedure Rules 1998, S.I. 1998/3132, r. 19-19.15 (UK).

27 Class Proceedings Act, S.O. 1992, c. 6 (Can.); Class Proceedings Act 1996, R.S.B.C. 1996, c. 50 (Can.); Class Actions Act, S.N.L. 2001, C-18.1 (Can.); Class Actions Act, S.S. 2001, c. C-12.01 (Can.); Class Proceedings Act, S.M. 2002, c. 14 (Can.); Class Proceedings Act, S.A. 2003, c. C-16.5 (Can.).

28 The English case law concerning the application of civil procedure rules to group litigation was influential, among others, in Australian and Canadian statute law going back to the Supreme Court of Judicature Act 1873. The role of the English Court of

Appeal in developing appropriate procedures for multi-party litigation has been noticed by legal scholars. In this matter, see the discussion by Rachael Mulheron, *The Class Action in Common Law Legal Systems* (Oxford: Hart 2004).

29 Australia has no Bill of Rights. Individual rights have been expanded by the case law of the Australian High Court. See generally James Allan, 'You Don't Always Get What You Pay For: No Bill of Rights for Australia' (2010) 24 *New Zealand Universities Law Review* 179.

30 Bill of Rights, 1689, 1 W & M., c. 2 (Eng.); Human Rights Act, 1998, c. 42 (Eng.); see David Erdos, 'Ideology, Power Orientation and Policy Drag: Explaining the Elite Politics of Britain's Bill of Rights Debate' (2009) 44 *Government and Opposition* 20 (framing the Human Rights Act as part of a Bill of Rights agenda).

31 US Const. amends I–X.

32 Canadian Charter of Rights and Freedoms, Part I of the Constitution Act, 1982, being Schedule B to the Canada Act, 1982 (UK).

33 New Zealand Bill of Rights Act 1990; see David Erdos, 'Aversive Constitutionalism in the Westminster World: The Genesis of the New Zealand Bill of Rights Act' (1990) (2007) 5 *International Journal of Constitutional Law* 343 (demonstrating the aversive model of constitutionalization of rights in established democrasies); David Erdos, 'Judicial Culture and the Politicolegal Opportunity Structure: Explaining Bill of Rights Legal Impact in New Zealand' (2009) 34 *Law and Social Inquiry* 95 (arguing that New Zealand bill of rights case law has been largely confined to criminal or freedom of speech issues, a culture established from British judicial norms).

34 Robert Cooter and Thomas Ulen, *Law and Economics* 3rd ed. (New York: Pearson Addison Wesley 2011).

35 Theodore B.F. Ruoff, *An Englishman Looks at the Torrens System* 1–2 (Sydney: Law Book Company of Australasia 1957).

36 John L. McCormack, 'Torrens and Recording: Land Title Assurance in the Computer Age' (1992) 18 *William Mitchel Law Review* 61, 95.

37 Ibid. 129.

38 Benito Arruñada, 'Property Enforcement as Organized Consent' (2003) 19 *Journal of Law, Economics and Organisation* 401, 420–421; Benito Arruñada and Nuno Garoupa, 'The Choice of Titling System in Land' (2005) 48 *Journal of Law and Economics* 709, 711; Benito Arruñada, 'Property Titling and Conveyancing' in Harry Smith and Ken Avotte eds *Research Handbook on the Economics of Property Law* (Cheltenham: Edward Elgar, 2010) 237, 240–244; see also chapter 6 on titling of property.

39 Ruoff (n35).

40 Land Registration Act, 1925, 15 & 16 Geo. 5, c. 21 (Eng.); Land Registration Act, 2002, c. 9 (Eng.).

41 Thomas J. Miceli and C.F. Sirmans, 'An Economic Theory of Adverse Possession' (1995) 15 *International Review of Law and Economics* 161 (discussing the underlying economic rationale of the adverse possession doctrine); Todd Barnet, 'The Uniform Registered State Land and Adverse Possession Reform Act, a Proposal for Reform of the United States Real Property Law' (2004) 12 *Buffalo Environmental Law Journal* 1 (analysing the Land Registration Acts of 1925 and 2002 and other aspects of the UK registration system); Barbara Bogusz, 'Bringing Land Registration into the Twenty-First Century: The Land Registration Act 2002' (2002) 65 *Modern* Law *Review* 556 (analysing the effects of the Land Registration Act of 2002); Amnon Lehavi, 'The Property Puzzle' (2008) 96 *Georgetown Law Journal* 1987 (analysing the effects of the Land Registration Act of 2002).

42 Priya P. Lele and Mathias M. Siems, 'Diversity in Shareholder Protection in Common Law Countries' (2007) Spring 2007 *Journal of Institutional Comparisons* 1, 3 (discussing differences in shareholder protection law among common law countries).

43 Andreas Engert and D. Gordon Smith, 'Unpacking Adaptability' (2009) *Brigham Young University Review* 1533, 1562 (stating that 'increasing the adaptability of the law

– and hence making the law less predictable – is not a general policy advice to enhance overall efficiency').

44 Michael A. Crew and Charlotte Twight, 'On the Efficiency of Law: A Public Choice Perspective'. *Public Choice*, vol. 66, 1990; Paul H. Rubin, 'Micro and Macro Legal Efficiency: Supply and Demand' (2005) 13 *Supreme Court Economic Review* 19. The most devastating criticisms are Gordon Tullock, *The Case Against the Common Law* (Durham: Carolina University Press 1997) and Gordon Tullock, Rent-Seeking and the Law'. In *The Selected Works of Gordon Tullock: The Organization of Inquiry, Volume 3*, Charles K. Rowley ed. Liberty Fund 2005. See also Todd J. Zywicki, 'The Rise and Fall of Efficiency in the Common Law: A Supply-Side Analysis' (2003) 97 *Northwestern University Law Review* 1551 (examining comparative attributes of the common and civil law systems).

45 Mark W. Crain and Robert D. Tollison, 'Constitutional Change in an Interest-Group Perspective'. *Journal of Legal Studies*, vol. 8, 1979; Mark W. Crain and Robert D. Tollison, 'The Executive Branch in the Interest-Group Theory of Government'. *Journal of Legal Studies*, vol. 8, 1979; William M. Landes and Richard A. Posner, 'The Independent Judiciary in an Interest-Group Perspective' (1975) 18 *Journal of Law and Economics* 875; Fred S. McChesney, 'Rent Extraction and Rent Creation in the Economic Theory of Regulation'. *Journal of Legal Studies*, vol. 16, 1987; Thomas W. Merrill, 'Does Public Choice Theory Justify Judicial Activism After All?' *Harvard Journal of Law and Public Policy*, vol. 21, 1997; Thomas W. Merrill, 'Institutional Choice and Political Faith'. *Law and Social Inquiry*, vol. 22, 1997, p. 959.

46 A. C. Pritchard and Todd J. Zywicki, 'Finding the Constitution: An Economic Analysis of Tradition's Role in Constitutional Interpretation'. *North Carolina Law Review*, vol. 77, 1999.

47 For a technical model, see Giacomo A. M. Ponzetto and Patricio A. Fernandez, 'Case Law Versus Statute Law: An Evolutionary Comparison' (2008) 37 *Journal of Legal Studies*; Carmine Guerriero, 'Democracy, Judicial Attitudes, and Heterogeneity: The Civil Versus Common Law Tradition' (2009) University of Cambridge Working Paper 0917.

48 Paul H. Rubin, 'Why is the Common Law Efficient?' (1977) 6 *Journal of Legal Studies* 51 (noting that the common law might have been more efficient in the past when the organization of interests was more costly, but not now). Also, these arguments face a serious challenge in areas such as antitrust law that might be statute law precisely because the traditional principle of fair trade in common law did not protect market competition and courts were excessively deferential to monopolies. Fred S. McChesney and William F. Shughart, *The Causes and Consequences of Antitrust* 2nd ed. (Chicago: The University of Chicago Press 1995).

49 Zywicki (n44). A more comprehensive discussion is provided by Daniel Klerman in 'Jurisdictional Competition and the Evolution of the Common Law' (2007) 74 *University of Chicago Law Review* 1179, who argues that institutional structures that were able to produce more innovative legal rules tended to prevail in English law. However, he challenges the efficiency of the supply-side competition between these courts. He notes that there was a pro-plaintiff bias that generated certain (hardly efficient) rules given the way judges were paid. Important changes to judicial compensation and salaries corrected the pro-plaintiff bias in the nineteenth century.

50 Esin Örücü ed., *General Introduction: Mixed Legal Systems at New Frontiers* in *Mixed Legal Systems at New Frontiers* (London: Wildy, Simmonds & Hill 2010); Vernon Valentine Palmer, 'Two Rival Theories of Mixed Legal Systems'. In *Mixed Legal Systems at New Frontiers*, Esin Örücü ed. (London: Wildy, Simmonds & Hill 2010).

51 Richard A. Posner, 'Utilitarianism, Economics, and Legal Theory' (1979) 8 *Journal of Legal Studies* 10.

52 Barry Friedman, 'The Politics of Judicial Review' (2005) 84 *Texas Law Review* 257 (arguing political ideology of members of the judiciary help explain judicial behaviour).

53 Rubin (n48).
54 George L. Priest, "The Common Law Process and the Selection of Efficient Rules" (1977) 6 *Journal of Legal Studies* 65.
55 Francesco Parisi and Vincy Fon, *The Economics of Lawmaking* (Oxford and New York: Oxford University Press 2009); Rubin (n47); Maxwell L. Stearns and Todd J. Zywicki, *Public Choice Concepts and Applications in Law* (St Paul, MN: West 2009); Robert Cooter and Lewis Kornhauser, 'Can Litigation Improve the Law Without the Help of Judges?' (1980) 9 *Journal of Legal Studies* 139 (arguing 'the law can improve by an unguided evolutionary process'); Vincy Fon and Francesco Parisi, 'Judicial Precedents in Civil Law Systems: A Dynamic Analysis' (2006) *International Review of Law and Economics* 26; Vincy Fon and Francesco Parisi, 'Litigation and the Evolution of Legal Remedies: A Dynamic Model' (2003) *Public Choice* 116, 2003; Vincy Fon, Francesco Parisi and Ben Depoorter, 'Litigation, Judicial Path-Dependence, and Legal Change' (2005) *European Journal of Law and Economics*, vol. 20); John C. Goodman, 'An Economic Theory of the Evolution of the Common Law' (1978) 7 *Journal of Legal Studies* (arguing that the probability that a particular litigant will win a favourable decision); Peter R. Terrebonne, 'A Strictly Evolutionary Model of Common Law' (1981) *Journal of Legal Studies* 10; Georg von Wangenheim, 'The Evolution of Judge-Made Law' (1993) 13 *International Review of Law and Economics* 381; Anthony Niblett et al. 'The Evolution of a Legal Rule'. *Journal of Legal Studies*, vol. 39, 2010, 325 (showing empirically that rules fail to converge with significant inconsistencies across states); Anthony Niblett, 'Do Judges Cherry Pick Precedents to Justify Extra-Legal Decisions? A Statistical Examination' (2010) 70 *Maryland Law Review* 234. A critical view of this literature is provided by Frederick Schauer, *Thinking Like a Lawyer: A New Introduction to Legal Reasoning*. Cambridge, MA: Harvard University Press 2009.
56 William M. Landes and Richard A. Posner, 'Adjudication as a Private Good' (1979) 8 *Journal of Legal Studies* 235.
57 Gillian K. Hadfield, 'Bias in the Evolution of Legal Rules' (1992) 80 *Georgetown Law Journal* 583, 584–585.
58 Mark J. Roe, 'Chaos and Evolution in Law and Economics' (1996) *Harvard Law Review* 109. For an explanation of path dependence theory, see Oona A. Hathaway, 'Path Dependence in the Law: The Course and Pattern of Legal Change in a Common Law System' (2001) 86 *Iowa Law Review* 601, 606 (outlining what she considers to be three strands of path dependency).
59 Nicola Gennaioli and Andrei Shleifer, 'The Evolution of Common Law' (2007) 115 *Journal of Political Economy* 43 (discussing following precedent, distinguishing and overruling as leading or not leading to efficiency).
60 Ibid.; Nicola Gennaioli and Andrei Shleifer, 'Overruling and the Instability of Law' (2007) *Journal of Comparative Economics* 35 (noting that although inefficient laws are more easily litigated and replaced, which improves efficiency over time, this effect can still reduce the long run volatility of the law because it cannot ensure convergence to efficiency); Anthony Niblett, 'Case-By-Case Adjudication and the Path of the Law' (2013) 42 *Journal of Legal Studies* 303 (arguing that polarization concerning precedent depends on judicial preferences, cases that get litigated, and cost of adhering to precedent).
61 Thomas J. Miceli, 'Legal Change: Selective Litigation, Judicial Bias, and Precedent' (2009) *Journal of Legal Studies* 38 (stating 'binding precedent plays no role in enhancing the efficiency of the law, but it can play a potentially important role in limiting the ability of biased judges to drive the law in an inefficient direction'); Luca Anderlini, Leonard Felli and Alessandro Riboni, *Why Stare Decisis?* (CEPR Discussion Paper, 2013) (arguing that stare decisis guarantees ex ante efficient decisions).

62 Gennaioli and Shleifer, 'The Evolution of Common Law' (n59) 45 (referring to the Priest (n54) and Rubin (n53) theories 'that disputes involving inefficient legal rules are more likely to be taken to court' and thus replaced 'by better ones over time').

63 In particular, we focus on Gennaioli and Shleifer, 'The Evolution of Common Law'; Miceli (n61); Ponzetto and Fernandez (n47); Georg von Wangenheim, 'The Evolution of Judge-Made Law' (1993) 13 International Review of Law and Economics Wangenheim (n55).

64 Gennaioli and Shleifer, 'Overruling and the Instability of Law' 323–347.

65 Miceli (n61) (arguing that the rate of creation of inefficient rules depend upon the strength of governing precedent); Wagenheim (n55).

66 Roe (n58) 647–648 (stating that in applying a path dependency model when there are multiple results, one outcome need not be better than the other because each could have been good enough, where the author uses a weak-path dependency to indicate multiple equilibria); Hathaway (n58) 634–635 (using the rule against perpetuities as an example of how the rule developed because of history and that its existence, while explainable, was not necessarily a unique equilibrium, indicating that given other circumstances an equally efficient alternative rule may have been possible).

67 Friedman (n10).

68 Hathaway (n58) 634–635 (in explaining how the rule of perpetuities exemplifies increasing path dependence, stating that despite being able to ascertain how the rule of perpetuities came into existence, the final outcome selecting that approach would have been difficult to predict in advance and that given another set of historical circumstances the rules governing inheritance could have developed differently).

69 Gennaioli and Shleifer 'Overrruling and the Instability of Law' 316 (claiming that the optimal [efficient] legal rule should be unbiased and that unless all judges are unbiased [which they are not], judge made law cannot achieve this outcome).

70 Miceli (n61) 163 (assuming that precedent continues to be non-binding, judges will decide cases that come before theme based solely on these preferences, meaning pro-plaintiff judges will uphold pro-plaintiff cases and overrule pro-defendant cases and vice versa).

71 Gennaioli and Shleifer, 'Overruling and the Instability of Law' 311, 315.

72 Ibid. 313.

73 Ponzetto and Fernandez (n47) 398 (identifying that judges are subject to additional pressures like those from interest-groups and as a result their decisions are more variable than legislation because they depend not only society-wide general and special interests but also the interests of the parties appearing before them in court).

74 Ibid. 382 (claiming that in the long run the dynamic properties of judge-made law make it an average more efficient).

75 Richard A. Posner, *Law and Legal Theory in England and America* (Oxford and New York: Clarendon Press; Oxford University Press), comparing and contrasting the divergent evolution of the common law in the UK and US).

76 Miceli (n61) 165 ('[T]he law will converge on the efficient rule (or diverge from it) more quickly as (…) the cost of abandoning precedent (…) becomes small.'); Gennaioli and Shleifer, 'The Evolution of Common Law' 56 (arguing that if the initial legal precedent is precise, the subsequent legal rules become more, and not less precise).

77 Wagenheim (n55).

78 Posner (n75); E.M. Wise, 'The Doctrine of Stare Decisis' (1975) 21 *Wayne Law Review* 1043, 1045–1046 (finding that the American judiciary congratulated itself from moving away from the strict English doctrine of precedent); Thomas R. Lee, 'Stare Decisis in Historical Perspective: From the Founding Era to the Rehnquist Court' (1999) 52 *Vanderbilt Law Review* 647, 664 n.84 (explaining that the US Supreme Court would have the power to overrule itself on the horizontal plane).

79 *Rylands v. Fletcher* [1868] 3 L.R.E. & I. App. 330 (H.L.).

80 For a general explanation on *Rylands v. Fletcher*, and other English cases related with the origins of the strict liability doctrine, see W. Page Keeton et al., *Prosser and Keeton on the Law of Torts* 5th ed. (St Paul, MN: West 1984) 545–548.

81 *Davies v. Mann*, (1842) 152 Eng. Rep. 588 (Ex.).

82 Keeton et al. (n80) 462–464 (laying out the affirmative defence of the last clear chance doctrine).

83 Sheila A.M. McLean ed., *Compensation for Damage: An International Perspective* (Aldershot and Brookfield VT: Dartmouth 1993) (giving general background on the law of damages); Bernard A. Koch and Helmut Koziol (eds), *Tort and Insurance Law Vol. 4: Compensation for Personal Injury in a Comparative Perspective* (Wien and New York: Springer 2003) (same); see also Jeffrey O'Connell and David Partlett, 'An America's Cup for Tort Reform? Australia and America Compared' (1988) 21 *University of Michigan Journal of Legal Reform* 443, 445–454 (detailing the different avenues of tort reform).

84 Ibid. 133.

85 For a general explanation of the evolution of the system, see G. Edward White, *Tort Law in America: An Intellectual History* (Oxford: Oxford University Press 2003). For a survey of New Zealand tort law, see Rosemary Tobin and Elsabe Schoeman, 'The New Zealand Accident Compensation Scheme: The Statutory Bar and the Conflict of Laws' (2005) 53 *American Journal of Comparative Law* 493 (detailing the New Zealand accident compensation scheme).

86 Frank B. Cross, 'Tort Law and the American Economy' (2011) 96 *Minnesota Law Review* 28, 47–50 (noting that the studies of tort law reform have been flawed). For a survey of judicial opinions on tort law and reform, see Larry Lyon et al., 'Straight from the Horse's Mouth: Judicial Observations of Jury Behavior and the Need for Tort Reform' (2007) 59 *Baylor Law Review* 419.

87 For example, see *Liebeck v. McDonald's Restaurants*, No. CV-93-02419, 1995 WL 360309 (N.M. Dist. Aug. 18, 1994), the so-called 'McDonald's Coffee Case', where the jury awarded $2.86 million to a woman who burned herself with a cup of coffee she purchased at a McDonald's restaurant. See Thomas S. Ulen, 'The View from Abroad: Tort Law and Liability Insurance in the United States' in Gerhard Wagner, ed. *Tort Law and Liability Insurance* 207–238 (Wien and New York: Springer 2005).

88 American Tort Reform Association, Judicial Hellholes (2011), available at www.judicialhellholes.org/wp-content/uploads/2011/12/Judicial-Hellholes-2011.pdf (accessed 1 October 2015). The American Tort Reform Association was founded in 1986. Since then it has focused on promoting the control – even statutorily – of the damages award to plaintiffs in civil tort cases.

89 A complete study on the initial consequences of the reform can be found in Geoffrey Palmer, *Compensation for Incapacity: A Study on Law and Social Change in New Zealand and Australia* (Oxford: Oxford University Press 1979).

90 See generally Peter H. Schuck, 'Tort Reform, Kiwi-Style' (2008) 27 *Yale Law and Policy Review* 187 (describing New Zealand's tort reform).

91 Some jurisdictions, including civil law countries, have followed the New Zealand example. Spain, for instance, has since 1995 implemented a statutory cap system for calculating damages for personal injuries caused by traffic accidents. Jesús Pintos Ager, 'Damage Schedules and Tort Litigation in Spain' (2003) InDret, Working Paper No. 131. Online at www.raco.cat/index.php/InDret/article/download/82542/107388 (accessed 1 October 2015).

92 Palmer (n89); Schuck (n90) 188; Tobin and Schoeman (n85) 493.

93 Australia tried to enact a similar system. The proposal was more comprehensive than the New Zealand system, since Australians aimed to cover the whole population from any personal injury. The proposal never reached the necessary parliamentary majority. For more references on the New Zealand reform and the Australian proposals, see John

G. Fleming, *The Law of Torts* 8th ed, (Sydney: LBC Information Services 1992) 374–378.
94 Ibid.
95 McLean (n83); Koch and Koziol eds (n83).
96 Yoram Barzel, 'Dispute and its Resolution: Delineating the Economic Role of the Common Law' (2000) 2 *American Law and Economics Review* 255 (noting that tort law, as a means to delineate rights, tends towards inefficiency but never maintains a constant level of efficiency).
97 Henry Coleman Folkard, *The Law of Slander and Libel* 7th ed. (London: Butterworth 1908).
98 Ibid.
99 Ibid.
100 Restatement (Second) of Tort: Witnesses in Judicial Proceedings § 558 (2011).
101 376 US 254 (1964).
102 Ibid. 279.
103 Ibid. 283.
104 Defamation Act, 1952, 15 & 16 Geo. 6 & 1 Eliz 2, c. 66, § 6 (Eng.). Online at http://www.legislation.gov.uk/ukpga/Geo6and1Eliz2/15-16/66 (accessed 1 October 2015).
105 Milner Frankum et al. 'United Kingdom' in Andrew B. Ulmer ed. *Media, Advertising and Entertainment Law* (London: Multilaw 2010) ch. 36).
106 Ibid.
107 Defamation Act, 1996, c. 31 (Eng.), www.legislation.gov.uk/ukpga/1996/31/contents accessed 1 October 2015; Electronic Commerce Regulations (2002) S.I. 2002/2555 (UK). Online at www.legislation.gov.uk/uksi/2002/2013/contents/made (accessed 1 October 2015).
108 Defamation Act 1992 (NZ). Online at www.legislation.co.nz/act/public/1992/0105/latest/DLM280687.html (accessed 1 October 2015); Defamation Act 2009 (Act No. 31/2009) (Ir.). Online at http:/www.irishstatutebook.ie/pdf/2009/en.act.2009.0031.pdf (accessed 1 October 2015); *Defamation Act 2006* (NT) s. 25 (Austl.). Online at www.austlii.edu.au/au/legis/nt/num_act/da2006802006145/ (accessed 1 October 2015).
109 *Oceanic Sun Line Special Shipping Co. v Fay* [1988] 165 CLR 197 (Austl.); *Down Jones & Co. v Gutnick* [2002] HCA 56 (Austl.).
110 *Hill v. Church of Scientology of Toronto* [1995] 2 S.C.R. 1130 (Can.).
111 Frankum et al. (n105). In the same volume and volume 2 of Ulmer, ed., *Media, Advertising and Entertainment Law*, see also the following chapters: Northcote and Schiffmann, 'Canada'; Kirton and Paul, 'Australia'; Fawcett et al., 'New Zealand'; Kelly et al., 'Ireland'.
112 Nuno Garoupa, 'The Economics of Political Dishonesty and Defamation' (1999) 19 *International Review of Law and Economics* 167 (arguing that tabloids are better informed than society and can provide an auditing role in preventing political corruption so long as they are deterred from defamation); Nuno Garoupa, 'Dishonesty and Libel Law: The Economics of the "Chilling" Effect' (1999) 155 Journal *Institutional and Theoretical Economics* 284 (arguing that the plaintiff winning a defamation suit is not a problem if the media can distinguish between honesty and dishonesty); Oren Bar-Gill and Assaf Hamdani, 'Optimal Liability for Libel' (2003) 2 *B.E. Journal of Economic Analysis and Policy* 1 (demonstrating an alternative model of libel); Manoj Dalvi and James F. Refalo, 'An Economic Analysis of Libel Law' (2008) 34 *Eastern Economic Journal* 74 (describing another model of liberal law); Ido Baum et al., 'Reporter's Privilege and Incentives to Leak' (2009) 5 *Review of Law and Economics* 701 (demonstrating that reporters have demonstrable incentives to report leaks, as defamation lawsuits rarely succeed).
113 [1960] 1 A.C. 191 (H.L.).
114 [1980] A.C. 198 (H.L.).

115 *Arthur J. S. Hall & Co. v Simons* [2002] 1 A.C. (H.L.) 615.
116 *D'Orta-Ekenaike v Victoria Legal Aid* [2005] 223 HCA 12 (Austl.).
117 See also discussion by Paul Hopkins, *The Success of Mediation in the UK* in *ADR Client Strategies in the UK: Leading Lawyers on Preparing Clients, Navigating the Negotiation Process, and Overcoming Obstacles* (Eagan, MN: Aspatore 2008).
118 Civil Procedure Rules and Directions, pt 44 (UK). Online at www.justice.gov. uk/courts/procedure-rules/civil/pdf/parts/part44.pdf (accessed 2 October 2015).
119 Rules of Civil Procedure, R.R.O. 1990, Reg. 194, r 57 (Can.).
120 Ian Freckelton, 'Judicial Attitudes Toward Scientific Evidence: The Antipodean Experience' (1997) 30 *University of California Law Review* 1137, 1142.
121 Melody Buckley, *Civil Procedure and Practice: An Introduction* (Dublin: Thomson Round Hall 2004).
122 Ibid.
123 Langbein et al. (n11) 1050.
124 Ibid.
125 Ibid.
126 Harry Woolf, *Access to Justice* (New York: Oxford University Press 1996).
127 For some versions of fee-shifting in specific circumstances, see Federal Rules of Civil Procedure 11(c)(4), 26(g)(3), 37, 41(d)(1).
128 Hugh Gravelle, 'The Efficiency Implications of Cost-Shifting Rules' (1993) 13 *International Review of Law and Economics* 3, 3; see also Ronald Braeutigam, Bruce Owen and John Panzar, 'An Economic Analysis of Alternative Fee Shifting Systems' (1984) 47 *Law and Contemporary Problems* 173, 181–182 (explaining that the glut of assumptions required by fee-shifting analysis make reaching clear conclusions difficult).
129 Lucian Arye Bebchuck, 'Litigation and Settlement Under Imperfect Information' (1984) 15 RAND *Journal of Economics* 404.
130 Steven Shavell, 'Suit, Settlement, and Trial: A Theoretical Analysis Under Alternative Methods for the Allocation of Legal Costs' (1982) 11 *Journal of Legal Studies* 55, 72 (explaining that British and American rules may interact with other factors to influence 'social welfare relative to the goal of achieving an appropriate volume of litigation').
131 Lucian Arye Bebchuck and Howard F. Chang, 'An Analysis of Fee Shifting Based on the Margin of Victory: On Frivolous Suits, Meritorious Suits, and the Role of Rule' (1996) 25 *Journal of Legal Studies* 371, 372.
132 Keith N. Hylton, 'An Asymmetric-Information Model of Litigation' (2002) 22 *International Review of Law and Economics* 153.
133 Shavell (n130) 57–58.
134 Hylton (n132) 154.
135 Brian G.M. Main and Andrew Park, 'The Impact of Defendant Offers into Court on Negotiation in the Shadow of the Law: Experimental Evidence' (2002) 22 *International Review of Law and Economics* 177, 178 (noting the existence of procedural arrangements specifically designed to influence settlement that can influence the choice of cost-shifting rule); Jennifer F. Reinganum and Louis L. Wilde, 'Settlement, Litigation, and the Allocation of Litigation Costs' (1986) 17 *RAND Journal of Economics* 557; John C. Hause, 'Indemnity, Settlement, and Litigation, or I'll Be Suing You' (1989) 18 *Journal of Legal Studies* 157; Louis Kaplow, 'Shifting Plaintiffs' Fees Versus Increasing Damage Awards' (1993) 24 *RAND Journal of Economics* 625; A. Mitchell Polinsky and Daniel L. Rubinfeld, 'Optimal Awards and Penalties When the Probability of Prevailing Varies Among Plaintiffs' (1996) 27 *RAND Journal of Economics* 269; A. Mitchell Polinsky and Daniel Rubinfeld, 'Does the English Rule Discourage Low-Probability-of-Prevailing Plaintiffs?' (1998) 27 *Journal of Legal Studies* 519.
136 Compare Edward A. Snyder and James W. Hughes, 'The English Rule for Allocating Legal Costs: Evidence Confronts Theory' (1990) 6 *Journal of Economics and*

Organization 345, 377–378 (concluding that the English rule reduces overall litigation and encourages settlement), and Main and Park (n238) 188 (concluding that the English rule has little impact on 'propensity to settle'), with Brian G. M. Main and Andrew Park, 'An Experiment with Two-Way Offers into Court: Restoring the Balance in Pre-Trial Negotiation' (2003) 30 *Journal of Economic Studies* 125, 139–140 (concluding that English rule may reduce settlement but ultimately has highly variable effects).
137 Herbert M. Kritzer, 'Lawyer Fees and Lawyer Behavior in Litigation: What Does the Empirical Literature Really Say?' (2002) 80 *Texas Law Review* 1943, 1946.
138 Langbein et al. (n11) 105.
139 Martin Davies, 'Time to Change the Federal Forum Nonconveniens Analysis' (2002) 77 *Tulane Law Review* 309, 346.
140 The consideration of variants does not change the conclusions of our analysis. For examples of such variants, consider Janice Toran, 'Settlement, Sanctions, and Attorney Fees: Comparing English Payment into Court and Proposed Rule 68' (2007) 35 *American University Law Review* 301, 304 and 308, citing US Federal Rule 68 and the English practice of payment into court as rules that shift costs based on the failure to achieve settlement; or Bebchuck and Chang (n234) 372, citing Federal Rule 11 as a rule shifting costs based on the margin of victory. Also, the fact that American states have variants of the English rule under some conditions; see for example Main and Park (n136) 178 and n3, does not undermine our conclusion.
141 Sally-Lloyd Bostock and Cheryl Thomas, 'Decline of the "Little Parliament": Juries and Jury Reform in England and Wales' (1999) 62 *Law and Contemporary Problems* 7, 7.
142 Michael Chesterman, 'Criminal Trial Juries in Australia: From Penal Colonies to a Federal Democracy' (1999) 62 *Law and Contemporary Problems* 69, 69 n1.
143 Neil Cameron, Susan Potter and Warren Young, 'The New Zealand Jury' (1999) 62 *Law and Contemporary Problems* 103, 138.
144 W. A. Bogart, '"Guardian of Civil Rights. Medieval Relic": The Civil Jury in Canada' (1999) 62 *Law and Contemporary Problems* 305, 305.
145 John D. Jackson, Kate Quinn and Tom O'Malley, 'The Jury System in Contemporary Ireland: In the Shadow of a Troubled Past' (1999) 62 *Law and Contemporary Problems* 203, 203.
146 Bostock and Thomas (n141) 9.
147 Neil Vidmar, 'A Historical and Comparative Perspective on the Common Law Jury' in Neil Vidmar ed., *World Jury Systems* (Oxford and New York: Oxford University Press 2000) 1, 7; Oscar G. Chase, 'American "Exceptionalism" and Comparative Procedure' (2002) 50 *American Journal of Comparative Law* 227, 288–289.
148 Bostock and Thomas (n141) 13; Marc Galanter, 'The Civil Jury as Regulator of the Litigation Process' (1990) 1990 *University of Chicago Legal Forum* 201, 202 ('In England, a series of restrictions reduced the use of juries from 100 percent of civil trials in 1854 to two percent a century later').
149 Bostock and Thomas (n141) 13.
150 *Ward v. James* [1966] 1 Q.B. 273 (Eng.).
151 [1997] Q.B. 586 (Eng.).
152 Defamation Act, 1996, c. 31, §§ 8–9.
153 *Thompson v. Comm'r of Police of the Metropolis*, [1997] 2 All E.R. 762 (Eng.).
154 Lewis N. Klar, 'The Impact of the U.S. Tort Law in Canada' (2011) 38 *Pepperdine Law Review* 359, 366; see also Senior Courts Act, 1981, § 69 (UK) (limiting trial by jury to judicial acknowledgement of a claim of fraud, libel, slander, malicious prosecution, or false imprisonment). Although the frequency of civil jury trials has been reduced, Scotland utilizes civil juries most frequently. Civil juries were abolished in the Sheriff Court, which is the lower of the civil courts. In the Court of Session, the higher civil court, some civil actions for personal injury damages and defamation are

still tried by jury. Court of Session Act (1988) § 11 (UK). Section 11 replaced its outdated counterpart in the Court of Session Act (1825) § 11 (UK), and removed from the ambit of jury trial a large number of types of actions, which, in practice, never went to a jury. Peter Duff, 'The Scottish Criminal Jury: A Very Peculiar Institution' (1999) 62 *Law and Contemporary Problems* 173, 174.

155 Michael Tilbury and Harold Luntz, 'Punitive Damages in Australian Law' (1995) 17 *Loyola of Los Angeles International and Comparative Law Journal* 769, 775–776.

156 S. Stuart Clark, 'Thinking Locally, Suing Globally: The International Frontiers of Mass Tort Litigation in Australia' (2007) 74 *Defense Counsel Journal* 139.

157 Kylie Burns, 'The Role of the Judiciary: Passive or Active?' (2006) 18(2) *Legaldate* 4, 4 ('Judges now decide the vast majority of court cases in Australia'); Jacqueline Horan, 'Perceptions of the Civil Jury System' (2005) 31 *Monash University Law Review* 120 (noting that '[t]here is an Australia-wide trend of reducing the right to civil jury trial'); Tilbury and Luntz (n155) 776 (stating 'the majority of civil actions [in Australia] do not use juries').

158 Burns (n157).

159 Tilbury and Luntz (n155) 775–776; see also *Gerlach v Clifton Bricks Pty Ltd.* (2002) 2009 CLR 478, 507 (Austl.) (disputing that civil jury trials cost more and take longer).

160 Lucille M. Ponte, 'Reassessing the Australian Adversarial System: An Overview of Issues in Court Reform and Federal ADR Practice in the Land Down Under' (2000) 27 *Syracuse Journal of International Law and Commerce* 335, 340 n38.

161 William Gummow, 'The Injunction in Aid of Legal Rights: An Australian Perspective' (1993) 56 *Law and Contemporary Problems* 83, 85.

162 Burns (n157).

163 Caroline Forell, 'Statutes and Torts: Comparing the United States to Australia, Canada, and England' (2000) 36 *Williamette Law Review* 865, 872 (noting that Australia appears to be headed in the direction of eliminating jury involvement in nearly all tort claims); Steven T. Masada, 'Australia's "Most Extreme Case": A New Alternative for U.S. Medical Malpractice Liability Reform' (2004) 13 *Pacific Rim Law and Policy Journal* 163, 180 and 193 (suggesting that the US legal system should adopt several reforms modeled after the Australian legal system, including the Australian approach to civil juries: 'Australia does not use civil juries and attorneys are compensated according to an hourly wage – two features that help reduce litigation, judicial backlog, and the high costs associated with the American civil system'); Gerald Walpin, 'America's Failing Civil Justice System: Can We Learn from Other Countries?' (1997) 41 *New York Law School Law Review* 647, 652 (comparing the approach of Australian and American legal systems to civil jury trials very briefly).

164 Cameron et al. (n143) 103.

165 Supreme Court Act 1841, § 19 (NZ).

166 Supreme Court Act 1860, § 22 (NZ).

167 Supreme Court Act Amendment Act 1862, § 8 (NZ) ('The following classes of [c]ases may be tried at the "Minor Jury Sittings" [for] [i]nquiries of damages not exceed[ing] One hundred pounds'); *id.* § 10 ('At any such "Minor Jury Sittings" the Judge presiding may try and decide any issue of fact which he is by law empowered to try'); *id.* § 12 ("The Jury at such Sittings shall consist of six Jurors."); Judicature Amendment Act 1977, § 9 ('Juries of 4 abolished').

168 Judicature Act 1908, §§ 19A, 19B (NZ).

169 Neil Cameron et al., 'The New Zealand Jury: Towards Reform' in Vidmar ed., *World Jury Systems*, 167, 178.

170 Scott Brister, 'The Decline in Jury Trials: What Would Wal-Mart Do?' (2005) 47 *Texas Law Review* 191, 194.

171 Cameron et al. (n169) 112.

172 Galanter (n148) 202.

56   *Legal origins in a nutshell*

Bogart (n144) 305; see also Neil Vidmar, 'Foreword' (1999) 62 *Law and Contemporary Problems* 1, 1–2 (recognizing the existence of the civil jury system in Canada).
174 *Babyn v. Patel* [1997] A.J. No. 261 (Alta. QB) (striking the jury because of difficult issues of causation and the likelihood of conflicting expert testimony); *Taguchi v. Stuparyk* [1993] A.J. No. 843 (Alta. Q.B.) (striking the jury because the trial would involve lengthy examination of documents and actuarial reports as well as much conflicting expert testimony).
175 Bogart (n144) 310.
176 Ibid. 318.
177 Ibid. 305.
178 Court Rules Act, B.C. Reg. 168/2009, Rule 12-6(5)(a)(i), (ii) (Can.) (permitting the Court to strike out a civil jury where the 'issues require prolonged examination', 'scientific investigation' or 'are of an intricate or complex character'); Walpin (n163) 652.
179 *Hamstra v. British Columbia Rugby Union*, [1997] 1 S.C.R. 1092, 1096 (Can.) (overturning *Theakston v. Bowhey*, [1951] S.C.R. 679, 683 (Can.), granting judges the discretion to release the jury if the jury can reasonably infer that a defendant is insured against a finding of liability); *Thomas-Robinson v. Song*, [1997] 34 O.R.3d 62 (Ont. Gen. Div.) (holding that the right to challenge potential jurors for cause, whether for racial bias or otherwise, does not exist in civil cases). While questions of law are rarely reserved for judges, Canadian courts often hold that complicated issues of law in a civil case are cause for striking the jury. See, e.g., *MacDougall v. Midland Doherty Ltd.*, [1984] 48 O.R.2d 603 (Ont. H.C.J.) (striking jury); *Fulton v. Fort Erie*, [1982] 40 O.R.2d 235 (Ont. H.C.J.) (striking jury); *Damien v. O'Mulvenny*, [1981] 34 O.R.2d 448 (Ont. H.C.J.) (striking jury).
180 Jackson et al. (n145).
181 Ibid. 203–204 and n3 ('The most significant recent change occurred when personal injury claims were taken out of the control of juries, first in Northern Ireland in 1987 and shortly afterward in the Republic of Ireland in 1988').
182 Vidmar (n147) 3.
183 Walpin (n163) 648–649.
184 Neil Vidmar and Valerie P. Hans, American Juries (New York: Pr)ometheus 2007) 346 (concluding that, on balance, juries are adequate). For a more technical analysis, see Luke M. Froeb and Bruce H. Kobayashi, 'Naive, Biased, Yet Bayesian: Can Juries Interpret Selectively Produced Evidence?' (1996) 12 *Journal of Law, Economics and Organization* 257.
185 Kevin M. Clermont and Theodore Eisenberg, 'Trial by Jury or Judge: Transcending Empiricism' (1992) 77 *Cornell Law Review* 1124; Neil Vidmar, 'The Performance of the American Civil Jury: An Empirical Perspective' (1998) 40 *Arizona Law Review* 849; Roselle Wissler, Michael J. Saks and Allen J. Hart, 'Decisionmaking about General Damages: A Comparison of Jurors, Judges, and Lawyers' (1999) 98 *Michigan Law Review* 751; Cass R. Sustein et al., *Punitive Damage: How Juries Decide* (University of Chicago Press 2002); Joni Hersch and W. Kip Viscusi, 'Punitive Damages: How Judges and Juries Perform' (2004) 33 *Journal of Legal Studies* 1; Seth A. Seabury, Nicholas M. Pace and Robert T. Reville, 'Forty Years of Civil Jury Verdicts' (2004) 1 *Journal of Empirical Legal Studies* 1; Margo Schlanger, 'What We Know and What We Should Know about American Trial Trends' (2006) *Journal of Dispute Resolution* 35; Theodore Eisenberg et al., 'Juries, Judges, and Punitive Damages: Empirical Analyses Using the Civil Justice Survey of State Courts 1992, 1996, and 2001 Data' (2006) 3 *Journal of Empirical Legal Studies* 263.

Part II

Piercing the veil – application of legal origins to specific legal institutes

6 Contrasting common and civil law

Private law

Given the dominance of statute over case law, the interest group or rent-seeking theories reviewed in chapter 3 should apply to civil law (especially French law). However, we have already identified several caveats with this line of reasoning. The pro-market bias of the common law (the idea of some Hayekian bottom-up efficiencies in the English legal system and top-down inefficiencies in the French legal system) might be an important argument, but the existence of some anti-market bias in French law is debatable.[1] It could be that traditional French legal scholarship has been less concerned with efficiency arguments. However, the lack of interest exhibited by French legal scholars concerning pro-market legal policies does not constitute strong evidence that French law itself is contrary to efficiency.[2] The lack of inclination for efficiency exhibited by French legal scholars has little bearing for the efficiency of French law.[3]

Even the thesis that French law is less effective than the common law in protecting property rights from state predation has been disputed.[4] In fact, current models developed to explain these differences have been subject to serious criticism.[5] Stability of the law is another argument in favour of judge-made law with deference to precedent against systematic and chaotic legislative production.[6] In this respect, however, the existence and importance of dissenting opinions cannot be seen as a contribution to the stability of the law. Furthermore, it is not empirically clear that case law is more stable and less ambiguous than legislation.[7] Another possibility is the enhanced willingness in common law jurisdictions to allow choice of law. But globalization of business transactions has exerted enormous pressure for change in civil law jurisdictions in this respect.[8] Overall, it might be that the common law is more efficient and positively correlated with economic growth, but that the causation is definitely under-theorized to a larger extent.[9]

The mechanism for the efficiency of the common law versus French civil law is intrinsically convoluted and debatable.[10] Furthermore, the competition between common law and civil law in hybrid systems does not provide an empirical answer as to which legal system prevails in the long run, because we would expect the most efficient legal system to be chosen by the relevant legal actors in a hybrid system, as we will discuss in chapter 8.[11] Finally, if indeed the common law was more efficient and more conducive to economic growth, the question of how to move from one to the other remains largely unaddressed. Legal culture, rent-seeking and accumulated human capital raise the costs of such transplantation.[12]

The analysis is complicated by the fact that the economic superiority of the common law is now the model for legal reform, as shown in chapter 4, as embodied by the *Doing Business* reports promoted by the World Bank.[13] There are good reasons to be careful about the implications of the *Doing Business* reports in the economy since they could be detrimental.[14] Furthermore, the basic rationale begs for a more theorized framework. The idea that ex ante regulation or administrative intervention always produces inefficient outcomes whereas ex post litigation always produces efficient outcomes is inconsistent with the recognized trade-off between these two alternatives.[15] The choice between ex ante control and ex post liability depends on several possible variables of the economic model, including determination of damages, timing, asymmetric information and enforcement costs. It is here that we identify an efficiency syndrome of the literature on the common law: the suggestion that the common law choice of institutional response is optimal, and therefore the French choice of institutional design is necessarily detrimental. This suggestion cannot hold, because it is unclear from the economic models that one or the other is the appropriate response.[16] Second, the suggestion implicitly assumes that the variables are the same in every jurisdiction and therefore there is only one right answer (a one-size-fits-all approach).[17] The prevailing preference for ex ante administrative intervention in French law, as opposed to the overall preference for ex post litigation in common law, might respond efficiently to different local problems and constraints.

A careful examination of rules and legal institutions shows that the inefficiency hypothesis of French law is not sustainable under the current framework of comparative law and economics, not least because many areas of French law, such as torts, commercial, and administrative review, are judge-made law.[18] Moreover, general cross-country comparisons are informative, but can also be badly formative processes if they are used to inadequately shape legal reform based on misguided and unsafe generalizations.[19]

As we have emphasized before, it is important to bear in mind that our goal is not to argue that French law is more efficient than common law. Our criticism is essentially methodological. Robust micro-based assessments of rules and legal institutions should prevail over macro generalizations that lack a serious theoretical framework. The obsession with the efficiency of the common law should not overcome the detailed study of legal institutions around the world. Successful legal reforms need to address local problems under local restrictions. Legal reforms based on misperceptions and generalizations could be more detrimental than doing nothing.

Surely there are many examples of rules and institutions that are more efficient in the common law world than in the French traditions. They have been successfully identified by the literature we have reviewed.[20] There are also many doctrines in the common law that an efficiency perspective cannot easily explain. There is no doubt that, within each legal system, we can find efficient doctrines as well as inefficient legal rules – but, at the end of the day, the goal must be to identify which legal system performs better overall.

Sophisticated indicators must be constructed in order to understand which legal system performs better overall. These indicators must balance the relevant aspects of substantive law, procedure, enforcement and legal institutions, while also taking local determinants into account. Inevitably, we need a micro theory where aspects and determinants are relevant to support the viability of these indicators. Without such a sophisticated theory, the indicators will be based on a mere 'cherry-picking' of examples and doctrines conveniently assembled to support a particular inclination concerning the relative efficiency of a particular legal system.

Traditional 'cherry-picking' approaches have reinforced the view that the common law is more efficient. But that is only part of the story, and our chapters on contrasting the common and civil law provide the other part. We describe some examples where French law is likely to be more adequate than common law from an efficiency perspective, or at least as efficient.

With no micro theory (and we doubt one can be easily developed), we are left with the alleged superiority of the common law based on mere cross-section regressions. Our examples are sheer illustrations of the methodological problems of such an approach. That is why we have opted for a relatively brief discussion of several relevant examples in multiple relevant fields, rather than a detailed analysis of a particular case.[21] Our examples are intended 'cherry-picking' much in the same way previous authors have defended the superiority of the common law. We believe this 'cherry-picking' exposes the flaws of an incomplete economic analysis.

We discuss two fundamental illustrations that correspond to the two main lines of reasoning against French law.[22] We start with examples that look at substantive law and procedure in the core areas of property, contracts and torts. Economists have argued these are the relevant areas to foster economic growth.[23] Our 'cherry-picking' approach challenges the traditional focus on specific efficiencies of the common law doctrines by presenting alternative efficiencies of French law.

Our second set of examples looks at the organization of the legal system and governance.[24] In particular, they focus on decision-making processes and thus identify the conditions under which the common law courts are more prone to produce efficient case results than French courts.[25]

Bona fide purchase

Consider the following situation: a farmer buys cattle from a person who does not have a good title. The true owner wants the cattle back after this transaction has taken place. At this point, both the farmer, who has paid for the cattle in good faith, and the true owner seem to have strong claims of ownership.

In French law, like most civil law systems, good faith possession of movables produces a good title, even in situations where the *bona fide* purchaser acquires his right from someone without any right (in cases of *adquisitio a non domino*).[26] The traditional common law rule has been that no one can have a better title than the title one rightfully owns (*nemo plus iura in alium transferre potest quam ipse habet* or *nemo dat quod non habet*).[27] Therefore, mere current possession of property is not conclusive of title under English law, although it could be under French law and other civil law systems. Such a rule protects the interests of the current rightful owner against the fraud committed by third parties who sell a good lacking rightful authorization. The rule entitles the owner to recover the property from an innocent purchaser. As a consequence, the innocent purchaser cannot rely on the fact of having acquired the good from a seller under good faith.

In English law, the original owner seems to be in a better position to claim ownership than the farmer; in French law, by contrast, the farmer could have an advantage. These two rules generate a very different ex ante allocation of property rights and incentives. The *nemo dat* rule, followed by traditional English law, avoids theft, since the person who acquires from the thief has no possible action against the true owner's claim.[28] The French rule, which protects the *bona fide* purchaser independently of the origin of the movable, reduces the investigation costs the potential purchaser must carry out.[29] Under French law, the original owner has to bear higher prevention costs to avoid the cattle being taken; otherwise, the likelihood of recovery is low.[30] Under English law, the farmer has to spend more resources in investigating the quality of the ownership status of the seller.[31] When the costs of prevention of theft are high, the English rule (*nemo dat*) is more efficient. By the same token, if the information costs concerning the right of the conveyor are significant, the French solution is more desirable.

In general, we expect prevention costs to be lower than title quality investigation costs.[32] Thus, we could argue that the French rule promotes market exchange, whereas the English rule delays or deters that exchange. This is a good micro example where the French rule is presumably more efficient (or at least more market friendly) than common law.[33]

The effect of such a rule seems to be clear. Under the traditional common law rule, owners can be confident in their ability to recover property that has been conveyed without their allowance.[34] At the same time, potential purchasers of goods have to always be aware of the identity of the seller and the validity of her right to sell.[35] Obviously, the problem is more acute with movable property.

The weaker the protection that the *bona fide* purchaser has, the more important the proof and quality of title is to the purchaser. This increases the cost of each purchase in the economy, which potentially hurts trade. Such effect has forced many common law jurisdictions to restrict the extent to which current owners are protected. The nature of the market and the necessity of conducting quick and secure deals have introduced corrections to the protection of owners, and have effectively brought the common law rule closer to the French solution.

The best example of the aforementioned evolution is provided by section 2-403 of the Uniform Commercial Code ('UCC'). It provides an instructive exception to the historical common law tradition:

1   A purchaser of goods acquires all title which his or her transferor had or had power to transfer except that a purchaser of a limited interest acquires rights

only to the extent of the interest purchased. A person with voidable title has power to transfer a good title to a good faith purchaser for value. When goods have been delivered under a transaction of purchase the purchaser has such power even though

a   the transferor was deceived as to the identity of the purchaser, or
b   the delivery was in exchange for a cheque, which is later dishonoured, or
c   it was agreed that the transaction was to be a 'cash sale', or
d   the delivery was procured through fraud punishable as larcenous under the criminal law;

2   Any entrusting of possession of goods to a merchant that deals in goods of that kind gives him power to transfer all rights of the entruster to a buyer in ordinary course of business.[36]

Therefore, the situation is that only under some special circumstances the rightful original owner is entitled to a claim against the person who bought with good faith.[37] In any other case, the *bona fide* purchaser is protected against the claims from the original owner. Hence, the UCC adopts an exception to the general common law principle. The UCC also seems to arrive at the general solution stated in section 2230 of the French Civil Code, according to which: '[o]ne is always presumed to possess for oneself, and in the capacity of an owner, where it is not proved that one has begun by possessing for another.'[38]

We now add the observation of the legal origins literature to this analysis: the French rule is enforced less effectively than the traditional English rule. The true original owner is the individual who needs an enforceable rule since the buyer has the possession of the good. Therefore, less effective enforcement of the French rule does not generate a major loss of efficiency, whereas more effective enforcement of the English rule increases the costs of investigation for the buyer. In fact, weaker enforcement is not a good method for ranking the efficiency of property law across legal families because it implicitly assumes that the substantive rules are equivalent, and only the degree to which they are enforced makes a difference. As we have seen with the example of *bona fide* purchasing, that is a misguided assumption.

Titling of property

Property rights are conveyed as a result of an exchange among people. As a consequence, it is crucial to determine who owns the right to control a certain resource or a specific good. At the same time, it is important to discover the ability of the owner to transmit or limit the use of the resource. This problem is common to movable property, as well as real estate property. In the latter case, given its costs and use as collateral in modern economics, it is more relevant to identify the owner and to know the legal status of the property in order to protect purchasers.[39] It is easy to understand that, in every legal system, a great part of the rules governing real estate property are intended to promote a reliable way to convey and exchange property.[40] The main goal involves the protection of potential purchasers and their ability to get loans.[41] As it is well known, real estate security and stability play a role of the utmost importance in economic growth.[42]

In this context, another good example in property law of the critical difference between common and civil law systems is the titling system of land recording versus registration.[43] In very broad terms, France uses a recording system, whereas registration prevails in England.[44] The main difference between the two is that registration generates a provisional priority for claims, whereas recording does not.[45] As a consequence, in the case of a valid claim by a third-party, the current owner keeps the land under registration (the rightful claimant gets compensated by the public system of registration), whereas under recording, the current owner loses the land (but usually receives compensation if an insurance mechanism is in place).[46]

In this context, the American case does not provide a good benchmark. Both systems co-exist in the United States (for example, Cook County in the state of Illinois). Each state has adopted a register of deeds that aims to give potential purchasers and lenders constructive notice about the legal status of the property.[47] More generally, the American legal system, based on the general principle of the relativity of titles,[48] does not provide any kind of previous control or examination of the registered deeds.[49] Under the traditional rule of the common law, however, the superiority of one claim to another should be determined by temporal ordering.[50] The situation is quite different in many civil law systems, such as Germany or Spain, where land registries and ex ante controls over the legality and validity of deeds promote a safer system to convey real estate property.[51]

The alleged superiority of the registration system is not immune to criticism. Registration helps property transactions, as well as the use of property as collateral, by reducing uncertainty.[52] However, it is a more expensive and demanding system because the cost of purging titles is not negligible.[53] Consequently, it could be that a more expensive system, such as registration, expels an important fraction of property from the public system. On the other hand, recording is a cheaper titling system, and therefore the fraction of property expelled from the public system is presumably lower.[54] Clearly, there is a trade-off between the assurance of quality of titling in land and the expulsion of property from the public system. From a theoretical perspective, it is not clear which titling system is better for the enforcement of property rights. Given the economic importance of titling systems for property and credit markets, there are good reasons to be cautious about endorsing the view that French law is inadequate.[55] In this context, the pure common law versus civil law distinction does not seem to be a relevant dimension for assessing the quality of titling of property.[56]

Principle of *non-cumul* in torts and contracts

Suppose a certain breach of contract configures a potentially tortious wrongdoing. A relevant legal question is the extent to which this breach of contract can be a cause of action concurrently in torts and contracts.[57] For example, this is the case in situations where breach of contract causes physical or emotional harm to the injured party.[58] Historically, product liability claims have generated the need for such a legal solution.[59] Such situations posed the problem that the existence of a contract might ban the application of tort remedies. Tort remedies were designed for the absence of a previous relation among the tortfeasor and the injured party.[60] At the same time, legal remedies for breach of contract might be insufficient because the physical and emotional harm suffered by the victim is not one of the foreseeable outcomes in the context of a typical contractual relation.[61]

There are a few cases where the injured party can strategically choose to pursue breach of contract under contractual liability or tort liability (for example, in restitution).[62] However, in most cases, when the same harm or impairment can be regarded as either contract or tort, there are no general legal provisions.[63] Nevertheless, a contract cannot always generate a tort claim.[64] For purposes of the present study, we assume that there are particular situations when an injured party could strategically choose between pursuing compensation by contractual liability or by tort liability: a 'picking the theory' choice.

Such situations raise two different, though related, questions. First, does the victim have two different claims against the same agent, one based on contractual remedies for breach of contract and another based on tort liability rules? If so, then can the victim claim both in the same cause of action? It is universally accepted that, in any case, the victim cannot recover twice for the same harm or detriment.[65]

Traditional civil law codes have disregarded these complex questions. Therefore, they have been addressed by case law.[66] In that respect, the problems related to the coexistence of tort and contract claims are a good field to compare the approaches by civil and common law. In both cases, the rules have their origin in judge-made law; hence, there are no structural differences in the process used to reach the legal solution – common law courts, as well as civil law judges, have selected the best solution in their own understanding. The latter, like the former, have done so without a general and preceding statutory rule.

Apparently, the American and English regimes are more flexible in that respect.[67] The American approach is well stated by §378 of the Second Restatement of the Law on Contracts, according to which:

> If a party has more than one remedy under the rules stated in this Chapter, his manifestation of a choice of one of them by bringing suit or otherwise is not a bar to another remedy unless the remedies are inconsistent and the other party materially changes his position in reliance on the manifestation.[68]

The traditional English rule, which holds that contractual and tort claims should not be filed in the same cause of action, was overruled by *Henderson v. Merrett Syndicates Ltd.* in 1995.[69] Before this decision, concurrent liability in both contract and tort had been accepted in claims for physical injury only.[70] The ruling opened the possibility for financial losses to the plaintiff. This ruling thus allowed one party to the contract to sue the other party for negligence in performing the contract, in addition to contractual remedies for breach of contract.[71]

In the same way, German[72] and Italian solutions[73] tend to consider tort and contract rules on damages as mutually complementary. The case is clearer in

Germany, where the doctrine and case law have defined the situation as an *Anspruchkonkurrenz* – that is to say, the coexistence of different rules aiming at a similar goal (although not identical since the same type of damage cannot be recovered twice).[74]

The problem is not only a formal one regarding how to sum up a specific claim. The problem relates to the boundaries of the right of the victim (either of harm or of breach of contract) to recover damages, due to the different ways to consider contractual and tort damages in most of the legal systems.[75] Thus, it is clear that the wider the definition of tort is, the more important it is to limit it in order to avoid its accumulation with other claims, significantly those related with a contract.[76] From this point of view, it seems obvious that the French system has developed the opposite solution.[77] Different from the aforementioned solutions, under the French principle of *non-cumul*, a victim of breach of contract cannot pursue a tort claim concurrently; when an obligation exists by virtue of a contract, it cannot also exist in tort.[78]

As stated, the doctrine of *non-cumul* is a natural consequence of the definition of a tort under article 1382 of the French Civil Code: 'Any act whatever of man, which causes damage to another, obliges the one by whose fault it occurred, to compensate it.' Independent of doctrinal and historical explanations, however, it is disputable that the common law rule of accumulation of contractual and non-contractual claims (also followed by some civil law jurisdictions) promotes more efficient results than the French doctrine of *non-cumul*.[79]

An efficiency approach should consider obligations contracted by mutual consent over other obligations. This principle underlies both the efficient formation and efficient breach of contracts. As a general principle, the use of tort law concurrently with contract law should be limited to specific situations where, for different reasons, we suspect contractual damages are unable to achieve the correct outcome. In other words, the efficient solution should look like a general principle of non-cumulative contractual and tort obligations with some particular derogation. Those familiar with contract law around the world will immediately recognize that this general rule looks more similar to French law than to English or American or German law.[80]

The option for a principle of *non-cumul* seems wise from an economic point of view. First, obligations freely negotiated should supersede potential tortious wrongdoings. Second, the possibility that breach of contract could generate a tort claim undermines efficient breach.[81] Third, ex ante facto, a potential tort claim could deter formation of contracts or increase negotiation costs to overcome potential future tort claims.[82] As a consequence, allowing tort claims concurrent with breach of contract claims can only be efficient in very exceptional conditions. One example is when contractual damages are unable to internalize the losses of non-performance due to externalities or the existence of serious asymmetries of information that undermine the optimality of contractual rules.[83]

We can also consider the long-run effects of the different rules. Suppose there is an important type of breach of contract that generates significant losses of a tortious nature. If they can never be the subject of action concurrently in torts and in contracts, we expect the evolution of the law to be in such a way as to have this class included in a broader scope of contract law. Even if they are tortious in nature, the fact that they are a by-product of a contract, and should only be cause of action in contract law, is likely to be appropriate because they are now subject to the mutual consent test.[84] If they can be causes of action concurrently in torts and in contracts, there would be no evolutionary pressure to subject them to a mutual consent test.

In French law, where *non-cumul* is the rule, a large body of law has evolved under contract law over the years to extend *responsabilité contractuelle* to include actions that are very substantively similar to tort law. Due to the *non-cumul*, such rules are housed within contract law. In other words, either the legal system sticks to the *non-cumul* under French law and accepts the growth of *responsabilité contractuelle* or the system decides that these cases must be dealt with as tort law cases despite the presence of a contractual relationship.

The expansion of *responsabilité contractuelle* as a consequence of the *non-cumul* is not without costs. The potential inclusion of actions of a tortious nature in *responsabilité contractuelle* creates a difficult balance for civil courts. They have to assure that *responsabilité contractuelle* is, by and large, moving along the same lines as *responsabilité délictuelle* to deal effectively with cases that look more like torts than anything else (e.g., an injury to a contracting party in the course of executing a contract). Developing and administering that body of law has a significant cost. Obviously, that cost can be minimized by keeping the two liability regimes close to one another; however, the basic rule of *non-cumul* is then unnecessary.

Recognizing that the inclusion of actions of a tortious nature is likely to raise important questions in contract law, we are inclined to argue that the route taken by French law seems better, even from a dynamic perspective.[85] Our view is based on the nature of explicit mutual consent in contracts. The only exceptions should be damage situations that require high transaction costs to achieve mutual consent ex ante. Inserting these cases into a broader contractual responsibility would raise the problems of so-called quasi-contracts, either by diluting the definition of mutual consent or by increasing the costs of contractual formation since those transaction costs become part of the costs of contract formation.[86]

From an economic perspective, our conclusion is that the French model of a general principle of *non-cumul*, subject to particular derogations in order to address significant externalities, is more appropriate from both a static and dynamic perspective when compared to the solutions developed in the common law and civil law jurisdictions.

The Good Samaritan Rule

The Good Samaritan Rule provides another example of how the common law and civil law differ in their approaches and effects on efficiency.[87] The relevance of this example is probably marginal since it does not have immediate economic effects. However, it provides a good exercise in the context of our book. For example, the approach towards a duty to rescue varies under the common and civil law; while civil law systems tend to impose a duty to rescue to everyone, the traditional common law solution foresees a no-duty-to-rescue rule.[88]

Under the realm of traditional common law rules, there is no affirmative duty to rescue another person from a situation of danger; Anglo-American courts do not impose a duty to rescue on bystanders.[89] The rule has few exceptions and is almost universally accepted – exceptions are roughly related to situations of risk negligently created by the potential rescuer or with the existence of a special relationship between the potential rescuer and the rescuee.[90] In the vast majority of cases, no person has an obligation to save another, even when the probability of salvation is high and its costs are small. Therefore, the lack of a duty to rescue creates an immediate disincentive to rescue: those who might want to rescue somebody in a risky situation may not carry out those dangerous activities after all. Those risky activities, however, can be socially beneficial.[91]

The traditional civil law approach differs from the traditional common law rule. Under the civil law, there is a general duty to rescue persons in danger, but the rescuee has to pay the rescuer for the expenses of the salvation.[92] The duty to rescue, the Good Samaritan Rule, is even enforced in the context of criminal law.[93] This general rule has few exceptions, and all of them relate to situations where it is more than foreseeable that the rescue will be unsuccessful.[94] The duty is not imposed where the cost of the rescue is excessive, although this exception is seldom used when the danger involves a natural person.[95] In doing so, civil law systems impose a liability rule on the potential rescuer, who will be liable if the rescue is not performed. It also imposes another liability rule to the rescuee, who has to reward or reimburse the rescuer with the expenses of the rescue.

Clearly, the civil law solution is superior and provides a more efficient framework to secure an implicit negotiation with high transaction costs.[96] The two-sided liability rule promotes rescues that can be performed at a low cost, but at the same time generates incentives for taking precautionary action, since the person in peril knows that she has to pay for the costs of her own rescue.[97] Both actors are fully incentivized to perform adequately, from both individual and social perspectives.[98]

Notes

1   We do not discuss here that, in some particular areas of the law or concerning some specific statutes, French law might have some anti-market bias whereas common law takes a pro-market position. The opposite is also true, as we show with our examples later in the book. Here, we refer to a general bias in the legal system. See Benito Arruñada and Veneta Andonova, 'Common Law and Civil Law as Pro-Market Adaptations' (2008) 26 *Washington University Journal of Law and Policy* 81; Benito Arruñada and Veneta Andonova, 'Judges' Cognition and Market Order' (2008) 4 *Review of Law and Economics* 665. The alleged business bias of the 1804 French civil code as understood by contemporary legal scholars is discussed by Jean-Louis Halperin, *The French Civil Code*, Basil Markesinis and Jörg Fedtke eds, 2nd ed. (London: UCL Press 2006) 59–60. A more general discussion can be found at John Henry Merryman, 'The French Deviation' (1996) 44 *American Journal of Comparative Law* 109.

2 Catherine Valcke, 'The French Response to the World Bank's *Doing Business* Reports' (2010) 60 *University of Toronto Law Review* 197; see also Bénédicte Fauvarque-Cosson and Anne-Julie Kerhuel, 'Is Law an Economic Contest? French Reactions to the *Doing Business* World Bank Reports and Economic Analysis of Law' (2009) 57 *American Journal of Comparative Law* 811. There is also an interesting discussion concerning the shortcomings of law and economics in France in Michel de S.-O.-l''E. Lasser, *Judicial Transformations: The Rights Revolution in the Courts of Europe* (Oxford and New York: Oxford University Press 2009).

3 Valcke (n2); Fauvarque-Cosson and Kerhuel (n2).

4 Compare Simeon Djankov et al., 'The New Comparative Economics' (2003) 31 *Journal of Comparative Economics* 595 with Benito Arruñada, 'Property Enforcement as Organized Consent' (2003) 19 *Journal of Law, Economics and Organisation* 401, 420–4421

5 For the economic models, see Ron Harris, 'Law, Finance and the First Corporations' in James J. Heckman, Robert L. Nelson and Lee Cabatingan eds, *Global Perspectives on the Rule of Law* Oxford: Routledge 2009); Edward L. Glaeser and Andrei Shleifer, 'The Rise of the Regulatory State' (2003) 41 *Journal of Economic Literature* 401, 408; Edward L. Glaeser and Andrei Shleifer, 'Legal origins' (2002) 117 *Quarterly Journal of Economics* 1193. For discussion, see Mark J. Roe, 'Legal origins, Politics, and Modern Stockmarkets' (2006) 120 *Harvard Law Review* 460; Frank B. Cross, 'Identifying the Virtues of the Common Law' (2007) 15 *Supreme Court Economic Review* 21; Daniel Klerman and Paul G. Mahoney, 'Legal Origin?' (2007) 35 *Journal of Comparative Economics* 278; Mark J. Roe, 'Juries and the Political Economy of Legal Origin' (2007) 35 *Journal of Comparative Economics* 294; Howard Rosenthal and Eric Voeten, 'Measuring Legal Systems' (2007) 35 *Journal of Comparative Economics* 711; Ralf Michaels, 'Comparative Law by Numbers? Legal Origins Thesis, *Doing Business* Reports and the Silence of Traditional Comparative Law' (2009) 57 *American Journal of Comparative Law*; Curtis J. Milhaupt, 'Beyond Legal Origin: Rethinking Law's Relationship to the Economy – Implications for Policy' (2009) 57 *American Journal of Comparative Law* 831; John Reitz, 'Legal Origins, Comparative Law, and Political Economy' (2009) 57 *American Journal of Comparative Law* 847.

6 Cross (n5).

7 For mixed evidence, see ibid. 41–46.

8 Erin O'Hara and Larry E. Ribstein, 'From Politics to Efficiency in Choice of Law' (2000) 67 *University of Chicago Law Review* 1151; Erin O'Hara and Larry E. Ribstein, *The Law Market* (Oxford: Oxford University Press 2009) (proposing jurisdictional competition to improve efficiency). Traditionally, there has been more freedom of choice of law in common law systems (for example, in the area of corporate law).

9 Cross (n5); Kenneth W. Dam, *The Law-Growth Nexus: The Rule of Law and Economic Development* (Washington: Brookings Institution Press 2006); Klerman et al. (n5) showing that legal origins does not seem to explain growth once legal and colonial origins are included in the regression analysis. Moreover, alternative theories might explain why certain institutions, related or unrelated to legal origin, cause economic growth. See, e.g., Robin M. Grier, 'Colonial Legacies and Economic Growth' (1999) 98 *Public Choice* 317; Daron Acemoglu, Simon Johnson, and James A. Robinson, 'Colonial Origins of Comparative Development: An Empirical Investigation' (2001) 91 *American Economic Review* 1369; Daron Acemoglu and Simon Johnson, 'Unbundling Institutions' (2005) 113 *Journal of Political Economy* 949; Daron Acemoglu and Simon Johnson, 'Disease and Development: The Effect of Life Expectancy on Economic Growth' (2007) 115 *Journal of Political Economy* 925; Daron Acemoglu et al., 'The Consequences of Radical Reform: The French Revolution' (2009) National Bureau of Economic Research, Working Paper No. 14831.

10 Anthony Ogus, 'Economic Approach: Competition Between Legal Systems' in Esin Örücü and David Nelken eds, *Comparative Law: A Handbook* (Oxford: Hart 2007) 155.

According to Professor Ogus, common law might be particularly appropriate for economic growth due to more freedom of choice of applicable legal regime, better facilitative law due to competition, and a decentralized and less bureaucratized administration of justice. In particular, the administration of justice in common law includes non-career judges, greater use of juries and non-professional judges, greater reliance on precedent and customary law, less reliance on legislation and codification, and oral rather than written procedures. All these characteristics produce two important advantages. First, mutual trust in commercial relations and enforcement of property rights is more effective. Second, common law is closer to preferences of citizens because it is bottom-up. But see David Nelken, 'Comparative Law and Comparative Legal Studies' in Örücü and Nelken eds, *Comparative Law* 3 (defending the proposition that more bureaucratized provisions of legal remedies could be more effective).

11 Ogus (n10) arguing that hybrid legal systems may benefit from competition of different legal cultures and, in that respect, that legal diversity is good. See also H. Patrick Glenn, 'Com-paring' in Örücü and Nelken eds, *Comparative Law* 91 (providing a good example in Quebec law, which has survived because the common law could not displace the written, substantive law of French origin already in place); Esin Örücü, 'A General View of Legal Families and of Mixed Systems' in Örücü and Nelken eds, *Comparative Law* 169 (providing a number of examples; one example is Malta, where French commercial law has survived the British influence even when exercised through constitutional law). Other examples include the colonial imposition of common law upon a civil law tradition that did not destroy it, as in Louisiana or South Africa. The evolution of the Scottish system provides a different angle, since the influence of common law is due to the proximity and need to promote commercial interaction and close cultural and political ties with England. Still, the civil law has prevailed.

12 Nuno Garoupa and Anthony Ogus, 'A Strategic Interpretation of Legal Transplants' (2006) 35 *Journal of Legal Studies* 339.

13 *Doing Business*, The World Bank. Online at www.doingbusiness.org, (accessed 3 October 2015).

14 Benito Arruñada, 'Pitfalls to Avoid When Measuring the Institutional Environment: Is *Doing Business* Damaging Business?' *Journal of Comparative Economics*, vol. 35, 2007; Kevin E. Davis and Michael B. Kruse, 'Taking the Measure of Law: The Case of the *Doing Business* Project' (2007) 32 *Law and Social Inquiry* 1095. A more comprehensive criticism is provided by Bertrand du Marais, 'Les Limites Méthodologiques des Rapports *Doing Business*' (2006) Programme de Recherches Attractivité Economique du Droit, Working Paper No. AED-2006-01; Didier Blanchet, 'Analyses Exploratoires des Indices Proposés par les Rapports *Doing Business* 2005 et 2006 de la Banque Mondiale' (2006) Programme de Recherches Attractivité Economique du Droit, Working Paper No. AED-2006-03; Bertrand du Marais et al., *Des Indicateurs Pour Mesurer Le Droit? Les Limites Methodologiques des Rapports* Doing Business (La Documentation Française 2006). The US Congress has now formally criticized the *Doing Business* project, and echoed some of the questions raised by legal economists, particularly with respect to employment law (House of Representatives, 111th Congress, Report 1st Session, Reform of the *Doing Business* Report of the World Bank, June 24, 2009, at 44-45). An internal evaluation of the World Bank has also identified further problems.

15 Steven Shavell, 'A Model of the Optimal Use of Liability and Safety Regulation' (1984) 15 *RAND Journal of Economics* 271. See also Donald Wittman, 'Prior Regulation Versus Post Liability: The Choice Between Input and Output Monitoring,' (1977) 6 *Journal of Legal Studies* 193; Jacob Nussim and Avraham D. Tabbach, 'Controlling Avoidance: Ex Ante Regulation Versus Ex Post Punishment' (2008) 4 *Review of Law and Economics* 45.

16 Shavell (n15).

17 Ibid.

18 According to Steiner, *French Legal Method* (Oxford: Oxford University Press 2002), 90–91, the landmarks of French case law are: (i) Administrative law: Blanco (1873) & Cadot (1889), developing state liability; and Administration des Douanes (1975), ruling the superiority of treaties over statutes; (ii) Contract law: Canal de Craponne (1876), limiting court interventionism in contract law; (iii) Commercial law: *Caisse Rurale Commune de Manigod v. Administration de l'Enregistrement* (1914), distinguishing between profit and non-profit commercial societies; and *Comité d'Etablissement de Saint-Chamond v Ray* (1954), granting legal personality to corporate bodies; (iv) Property law: *Clément-Bayard v Cocquerel* (1915), limiting *abus de droit* in property law; (v) Torts: Veuve Jand'heur (1930), establishing a principle of tort liability; (vi) Family law: *Proc. Gén. C. de Cass. v Madame X* (1991), regulating surrogate motherhood.
19 Misunderstandings about the role of courts in French law are common. Daniel A. Farber and Suzanna Sherry, *Judgment Calls: Principles and Politics in Constitutional Law* (Oxford: Oxford University Press 2009) 102–104 (arguing that the apparent formalism of French judges decreases transparency and concluding that the whole process is a scam, since the *rapports* include policy arguments but are not made public to keep the fiction that courts are not making law). Michel de S.-O.-l'E. Lasser, *Judicial Deliberations: A Comparative Analysis of Judicial Transparency and Legitimacy* (Oxford: Oxford University Press 2009) 299–321 (arguing that, under the American academic imagination, the French style of judicial deliberation stands for non-transparency because it lacks individual accountability and possesses an absence of democratic deliberation; American legal scholarship mistakenly considers that French judges have no individual responsibility on shaping doctrines and developing law).The author attributes the misunderstanding to the classical work by John P. Dawson, *The Oracles of the Law* (Ann Arbor: University of Michigan, 1968).
20 Frank Upham, 'Mythmaking in the Rule-of-Law Orthodoxy' in Thomas Carothers ed, *Promoting the Rule of Law Abroad: In Search of Knowledge* (Washington: Carnegie Endowment for International Peace 2006) 75 and 83–90, identifies shortcomings with this argument in the context of American law, particularly: (i) rule by politicized judges, or at least permeated by politics, and not by apolitical judges (US judges allow their preferences to overrule law when the opportunity arises); (ii) inconsistency in legal rules and in results are allowed, if not promoted; (iii) the jury system makes results and outcomes less predictable; and (iv) access to justice undermines equality which undermines the universality of legal norms. See also Ogus (n10) discussing two important aspects: (i) civil law seems to protect consumers more than traders unlike the common law and (ii) France has a more generous compensation for traffic accidents which inevitably results in higher transport costs that may undermine competitiveness).
21 Ugo Mattei, *Comparative Law and Economics* (Ann Arbor: University of Michigan Press 1996) 182–192 discussing comparative efficiency of penalty clauses in contracts, private trusts, and the path of legal change across legal families). For a discussion of efficient doctrines in contract law, see Aristides N. Hatzis, 'Civil Contract Law and Economic Reasoning: An Unlikely Pair?' in Stefan Grundmann and Martin Schauer eds, *The Architecture of European Codes and Contract Law* (Alphen aan den Rijn: Kluwer Law International 2006); Ejan Mackaay, 'The Civil Law of Contract' in Gerrit de Gees ed., *Encyclopedia of Law and Economics* 2nd ed. (Cheltenham: Edward Elgar 2011). The existence of penalty clauses in French contract law, a point we skip in our discussion given the existence of literature on the matter, is of particular importance. For a discussion of efficient rules in property law, see Norman Barry, 'Property Rights in Common and Civil Law' in Enrico Colombatto ed., *The Elgar Companion to the Economics of Property Rights* (Cheltenham: Edward Elgar 2004) 177 (observing some convergence in both legal systems). But see Dan Bogart and Gary Richardson, 'Making Property Productive: Reorganizing Rights to Real and Equitable Estates in Britain, 1660–1830' (2009) 13 *European Review of Economic History* 3 (suggesting that the

improvements in property law in Britain have been achieved by statute and not judge-made law).

22 Dam (n9) mentions (i) contracts and property (inspired by new institutional economics), (ii) enforcement in the broad sense (procedural rules), (iii) public law (although here the distinction between common law and civil law is incorrect in our view), in particular judicial review and administrative separate jurisdiction (allegedly less independent), and (iv) legal culture and governance.

23 Paul Mahoney, 'The Common Law and Economic Growth: Hayek Might Be Right' (2001) *Journal of Legal Studies* 30(2).

24 Ibid.

25 Maxwell L. Stearns and Todd J. Zywicki, *Public Choice Concepts and Applications in Law* (St Paul, MN: West 2009) concerning the case of the common law.

26 This example has been originally mentioned by Nuno Garoupa, 'Doing Comparative Law and Economics: Why the Future is Micro and Not Macro' in Michael Faure and Fran Stephen eds, *Essays in the Law and Economics of Regulation in Honour of Anthony Ogus* (Antwerp: Intersentia 2008) 63–70. For a general discussion on different legal treatments of *bona fide* purchase, see Saul Levmore, 'Variety and Uniformity in the Treatment of the Good-Faith Purchaser' (1987) 16 *Journal of Legal Studies* 43; Alan Schwartz and Robert E. Scott, 'Rethinking the Laws of Good Faith Purchase' (2011) 111 *Columbia Law Review* 1332; Ogus (n10).

27 John E. Cribbet et al., *Property: Cases and Materials* 8th ed. (New York: Foundation Press 2002) 122–132 (providing a classical explanation of the rule and its problems).

28 Anthony Ogus, *Costs and Cautionary Tales: Economic Insights for the Law* (Oxford: Hart 2006).

29 Ibid.

30 Ibid.

31 We do not take into account the protection against void or voidable contracts, that is to say, situations in which the law may refuse to give full effect to a contract on the ground of illegality, or on the ground of misrepresentation. Our point here is to show how the protection against acquisitions *a non domino* differs in civil law governed by the French rule and in common law. For more details on the protection in cases of void and voidable contracts, see Günther H. Treitel, *Law of Contract* Edwin Peel ed., 12th ed. (London: Sweet & Maxwell 2007) 470–473.

32 Ogus (n28).

33 Ibid. 45–47; Anthony Ogus, 'What Legal Scholars Can Learn from Law and Economics' (2004) 79 *Chicago-Kent Law Review* 383, 394–395. However, in the context of ownership of art, see the opposite conclusion being defended by William Landes and Richard A. Posner, 'The Economics of Legal Disputes Over the Ownership of Works of Art and Other Collectibles' in Pierre-Michel Menger and Victor A. Ginsburgh eds, *Economics of the Art: Selected Essays* (New York: Elsevier 1996).

34 Ogus (n28).

35 Ogus (n28).

36 U.C.C. § 2-403 (1952).

37 Joseph William Singer, *Property Law: Rules, Policies, and Practices* 3rd ed. (New York: Aspen Law & Business 2002) 103–104.

38 Code Civil [C. civ.] art. 2230 (Fr.).

39 Cribbet et al. (n27) 1070 ('The net effect of the system is to introduce by statute the equitable concept or bona fide purchaser for value without notice so that the b.f.p. takes free of prior deeds, mortgages, leases, etc., if they are not recorded as required by the particular act').

40 Arruñada (n4).

41 Ibid.

42 Ibid.

43 Klaus Deininger and Gershon Feder, 'Land Registration, Governance, and Development: Evidence and Implications for Policy' (2009) 24 *World Bank Research Observer* 233 (recognizing limitations to the literature that argues for land registration). See generally Arruñada (n17); Benito Arruñada and Nuno Garoupa, 'The Choice of Titling System in Land' (2005) 48 *Journal of Law and Economics*; Benito Arruñada, 'Property Titling and Conveyancing' in Harry Smith and Ken Avotte eds *Research Handbook on the Economics of Property Law* (Cheltenham: Edward Elgar, 2010)..
44 Arruñada and Garoupa, 'The Choice of Titling System in Land'.
45 Ibid.
46 Ibid.
47 See discussion by Arruñada, 'Property Titling and Conveyancing'.
48 Singer (n37) 99 ('The rules in force generally award both real and personal property to the prior peaceable possessor, even though she does not have title to the property. This result illustrates the concept of relativity of title').
49 For a critical approach to the system, see Cribbet et al. (n27) 1119–1122. See also ibid. at 1128. ('Most contracts for the sale of real estate require the vendor to convey a merchantable title to the purchaser. Unfortunately, this does not solve the buyer's problem because the ownership of real property is so complex a matter the seller frequently does not know whether his title is "good" or "bad". Moreover, once the deed is delivered the doctrine of merger ends most of the purchaser's rights under the contract, and he must assure himself that the deed in fact conveys what he wants.')
50 J. Gordon Hylton et al. *Property Law and the Public Interest: Cases and Materials* 3rd ed. (Newark, NJ: LexisNexis 2007) 358–359. ('If A sold Blackacre to B, and then one day later sold it again to C, B would always prevail against C (short of C establishing title by adverse possession), because B's claim was first in time. Similarly, if A executed a mortgage to B and then a second mortgage to C (which, unlike the first example, is perfectly legal), B would have first priority to any proceeds from the sale if it became necessary for her to foreclose against A.')
51 See discussion by Arruñada, 'Property Titling and Conveyancing'.
52 Arruñada and Garoupa, 'The Choice of Titling System in Land'.
53 Ibid.
54 Ibid.
55 Ibid.
56 See generally Arruñada, 'Property Titling and Conveyancing'.
57 For the main differences between English and French contract law, see Catherine Valcke, 'On Comparing French and English Contract Law: Insights from Social Contract Theory' (2009) 3 *Journal of Comparative Law* 69 (arguing that in French law, facts and norms tend to be delineated, with the norms ultimately prevailing, while in English law, the line between facts and norms is blurred and factual arguments are relatively more important and noting that contractual intention and contractual mistake are more practical concepts in English than in French law).
58 See generally Eric Descheemaeker, *The Division of Wrongs: A Historical Comparative Study* (Oxford: Oxford University Press 2009) (presenting an argument for incorporating this structure into the common law). For a general explanation on the *non-cumul*, see Geneviève Viney and Patrice Jourdain, 'Les conditions de la responsabilité' in Jacques Ghestin, Jérôme Huet and Stéphane Piedelièvre, *Traite de Droit Civil* 85, 85–93 (2nd ed. L.G.D.J. 1998). Civil law, unlike common law, includes contracts and torts in the law of wrongs which is determined by different degrees of culpability (*dolus, culpa* and *casus*).
59 *Donoghue v. Stevenson*, [1932] A.C. 562 (H.L.) (appeal taken from Scotland) (holding that the contractual relationship between the parties should not exclude a right of action based on negligence as between the same parties); Simon Deakin, Angus Johnston and Basil Markesinis, *Markesinis and Deakin's Tort Law* 5th ed. (Oxford: Clarendon Press 2003) 7–19; Tony Weir, *Economic Torts* (Oxford: Clarendon Press 1997) 25.

60 Descheemaeker (n58).
61 The problem derives from one particular perspective, which is otherwise general to common and civil law legal systems. According to this general understanding, the main categories in private law are those related to the obligations borne by agreement, and those imposed without any voluntary consent from both parties. There are other ways to understand the relation among individuals with legal effects. See Peter S. Atiyah, *Essays on Contract* (Oxford: Oxford University Press 1986) 10–15.
62 Stephen A. Smith, 'Concurrent Liability and Unjust Enrichment: The Fundamental Breach Requirement' (1999) 115 *Law Quarterly Review* 245. In particular, if the facts satisfy the elements of two causes of action, a breach of contract can also support an act in tort, or vice versa.
63 Descheemaeker (n58); Smith (n62).
64 Descheemaeker (n58), Deakin et al. (n59); Smith (n62).
65 See generally Tony Weir, 'Complex Liabilities' in André Tunc ed., *International Encyclopedia of Comparative Law* (Tübingen: Mohr 1976) pt.2.
66 Descheemaeker (n58); Viney and Jourdain (n58).
67 *Henderson v. Merrett Syndicates* [1995] 2 A.C. 145 (H.L.) (appeal taken from Eng.); Ogus (n26) 88; Raymond Youngs, *English, French and German Comparative Law* 2nd ed. (London and New York: Routledge-Cavendish 2007); see also Jack Beatson, 'Restitution and Contract: Non-Cumul?' (2002) 1 *Theoretical Inquiries in Law* 83; William Lloyd Prosser, S*elected Topics on the Law of Torts* (Ann Arbor: University of Michigan Law School 1953) 380–454.
68 Restatement (Second) of Contracts § 378 (1981).
69 Henderson 2 A.C. 145.
70 Ogus (n10) 92–94.
71 Donald Harris, David Campbell and Roger Halson, *Remedies in Contract and Tort* 2nd ed. (Cambridge: Cambridge University Press 2002) 575–578.
72 The German solution allows concurrent claims in contract and tort. There are several reasons supporting that approach, namely because damages for pain and suffering are not available in a contract suit. Gerhard Wagner, 'Unerlaubte Handlungen' in *Münchener Kommentar zum Bürgerlichen Gesetzbuch* Band 5, Auflage 4 (München: Beck 2004) 1495–1501. However, different limitations rules and a common reason for concurrent claims no longer hold after the 2002 changes.
73 In Italian law, a wide range of (contractual) damages can be recovered in torts (non-contractual liability); although the defendant is not liable for every single consequence of breach, damages are not limited to foreseeable losses. Indirect damages are recoverable when they can be attributed to breach through standard principles of causation. Even future losses can be recovered, if they are based on an inevitable situation. Guido Alpa and Vincenzo Zeno-Zenovich, *Italian Private Law* (London and New York: Routhledge-Cavendish 2007) 242–244.
74 Nigel Foster and Satish Sule, *German Legal System and Laws* 3rd ed. (Oxford: Oxford University Press 2002) 417–419.
75 Assunção Cristas and Nuno Garoupa 'On the Boundary between Torts and Contracts: An Economic View' in Pierre Larouche and Filomena Chirico eds, *Economic Analysis of the DCFR: The work of the Economic Impact Group within the CoPECL* (Munich: Sellier European Law 2010).
76 Ibid.
77 Ibid.
78 Anthony Ogus and Michael Faure, *Économie du Droit: Le cas Français* (Paris: Éditions Panthéon-Assas 2002) L.G.D.J. Diffuseur (explaining the principle of *non-cumul*); Denis Tallon, 'Contract Law' in George A. Bermann and Etienne Picard eds, *Introduction to French Law* (Alphen aan den Rijn and Frederick, MD 2008) 205, 231.

79 We should note the criticism received by the *non-cumul* doctrine from some prominent French authors. Jean Carbonnier, 'Droit Civil' in *Tome 4: Les Obligations* (Paris: Quadrige 2000) 514–518.

80 Ogus (n10) 86–92. For example, the rule does not apply when the breach is a consequence of a criminal action. See Tallon (n78).

81 Unless contractual damages are too low and therefore tort damages operate as a mechanism to achieve efficient breach, an argument that seems quite difficult to make in general terms since expectation damages and specific performance tend to prevail.

82 Ogus (n10) 92–94.

83 French law allows for derogation of the principle of *non-cumul* for reasons of public interest which could be interpreted as serious negative externalities. Ogus and Faure (n78) 104.

84 By mutual consent test, we understand that both sides agree voluntarily to the terms of the formalized contract.

85 Peter Schlechtriem, 'The Borderland of Tort and Contract: Opening a New Frontier?' (1988) 21 *Cornell International Law Journal* 467 (defending the benefits of the *non-cumul* doctrine in international trade on the grounds that it avoids the risk of large claims of damages to international investors).

86 Cristas and Garoupa (n75).

87 For a general overview of the French tort system, its influence on civil law, and its differences with the common law, see André Tunc, *La Responsabilité Civile* 2nd ed. (Paris: Économica 1989).

88 Kenneth S. Abraham, *The Form and Functions of Tort Law* 3rd ed. (New York: Foundation Press 2007) 234. ('As a matter of principle, the common law cares enough about individual liberty that typically it does not ask people to do more than mind their own business. If I have done nothing to put someone in a position of danger, I have no duty to rescue him from that position.') See generally James M. Ratcliffe ed., *The Good Samaritan and the Law* (Gloucester, MA: Peter Smith 1981) (discussing the traditional explanation of the rule and its implications); Saul Levmore, 'Waiting for Rescue: An Essay on the Evolution and Incentive Structure of the Law of Affirmative Obligations' (1986) 72 *Virginia Law Review* 879 (explaining the common law rule from a comparative perspective).

89 Such result obviously has some critics among common law scholars. Mary Ann Glendon, *Right Talks: The Impoverishment of Political Disclosure* (New York: Free Press 1991) 84 (arguing that the rule is the result of the 'extreme individualism typical of Anglo-Saxon legal thought'); Ernest J. Weinrib, 'The Case for a Duty to Rescue' (1980) 90 *Yale Law Journal* 247 (arguing in favour of the recognition by the courts of a general duty to rescue, and even noting that 'On the judicial side, many of the outposts of the doctrine that there is no general duty to rescue have fallen. Recognizing the meritoriousness of rescue and the desirability of encouraging it, the courts have increasingly accorded favorable treatment to injured rescuers'). In fact, some states in the US have passed statutes imposing a general Good Samaritan rule. There are only few exceptions to the rule according to which there is no general duty to rescue. Such exceptions imply a duty to affirmative action have been formalized by practice and judicial decisions over the years. The most comprehensive outlook is in the Restatement. See *Restatement (Second) Torts* (1979) §314A and 314B, recognizing five situations of an affirmative duty to rescue: (1) carrier–passenger, (2) innkeeper–guest, (3) landowner–invitee, (4) custodian–award, (5) employer–employee.

90 *Stockberger v. United States*, 332 F.3d 479, 481 (7th Cir. 2003). Judge Posner wrote that 'various rationales have been offered for the seemingly hardhearted common law rule: people should not count on nonprofessionals to rescue; the circle of potentially liable nonrescuers would be difficult to draw … altruism makes the problem a small one and liability might actually reduce the number of altruistic rescuers by depriving people of credit for altruism'. Ibid.

91 But cf. William M. Landes and Richard A. Posner, 'Salvors, Finders, Good Samaritans, and Other Rescuers: An Economic Study of Law and Altruism' (1978) *Journal of Legal Studies* 83, 126 (suggesting that 'the results under the common law, occasionally imposing liability but mostly denying it, may be consistent with efficiency'); Sophie Harnay and Alain Marciano, 'Should I Help my Neighbor? Self-Interest, Altruism and Economic Analyses of Rescue Laws' (2009) 28 *European Journal of Law and Economics* 103.

92 Landes and Posner (n91); Harnay and Marciano (n91).

93 F. J. M. Feldbrugge, 'Good and Bad Samaritans: A Comparative Survey of Criminal Law Provisions Concerning Failure to Rescue' (1966) 14 *American Journal of Comparative Law* 630.

94 Landes and Posner (n91); Harnay and Marciano (n91); Feldbrugge (n93).

95 Landes and Posner (n91); Harnay and Marciano (n91).

96 For an empirical analysis and discussion, see David A. Hyman, 'Rescue Without Law: An Empirical Perspective on the Duty to Rescue' (2006) 84 *Texas Law Review* 653.

97 Donald A. Wittman, *Economic Foundations of Law and Organization* (Cambridge: Cambridge University Press 2006) 176. ('The continental rule encourages low-cost rescues in two ways. First, the rescuer is compensated for the small cost of rescue; second, if the potential rescuer's costs are somewhat higher than the average so that the reward does not fully cover all rescuers' costs, then the threat of being liable for damage to the potential rescuee will motivate the person to the rescue. The rule also provides the appropriate incentives for those who might need rescue. By charging for the average of the rescue, the rescuee takes the appropriate level of care. A higher price for rescue would result in the potential rescuee being overly cautious and too few rescues.') For a study on the evolution of the different understandings of the civil law rule and its economic implications, see Harnay and Marciano (n91).

98 The critique by some scholars who argue that the Good Samaritan rule would require, as a natural extension, the duty to give charity to the poor is economic nonsense. Richard A. Epstein, 'A Theory of Strict Liability' (1973) 2 *Journal of Legal Studies* 151. Such a statement can be done only from the misunderstanding of the proximate causation doctrine.

7 Contrasting common and civil law

Legal governance and the specialization of courts

While the previous chapter looked at examples in substantive law that seem to be more appropriately addressed by French law rather than by common law (and with implications for economic performance), in this section we look at court structure and organization. As mentioned above, although the influence of these variables on economic growth is controversial, they have been part of the argument against the efficiency of French civil law. In particular, it has been suggested that the model of court specialization followed in France is not conducive to economic growth.[1]

The model

We start by developing a framework that will be used to assess the different degrees of specialization of courts and legal governance across legal families. We then assess applications to administrative, commercial and constitutional laws.

The main costs and benefits of specialized courts are summarized in Table 7.1. Obviously, a specialized jurisdiction could assure correct and legally coherent decisions in a complex area given the difficulties in establishing liability and the technical nature of the underlying facts. This argument only makes sense if the determination of one particular class of liability is substantively different from other existing types of liability, in particular, within private law.

A related argument is that the quality of decisions increases due to competitive pressure. A specialized jurisdiction in direct competition with regular courts should develop structural qualities to be more innovative and more persuasive, and to develop more appropriate legal doctrines.[2]

A different advantage is the uniformity of judicial decisions. Absent inter-circuit *stare decisis*, uniform interpretation of federal administrative law is usually presented as an argument for specialization. This is not an issue in French law given the position enjoyed by the *Conseil d'État*. It is plausible that uniformity over some areas of the law is more important than over other areas because of the social, political, economic, or budgetary implications of adjudicating liability.

Another argument is court workload, in particular when we have court congestion with an increased volume of litigation and a potential reduction in

Table 7.1 Costs and benefits of specialized courts[3]

Advantages	Disadvantages
Higher quality of decisions (in content and in timing)	Administrative costs of running a new network of courts
Legal coherence	Capture by specialized interests (including a specialized bar)
Uniformity of judicial decisions	Costs of coordination with regular courts (include losses to incoherence between different areas of the law and procedure)
Reduction of regular courts' workload	Development of vested interests by specialized judges and court services or the creation of new state agencies
	Costs of appeal from specialized courts to nonspecialized appeal courts (depending on the locus of specialization)
	Costs of less geographical proximity of courts to populations (since specialized courts are usually located in large cities)

quality in sentencing as a response.[4] In other words, the need to keep high-quality generalist courts might justify transferring jurisdiction of certain areas of the law to specialized courts.[5] In fact, one should note that by alleviating the docket loads of regular courts, one expects to increase the general understanding of the law (due to fewer people writing about the same law), and this leads to less litigation and less workload in the future.[6] The natural question is why transfer one particular area of the law but not other relevant areas? The answer seems to be that what should be transferred are cases characterized by a high volume of routine cases with significant workload for regular courts.

In addition to pure efficiency considerations of specialization, there might be political economy arguments as well. The standard justification for why administrative bodies cannot adjudicate administrative or constitutional liability is due to their lack of impartiality since they combine rulemaking, adjudication, and enforcement functions.[7] The creation of specialized courts to deal with this type of liability could be part of a broader course of action that effectively reverses the process of delegation of authority to administrative agencies.[8] Yet, it is not obvious why specialized courts would be willing to confront the administration more frequently than regular courts.[9] In other words, it could be that specialized courts are more willing to impose liability than traditional administrative or executive agencies, but the relevant comparison should be between specialized and generalist courts. Furthermore, if specialized courts are to be used as a mechanism to limit administrative authority, they could generate a backlash in terms of future delegation or new legislation. Another line of reasoning is to argue that specialized courts, by limiting and supervising agencies, reduce the need for further administration supervision, and therefore provide a good signal of which areas of the administration are more prone to generate liability.

Capture is the standard argument against specialization.[10] It can take place at the appointment level.[11] Dependence on a specialized bar or of a specialized judicial council might create devices by which the interests of the administration can make its influence felt in the appointment mechanism. Capture can also take place at the level of the adjudication.[12] There are very strong arguments to consider capture of specialized courts as a major issue.[13] The costs of capturing are lower given the specificity of the issues at stake and the relatively low chances of being exposed. On the other hand, the perspective of specialized judges forming a cohesive group, fairly insulated from other magistrates and less likely to be accountable, increases potential benefits. Finally, in the case of administrative and constitutional laws, we might suspect important structural biases. Indeed the influence of the government and of special interests will tend to align the profile of the state bureaucracy with that of the specialized bench.[14] We could say that many of the particularities of administrative procedure are in part consequences of this alignment.

There is also the possibility of internal capture or the development of vested interests.[15] Courts could behave strategically as any other bureaucracy and push for expansion of budgets and resources, attract new business to justify their existence, or develop confusing and incoherent procedures (discovery, pleading or trial methods) that make cross-relationships unproductive (therefore keeping the monopoly of specialized courts over a particular subject matter). A potential ratchet effect should also not be neglected. Specialized courts could push for idiosyncratic procedures, a specialized bar and hence a particular market for legal services. Thus, this might create a completely different legal environment for some areas of the law. Finally, the highly significant influence of specialized courts on a particular area of the law (both substantively and procedurally) reduces effective supervision by higher regular or generalist courts. For instance, such ineffective supervision increases the possibility of mistakes that will exacerbate the need for new legislation.

Many of the benefits and costs are exacerbated if adjudication is assigned to specialized courts on the basis of exclusivity and limitation.[16] Similarly, this may apply if specialized courts are staffed with specialized judges rather than generalist judges.[17] Increased collegiality of the specialized judiciary promotes faster learning in specific areas of the law, but generates two important drawbacks.[18] First, a specialized bench might not enjoy the reputation of being considered a generalist judiciary; hence, an adverse selection effect might take place (it could be harder for specialized courts to attract talent).[19] Second, a specialized bench might have to interact with higher courts staffed with generalist judges.[20] This hierarchical relationship might create serious conflicts, especially because the use of particular procedures in specialized courts (that is, procedures that are modified for specific goals) might disturb the whole court system.[21]

Having reviewed the general model, we turn now to three examples that are relevant in France, namely the administrative, commercial and constitutional courts.

Administrative courts

Some legal scholars consider the separation of jurisdiction between civil and administrative courts in the French tradition as an example of inefficiency in legal governance.[22] A standard criticism is that the administrative jurisdiction lacks true independence to review the acts of the executive effectively.[23] From an economic perspective, we can say that French-style administrative courts are likely to be captured by the government and therefore cannot effectively restrain the government from potentially undermining private property rights.[24] In fact, capture might simply result from some hindsight bias by which administrative courts have difficulties to envisage that the state might have overreached (in relation to the appropriateness of intervention), either because of a cognitive bias (e.g. the existence of the state is not to be questioned) or more simply because of self-preservation as state officials.[25]

Although such argument is subject to empirical controversy (for example, it is unclear that the *Conseil d'État* has a significant pro-government bias[26]), let us assume for the sake of discussion that this is true. Nevertheless, capture is one of the well-known costs of specialization as clarified by the general model.[27] Therefore, the French approach must be assessed and configured in a framework that recognizes the benefits of specialization versus the costs of capture, rather than a mere misguided *ceteris paribus* analysis of the potential losses of a dual jurisdictional organization.[28]

Better training, better particularized information, tailored procedures in court to deal with the special features of the state as defendant or as plaintiff, and better technology in evidence production are possible when judges have the training and the incentives to become specialists in administrative law.[29] On the other hand, separation makes capture by the government or by special interests easier.[30] Also, specialization makes accountability more difficult.[31] The knowledge of administrative law becomes a specific asset in human capital for the judges.[32] Therefore, they are more dependent on (or more easily constrained by) the government (state officials).[33] The marginal cost for a judge of deciding against the state or the government is much higher in administrative courts than in ordinary judicial courts.[34] If specialization is more important than capture – that is, the benefits from specialization outweigh the costs of capture – then administrative courts should exist for purposes of enforcing and interpreting administrative law.[35]

Some cases in administrative litigation share a substantial portion of legal issues with ordinary tort cases (causation, proximate causation, determination of fault, estimation of harm), thus decreasing the benefits of having specialized courts in administrative law deal with these cases.[36] It is true, however, that other cases share fewer issues with ordinary tort cases among private individuals or firms (for example, the illegal denial of permits or licenses).[37] The extent to which complexity in administrative law is intrinsic to determining liability when the state is the defendant or the plaintiff is inevitable in this context.[38] Necessarily, we do not consider this argument to be overwhelming. For example, a special treatment of state liability for provision of private goods does not seem to satisfy the argument for a specialized jurisdiction.

Once the costs and benefits are identified, the calibration of the cost-benefit analysis must take into account that the French approach is adequate under some conditions and inadequate under others.[39] It could be that a dual jurisdictional organization is the best solution in France, but not in England or America. If such analysis is true, then evaluating French-style administrative courts from an incomplete or partial cost-driven perspective is methodologically incorrect. The existing trade-off between specialization (better knowledge of administrative law and more adequate procedural rules) and capture (loss of independence) could have different optimal responses across legal families.

In our view, the striking difference between a specialized court system for administrative law of the French type and another one for the common law does not necessarily mean that one arrangement is superior to the other. We argue that there are certain characteristics of the French system that might justify its design being used for certain jurisdictions. The most immediate argument is the general complexity of administrative law.[40] Here, one should look not only at the overall complexity, but also at the variance within the field of administrative law. Administrative law has many subfields such as state liability, review of agency regulations and public employment rules. The variance of complexity across subfields is important to determine benefits. The higher the variance in the legal issues across different types of administrative law cases, the higher the benefits of specialization.[41] To this legal complexity, one needs to add the assessment of state actions that are market-oriented in economic nature but of legal public nature (public provision of public goods and services).

A second argument that distinguishes France (and other continental jurisdictions) from Britain or America is the strong state intervention in the economy (larger size of public sector) and in society (regulation of social life). A strong state intervention increases the complexity of administrative law and the likelihood of litigation between private citizens and the state, *ceteris paribus*.[42] Notice that the argument is positive, not normative, in the sense that we are not discussing the merits and demerits of a strong state intervention. We are merely arguing that a strong state intervention naturally leads to a more complex and relevant administrative law.[43]

A third related argument is strong and substantial public employment. It is likely that important conflicts between unionized public workers and the government (as an employer) require more effective administrative courts. Again, our argument is not normative (whether or not a large sector of unionized public employment is beneficial or detrimental for economic growth), but merely positive.

Finally, we need to add a weak system of independent regulatory agencies. These agencies play an important role in providing expertise on administrative law in their own fields of regulation.[44] They also provide informal review of administrative justice.[45] The judiciary would, in general, be less distrustful of an independent agency than of purely political decisions from an administrative agency.[46] Hence, where we find strong and independent expert agencies, we expect less need for specialized administrative courts. Independent expert agencies and specialized administrative courts are, to some degree, institutional substitutes, both in terms of enforcing administrative law and in their political independence from the executive.[47] Note that our conclusion looks at independent regulatory agencies and specialized courts as providers of high quality reviews of administrative decisions. A different viewpoint refers to accountability where the appeals process plays an important role in keeping independent regulatory agencies constrained.[48]

Altogether, there are good reasons to be cautious and not to jump to the conclusion that the French-style administrative courts are inefficient and detrimental to economic growth.[49] On the contrary, though, the abolition of a separate administrative jurisdiction without further profound legal reforms could be quite disastrous in civil law countries of the French tradition.

Commercial courts

The *lex mercatoria* and the consequent enforcement by specialized courts within the trade guilds have always attracted legal historians and economists.[50] The economic advantages of a specialized court system tailored and developed by businessmen to resolve their litigation according to their own laws have been documented.[51] They are easily framed in our model as summarized by Table 7.1, including specialization in substance and in procedure that provides high-quality decisions in a pro-market setting with little intervention by the state. The quality of business courts relies on reputation and self-regulating mechanisms that avoid the standard capture problem. The economic argument for these decentralized business or industry courts has been made not only in the context of the Middle Ages' *lex mercatoria*,[52] but also in relation to more recent experiences, where legal informality, a business background, and a significant experience with merchant practices tend to prevail after the gradual professionalization of the judiciary.[53]

The general appraisal by legal economists for merchant courts has neglected the French case of commercial courts (*Tribunaux de commerce*).[54] It is a system of courts that can be traced back to 1563 and survived the important reforms of the French court system.[55] The enforcement of the 1807 *Code du commerce* was entrusted to these courts, which are staffed only by litigation attorneys who deal with commercial matters. Members of the local chamber of commerce elect these lay judges for terms of four years after they have been practising as businessmen for at least five years.[56] In the court, they sit in panels of at least three.[57] Commercial litigation is dominated by oral proceedings, unlike the general arrangements in the civil law tradition.[58] They are considered to be reasonably fast as compared to the regular courts.[59] Finally, there are also few appeals to the *Cour d'appeal* and even fewer reversals.[60]

It is difficult to find a better example on a large scale of business courts than the French commercial courts. Yet legal economists have largely neglected their existence and importance in the context of French commercial law.[61] Notice that the existence of these specialized courts is not without problems, as shown in the context of our model. They also have their limitations since they are bound by substantive commercial law.[62] Nevertheless, they have the ability to effectively improve enforcement and to develop creative procedural rules.[63]

From an economic perspective, and relying on the enthusiasm for business courts promoted by legal economists, we can only say that the French commercial courts are certainly among the best institutional arrangements in the world to deliver commercial law.[64] A comprehensive assessment of the comparative quality of commercial law is inevitably compromised if it fails to recognize the significant advantages of the French commercial courts. We are not saying that French commercial courts are superior to the use of commercial arbitration in common law jurisdictions. We merely point out that a comparative analysis that neglects the role and the nature of the French commercial courts fails to recognize the advantages posed by this institutional design.

Constitutional courts

Constitutional law is a central element in determining the various dimensions of political and legal reform. This is because constitutional adjudication should be more responsive to long-run interests and less limited by political short-run opportunism.[65] Therefore, conformity with the constitution becomes an important instrument to achieve political and economic stability.[66] Moreover, empirical economic analysis supports the view that independent courts and constitutional review are factors that should be taken into account not only if the goal is to guarantee political freedom, but also to protect economic liberties and foster economic growth.[67]

The design of most constitutional courts in civil law countries has been influenced by the ideas and legal theories of Hans Kelsen.[68] Many countries have adopted his 'negative legislator' model.[69] In his view, ordinary judges are mandated to apply law as legislated or decided by the parliament.[70] There is a strict hierarchy of laws that makes judicial review by a constitutional court incompatible with the subordination of the ordinary judges to the legislator.[71] Hence, only an extrajudicial organ can effectively restrain the legislature and act as the guarantor of the will of the constitutional legislator. The Kelsenian model proposes a centralized body outside of the structure of the conventional judiciary to exercise constitutional review.[72] This body, conventionally called the constitutional court, operates as a negative legislator because it has the power to reject legislation (but not propose legislation).[73]

In fact, the centralization of constitutional review in a body outside of the conventional judiciary has been important to secure independence and the commitment to democratization after a period of an authoritarian government in many countries.[74] The judiciary is usually suspected of allegiance to the former regime, and hence, a new court is expected to be more responsive to the democratic ideals contemplated in the new constitution.[75]

The application of the Kelsenian model in each country has conformed to local conditions, and therefore, the competences and organization of constitutional courts are usually much broader than a simple 'negative legislator'.[76] Ex ante review of legislation (i.e., before promulgation) has been extended to ex post review (i.e., after promulgation) in many countries.[77] Abstract review (traditionally in France) has been conjugated with concrete review in Germany or Spain.[78] Most constitutional courts have expanded ancillary powers in different, but important, areas such as verifying elections, regulating political parties (illegalizing them or auditing their accounts), and performing other relevant political and administrative functions, such as performing as acting as a judicial council, as seen in Taiwan.[79]

The Kelsenian-type courts for constitutional review now exist now in most countries of the civil law tradition, with the Netherlands, the Scandinavian countries and most Latin American countries being the most striking exceptions.[80] Also, most Central and Eastern European former communist countries have now developed a similar institutional structure.[81] Nevertheless, the institutional design followed in Germany and in Spain broadens the initial Kelsenian model, whereas the traditional French model (before the 2008 reform), with narrower competences and almost exclusively preventive review, offers less than what is expected from a Kelsenian-type court.[82] Indeed, the Austrian model of the early 1920s limited constitutional review to abstract review of the legislation, but incidental referrals that effectively provided for concrete review were introduced soon after in the 1930s.[83]

It then becomes a question of cost-benefit analysis of the option for the Kelsenian model versus the American model.[84] The general nature of the costs and benefits of court specialization in constitutional law follow the model specified in Table 7.1 and discussed above. The Kelsenian model offers a specialized constitutional court that presumably can offer high-quality decisions in a more coherent and uniform way.[85] The cost is the detachment between the constitutional court and the rest of the court system, and the potential capture by special interests (in particular, the political actors).

Originally, the Kelsenian model was not defended in a cost-benefit framework. It is easy to see, however, that under the legal tradition of the civil law and the specific nature of a career judiciary, a cost-benefit argument can be made that the benefits enhanced by the Kelsenian model offset the potential costs of capture. In fact, current empirical results seem to show that the Kelsenian model is more adequate for growth.[86] Apparently, the benefits of specialization offered by the Kelsenian model certainly more than justify the costs.[87]

Notes

1 Paul Mahoney, 'The Common Law and Economic Growth: Hayek Might Be Right' (2001) 30(2) *Journal of Legal Studies*.
2 Richard Stith, 'Securing the Rule of Law Through Interpretive Pluralism: An Argument From Comparative Law' (2008) 35 *Hastings Constitutional Law Quarterly* 401 (arguing

that multiple higher courts provide a better framework for interpretation, and that, each high court has to persuade the other higher courts of the correctness of their arguments).

3 Nuno Garoupa, Natalia Jorgensen and Pablo Vasquez, 'Assessing the Argument for Specialized Courts: Evidence from Family Courts in Spain' (2010) 24 *International Journal of Law, Policy and the Family* 54, 55.
4 Richard L. Revesz, 'Specialized Courts and the Administrative Lawmaking System' (1989) 138 *University of Pennsylvania Law Review* 1111.i
5 Ibid.
6 Ibid.
7 Nuno Garoupa, Anthony Ogus and Andrew Sanders, 'The Investigation and Prosecution of Regulatory Offences: Is There an Economic Case for Integration?' (2011) 70 *Cambridge Law Journal* 229.
8 This is due to the fact it reallocates some of their competences to the benefit of the courts. Giuseppe Dari-Mattiacci, Nuno Garoupa and Fernando Gómez-Pomar, 'State Liability' (2010) 18 *European Review of Private Law* 773.
9 Under the capture hypothesis, specialized courts might be less willing to do so. See ibid.
10 Ibid.
11 Ibid.
12 Ibid.
13 For instance, court capture by interest groups has been considered one of the critical factors explaining the expansion of patent rights in the US, after the creation in 1982 of the US Court of Appeals for the Federal Circuit. The latter concentrates jurisdiction over appeals from the Patent and Trademark Office as well as from federal district courts in patent infringement cases. William M. Landes and Richard A. Posner, *The Economic Structure of Intellectual Property Law* (Cambridge, MA: Harvard University Press 2003) 334–353.
14 Dari-Mattiacci, Garoupa and Gómez-Pomar (n8).
15 Ibid.
16 Revesz (n4) discussing terminology; exclusivity means that specialized courts hear every case of a particular area of the law whereas by limitation we understand that specialized courts hear only cases of a particular nature.
17 Ibid.
18 Ibid.
19 Ibid.
20 Ibid.
21 Ibid.
22 Mahoney (n1); Dari-Mattiacci et al. (n8).
23 Dari-Mattiacci et al. (n8).
24 Ibid.
25 Ibid.
26 Ibid.
27 Ibid.
28 Ibid.
29 The institutional design is relevant in order to mitigate conflicts of jurisdiction and of law; an example is the French *Tribunal des Conflits*.
30 Dari-Mattiacci et al. (n8).
31 Ibid.
32 Ibid.
33 Ibid.
34 Ibid.
35 Richard Posner, 'Will the Federal Courts of Appeals Survive Until 1984? An Essay on Delegation and Specialization of the Judicial Function' (1983) 56 *Southern California Law Review* 761; Rochelle C. Dreyfuss, 'The Federal Circuit: A Case Study in Specialized Courts' (1989) 64 *New York University Law Review* 1.

36 Dari-Mattiacci et al. (n8).
37 Ibid.
38 John Bell, 'Administrative Law in a Comparative Perspective' in Esin Örücü and David Nelken eds, *Comparative Law: A Handbook* (Oxford: Hart 2007) 291–293, 299. Professor Bell recognizes that the major advantage of separate administrative courts is the possibility to develop a set of principles that accepts the specific nature of the state as defendant or as plaintiff (access to information, evidence produced by the administration, control over administrative discretion) balancing the interests of citizens and the ability of the administration to pursue the public interest. According to Professor Bell, the main disadvantages are potential conflicts of jurisdiction that require another special court to solve them, the *Tribunal des Conflits*.
39 Dari-Mattiacci, Garoupa and Gómez-Pomar (n8).
40 John Bell, Sophie Boyron and Simon Whittaker, *Principles of French Law* (2nd edn Oxford University Press 2008); John Bell, *Judiciaries within Europe: A Comparative Review* (Cambridge University Press 2006) 47–49. Professor Bell emphasizes that administrative law includes different rules within public law, including contract with public authorities, liability of public authorities, and employment within public administration. The substantial workload of administrative courts in France is partially explained by the principle of right to appeal in facts and in points of law.
41 Dari-Mattiacci et al. (n8).
42 Ibid.
43 This point was echoed by Kenneth W. Dam, *The Law-Growth Nexus: The Rule of Law and Economic Development* (Washington: Brookings Institution Press 2006) 118–120 (referring to the significant size of the public sector and the potential need for specialized administrative review). See also Bell (n38) 289–293 (discussing healthcare, education, housing, social security and infrastructure). It could be that a large public sector is negatively correlated with growth, but in this case the choice of court structure is a mere response to a political preference and not itself negatively correlated with growth. In fact, if our argument is correct, an alternative court structure on the lines of common law jurisdictions would be second-best and hence further contribute to the negative correlation between a large public sector and economic growth.
44 Dari-Mattiacci et al.n8).
45 Ibid.
46 Ibid.
47 Jean-Michel Josselin and Alain Marciano, 'The Paradox of Leviathan: How to Develop and Contain the Future European State?' (1997) 4 *European Journal of Law and Economics* 5 (emphasizing the advantages of the French type of administrative law in restraining the state).
48 Dari-Mattiacci et al. (n8).
49 Part of the argument against the French solution is derived from a general dislike of French administrative law by Anglo-American legal scholars. *See* J. W. F. Allison, *A Continental Distinction in the Common Law: A Historical and Comparative Perspective on English Public Law* (Oxford University Press 1996) 157–158 (arguing that the Anglo-American understanding of French administrative law and courts is flawed). Allison blames Dicey who, in 1885, wrote that administrative law is incompatible with the English tradition (in his Lectures Introductory to the Study of the Law of the Constitution). Dicey changed his mind later by recognizing the modern French administrative law addressed important concerns and was not necessarily incompatible with the rule of law. Ibid. 161. In fact, different constitutional law arrangements could demand stronger administrative law and Dicey ignored this point as do many recent Anglo-American scholars. Proposals for separate administrative courts in Britain were rejected in the mid-1930s (including an English *Conseil d'État*) but administrative tribunals have proliferated as governments got bigger, as we suggest they should.

50 J. H. Baker, 'The Law Merchant and the Common Law Before 1700' (1979) 38 *Cambridge Law Journal* 295; Richard A. Epstein, 'Reflections on the Historical Origins and Economic Structure of the Law Merchant' (2004) 5 *Chicago Journal of International Law* 1; Emily Kadens, 'Order Within Law, Variety Within Custom: The Character of the Medieval Merchant Law' (2004) 5 *Chicago Journal of International Law* 39; Celia Wasserstein Fassberg, 'Lex Mercatoria: Hoist with Its Own Petard?' (2004) 5 *Chicago Journal of International Law* 67; Roger B. Myerson, 'Justice, Institutions and Multiple Equilibria' (2004) 5 *Chicago Journal of International Law* 91; Avner Greif, 'Impersonal Exchange Without Impartial Law: The Community Responsibility System' (2004) 5 *Chicago Journal of International Law* 109; Avinash Dixit,'Two-Tier Market Institutions' (2004) 5 *Chicago Journal of International Law* 139.

51 Avner Greif, *Institutions and the Path to the Modern Economy: Lessons from the Medieval Trade* (Cambridge: Cambridge University Press 2006) 391–395; Bruce L. Benson, 'The Spontaneous Evolution of Commercial Law' (1989) 55 *Southern Economic Journal* 644; Avner Greif, Paul Milgrom and Barry R. Weingast, 'Coordination, Commitment, and Enforcement: The Case of the Merchant Guild' (1994) 102 *Journal of Political Economy* 745; Avner Greif, 'Institutions and Impersonal Exchange: From Communal to Individual Responsibility' (2002) 158 *Journal of Institutional and Theoretical Economy* 168.

52 Oliver Volckart and Antje Mangels, 'Are the Roots of the Modern *Lex Mercatoria* Really Medieval?' (1999) 65 *Southern Economic Journal* 427 (arguing that differences between law codes did not pose a substantial problem and that mercantile guilds developed, not to provide institutions comparable to the modern *lex mercatoria*, but rather to supply protection, as a result of which the importance of universally accepted commercial institutions in the Middle Ages has hitherto been vastly misperceived).

53 Robert D. Cooter, 'Structural Adjudication and the New Law Merchant: A Model of Decentralized Law' (1994) 14 *International Review of Law and Economics* 215; Robert D. Cooter, 'Decentralized Law for a Complex Economy: The Structural Approach to Adjudicating The New Law Merchant' (1996) 144 *University of Pennsylvania Law Review* 1643; Lisa Bernstein, 'Merchant Law in a Merchant Court: Rethinking the Code's Search for Immanent Business Norms' (1996) 144 *University of Pennsylvania Law Review* 1765; Leon E. Trakman, 'From the Medieval Law Merchant to E-Merchant Law' (2003) 53 *University of Toronto Law Journal* 265; Mark D. Rosen, 'Do Codification and Private International Law Leave Room for a New Law Merchant?' (2004) 5 *Chicago Journal of International Law* 83; Clayton P. Gillette, 'The Law Merchant in the Modern Age: Institutional Design and International Usages under the CISG' (2004) 5 *Chicago Journal of International Law* 157; Ralf Michaels, 'The True Lex Mercatoria: Law Beyond the State' (2007) 14 *Indiana Journal of Global Legal Studies* 447.

54 But see Amalia D. Kessler, *A Revolution in Commerce: The Parisian Merchant Court and the Rise of Commercial Society in Eighteen-Century France* (New Haven, CT: Yale University Press 2007) 286–297 (discussing the French commercial courts from an economic perspective).

55 Bell et al. (n40).

56 Only the court recorder (*greffier*) has legal training. See Bell et al. (n40) 62–63, 77.

57 Simple cases are heard by the president and around 30 per cent by the three judge panel. Ibid 45–48.

58 Bell et al. (n40).

59 Ibid.

60 Bell et al. (n40) 48.

61 On the development of judge-made commercial law in England and in France not being significantly different, see Gino Gorla and Luigi Moccia, 'A 'Revisiting' of the Comparison between 'Continental Law' and 'English Law' (16th–19th Century)' (1981) 2 *Journal of Legal History* 143, 149.

62 Nicholas H. D. Foster, 'Comparative Commercial Law: Rules or Context' in Örücü and Nelken eds, *Comparative Law* 271, 272. Professor Foster discusses the law regarding the facilitation and regulation of commerce. He acknowledges that both in common and civil law, commercial law is based on the *lex mercatoria*. However, the path taken is significantly different. With respect to English law, commercial law based on the *lex mercatoria* gradually disappeared and was inserted into common law by professional judges. In turn, such movement increased the need of merchants as juries or helping more directly the court. The system received statutory regulation by the Sale of Goods Act 1893, the Partnership Act 1890, the Bills of Exchange Act 1882 and Marine Insurance Act 1906, all influenced to some degree by Continental law. Statute law recognizes the autonomy of business law, the legal principle of encouraging commerce, and the conventional common law pragmatism with flexibility dominated by commercial lawyers. French law has followed a different path. Commercial law was developed separately from civil law influenced by the growing through trade within Europe. It was based on statutory law of Italian cities and Roman law, centralized by government with the ordinances of 1673 and 1681 (*Ordonnance sur le commerce de terre* and *Ordonnance sur la marine*). Before codification, French law was superior in terms of flexibility since it was subject only to lay commercial courts which were innovative. Influenced by civil law, the 1807 commercial code was based on the old ordinances but was outdated soon, and new legislation amended the code until its replacement in 2000.

63 In fact, proposals for professionalization of the commercial judges have failed so far. Bell et al. (n40) 48; Loïc Cadiet and Soraya Amrani-Mekki, *Civil Procedure in* George A. Bermann and Etienne Picard eds, *Introduction to French Law* (Alphen aan den Rijn Frederik, MD: Kluwer Law International 2008) 311 (noting proposals to convert the commercial courts into mixed courts with professional judges have been dropped). Most of the criticism directed at commercial courts was derived from a general perception that they were excessively captured by particular business interests in the context of bankruptcy litigation.

64 Notice that they are unique among countries of French legal tradition, thus also showing the problems of generalizations. Hans Ulrich Walder-Richli, *Law of Civil Procedure*, in François Dessemontet and Tuğrul Ansay eds, *Introduction to Swiss Law* 3rd ed. (The Hague and Frederick, MD: Kluwer Law International 2004) 289 (discussing the Swiss case); Jean Laenens and George Van Mellaert, *The Judicial System and Procedure*, in Hubert Bocken and Walter de Bondt eds, *Introduction to Belgian Law* (Bruxelles, The Hague and London: Kluwer Law International 2001) 86 (discussing the Belgian case). In four Swiss cantons (including those covering Zurich and Berne), there are specialized commercial courts if the action involves important transactions and at least the defendant is listed as a firm in the Swiss commercial register. They have two professional judges and three business assessors drawn from the local business community. They function as experts. In Belgium, there is a commercial court in every judicial district with jurisdiction over commercial litigation. They have professional judges (including the president of the court) and lay judges who assist the president of the court.

65 Rafael La Porta et al., 'Judicial Checks and Balances' (2004) 112 *Journal of Political Economy* 445.

66 Ibid.

67 Ibid.

68 Hans Kelsen, 'Judicial Review of Legislation: A Comparative Study of the Austrian and the American Constitution' (1942) 4 *Journal of Politics* 183. See generally Alec Stone Sweet, *Governing With Judges: Constitutional Politics in Europe* (Oxford and New York: Oxford University Press 2000).

69 Tom Ginsburg, *Judicial Review in New Democracies: Constitutional Courts in Asian Cases* (Cambridge and New York; Cambridge University Press 2003); Sweet (n68). The notion of a 'negative legislator' is based on the idea that the court expels legislation

from the system and therefore shares legislative power with the parliament. Kelsen (n68) 193–194.

70 Kelsen (n68) 194–197.
71 Sweet (n68).
72 Ibid.
73 Ibid.
74 Ibid. Examples include the cases of Portugal, Spain and most Central and East European countries.
75 Ginsburg (n69).
76 Ibid; Sweet (n68).
77 Ginsburg (n69), Sweet (n69).
78 Ibid.
79 Ginsburg (n69). More generally, see Tom Ginsburg, 'Beyond Judicial Review: Ancillary Powers of Constitutional Courts' in Tom Ginsburg and Robert A. Kagan eds, *Institutions and Public Law: Comparative Approaches* (New York: Peter Lang 2005) 225, 230.
80 Ginsburg (n69), Sweet (n68).
81 Ibid.
82 Ibid.
83 Ibid.
84 See generally Alec Stone Sweet, 'Constitutions and Judicial Power' in Daniele Caramani ed., *Comparative Politics* (Oxford and New York: Oxford University Press 2008) 218 (discussing the standard trade-offs).
85 Nicolas Marie Kublicki, 'An Overview of the French Legal System from An American Perspective' (1994) 12 *Boston University International Law Journal* 58 (arguing that the French experience demonstrates the sporadic and slowness of American constitutional review even if French constitutional review lacks the capacity to implement social and economic policy).
86 Lars P. Feld and Stefan Voigt, *Judicial Independence and Economic Growth: Some Proposals Regarding the Judiciary* in Roger D. Congleton and Birgitta Swedenbord eds, *Democratic Constitutional Design and Public Policy: Analysis and Evidence* (Cambridge, MA: MIT Press 2006).
87 Ibid. 251, 276–277 (finding that constitutional review powers vested in the highest judicial instance (the American model) reduce economic growth).

8   The puzzle of mixed law
jurisdictions

Legal systems are not randomly distributed around the world.[1] Most jurisdictions inherit their legal system from an invader, an occupier or a colonial power.[2] Few countries have actually chosen their legal system as the outcome of a conscious debate over the existing possibilities.[3] The standard examples arc Japan, Thailand and the Ottoman Empire, countries that by the end of the nineteenth century favoured civil law (German in the first case and French in the last two cases) over available alternatives at the time.[4] The reasons for their choice had less to do with economic efficiency and more to do with the perception of the fast growing French and later German power (military more than economic) and modernization.[5]

However, at the same time, one can hardly think that legal systems are merely correlated with the particular dominant culture.[6] In fact, being simplistic but nevertheless informative, Britain colonized the areas of the world that were relevant from the perspective of their economic and military interests[7]. The remaining European powers were essentially left with the regions that the British did not want.[8] Britain defeated all competing European colonial powers at one stage or another, so common law was developed in places Britain perceived to be important areas of the world.[9] Civil law was constrained and limited to regions that were not perceived significant for British interests.[10] As a consequence, the distribution of legal systems is necessarily correlated with British imperial perceptions of relevance.[11] And these perceptions are inevitably correlated with potential economic growth, thus creating a serious technical problem to the econometric estimations of the legal origins movement.[12]

Some areas of the world were initially colonized by European countries that have civil law (although in some cases their civil law predates the nineteenth century codification).[13] Due to the strategic role they played for the interests of the British Empire, Britain eventually defeated other European powers and acquired these territories.[14] Consequently these parts of the globe were subject to common law in a second wave of legal transplants.[15] In not a single case have we seen common law fully obliterating the civil law past.[16] In some jurisdictions, the civil law past has faded with time and is tenuously reflected in current legal institutions, the most obvious examples are the American Southern states.[17] However, in the vast majority of these jurisdictions, the civil law and the common law have coexisted.[18] Comparativists loosely refer to these institutional arrangements as mixed jurisdictions.[19]

In this chapter we take a different approach from our previous discussion. We focus on mixed, pluralist or hybrid jurisdictions. These are jurisdictions that mix elements of civil law and common law (and eventually elements from a third legal system). Given the alleged superiority of the common law system, one should expect the civil law to fade away. Moreover, the common law being the legal system of the later, stronger colonizer or occupier, we should suppose the civil law to be in a difficult position to survive.[20] Such predictions are, broadly speaking, inconsistent with reality.[21] We discuss the reasons for that with an economic model.

The comparative law literature does not provide for any precise definition of a mixed jurisdiction. The reason is that probably all jurisdictions are mixed in the sense that they are informed by indigenous legal tradition and transplants in relevant areas of the law.[22] Jurisdictions interact for multiple reasons and, as a consequence, conscious or not, by statute, by case law, or by legal practice, are influenced by other jurisdictions.[23] If every jurisdiction is mixed, then the classification of legal families must be based on a matter of degree.[24]

The first distinction is between those jurisdictions that mix legal systems in a systematic way and those that do not.[25] Within the jurisdictions that do not mix legal systems in a systematic way, we include the vast majority of the world that is usually affiliated to a particular legal family. They occasionally and opportunistically transplant laws and legal institutions from a different legal family, but overall they follow a particular dominant tradition.[26] Obviously such classification does not come without problems. Nevertheless, it fits with the traditional division between civil and common law legal families.[27] The focus of this chapter is on those jurisdictions that combine legal systems in a systematic way and therefore cannot be regarded as either civil or common law.

A second important distinction is between those jurisdictions that have a structured mix and those that have an unstructured mix.[28] By unstructured mixed legal system, comparativists understand an overlap of two traditions, with no clear or evident application of one or the other to all legal subjects.[29] There is no formal articulation or coordination between the two legal traditions. The obvious example is European law and aboriginal law in many African countries.[30]

Contrarily, by structured mixed legal system, there is some coordination.[31] Such coordination can take different complementary forms. It could be established by conceptual boundaries (such as private and public law).[32] It could be categorized even within areas where the overlap is unclear (such as commercial law or procedure).[33] Alternatively, a legal tradition could dominate in certain areas of the law with legislative pockets of the other legal family.[34] Finally, both legal traditions may coexist under a process of mutual recognition of structured boundaries and sources.[35]

Structured mixed legal systems can be pluralist (usually dualist) or hybrid.[36] By pluralist, we envisage the case where the different legal families operate side by side, in well-defined contained areas of the law.[37] For example, private law follows the civil law tradition whereas public law follows the common law tradition.[38] By hybrid, we consider the possibility of blending together those legal traditions.[39] A possibility is that contract law, or more generally private law, combines both common and civil law doctrines.[40]

The terminology in comparative law is not without problems. In fact, some comparitivists have criticized the standard vocabulary. For example, legal scholars refer to 'mixed jurisdictions' when they use common and civil law traditions, rather than 'mixed legal systems' as would be more appropriate.[41] The term 'mixed jurisdictions' seems to presuppose a degree of hybridism which is usually absent.[42] The term 'mixed legal systems' anticipates legal pluralism, which seems more frequent than hybridism.[43]

In this chapter we study structured mixed legal systems, in particular those that use both the common and the civil law traditions. Table 8.1 summarizes the jurisdictions we are considering. Notice that some relevant cases have been excluded from Table 8.1 (based on the work of comparativists) but can be easily framed in the context of our model. They are Japan, Korea and Taiwan that were pure civil law jurisdictions (all of German tradition) and have now been influenced by the US common law system.[44] We could add Hong Kong as a common law tradition now under the influence of Chinese law (which loosely speaking could be considered in the civil law tradition).[45] The European Union is a completely different case that blends the different civil law traditions with some elements of the common law (due to the United Kingdom, Ireland and more recently Malta and Cyprus).[46]

Table 8.1 Mixed legal systems[47]

Common and Civil Law	Common, Civil and Customary Law	Common, Civil and Muslim Law	Common, Civil and Talmudic Law
Botswana	Cameroun	Iran	Israel
Thailand	Djibouti	Jordan	
Cyprus	Eritrea	Saudi Arabia	
South Africa	Indonesia	Somalia	
Guyana	Lesotho	Yemen	
Seychelles	Sri Lanka		
Louisiana	Vanatu		
Scotland	Zimbabwe		
Malta			
Saint Lucia			
Mauritius			
Quebec			
Namibia			
Puerto Rico			
Philippines			

There is no formal model of mixed jurisdiction to the same extent that there is no formal model of common law or of civil law.[48] Any jurisdiction incorporating elements from both legal traditions has developed a particular institutional feature that makes any mixed system unique. In fact, jurisdictions of a mixed legal family were not originally founded as such.[49] Their mixed nature is the product of a later change. Following the insights of a famous legal scholar, we could define these jurisdictions as 'basically a civilian system that had been under pressure from the Anglo-American common law and has in part been overlaid by that rival system of jurisprudence'.[50] The civil law is not necessarily the original legal tradition (since many of these countries had some aboriginal or indigenous law before European colonization), but it was implemented before the arrival of British common law.[51]

All jurisdictions in Table 8.1 are fundamentally dualist (the first column) or pluralist (the remaining columns).[52] They have a legal system with a dual foundation. A large proportion of substantive law and procedure can be distinctly traced back to civil or common law systems.[53] Generally speaking, private law seems to be of civil tradition whereas public law (administrative, criminal, and constitutional) comes from Anglo-American influence.[54] The main reason is, broadly speaking, the earlier development of private law and later development of public law.[55]

Legal scholars have traced the combination of civil and common law back to two distinct possible historical reasons[56]:

i   *Intercolonial transfer* (losses from France, Spain, the Netherlands, or the Ottoman Empire; gains to Britain or the United States).[57] There is usually little influence of Anglo-American law before the transfer of sovereignty.[58] The transfer of sovereignty usually results from an event unrelated to the legal system (for example, war).[59] The new dominant political actor is established in a strong position but avoids or fails to effectively impose the common law because of a large non-Anglophonic community that is socially and economically dominant (but not politically).[60] The English speaking community initially is a minority that communicates in a different language that does not dominate the life of the jurisdiction.[61] Still, this English minority shapes the political process.[62] Not surprisingly, the common law expands due to a well-developed colonial administration and the local (business) interests of the small English speaking community.[63]

For example, consider the case of Malta.[64] Private law is essentially dominated by the civil law tradition but administrative and constitutional law is inevitably English.[65] Legal scholars have explained the enactment of Maltese codes in the nineteenth century as a mechanism to achieve consistency between the influence of Italian law and the realities of the political connection to Britain.[66] As a consequence, the pure civil law tradition has been blended with the practice of English oriented sources. However, even today, the combination of common and civil law is fundamentally more practical than doctrinal and fully theorized.[67]

Scholars can also use this model to understand Japan, Korea and Taiwan. They were initially influenced by German law after the reforms enacted following the Meiji restoration.[68] The American occupation after WWII promoted important legal reforms in Japan and Korea (the anti-monopoly laws being the standard example).[69] Taiwan's history after 1949 induced an approximation to the United States that had consequences in later legal reforms.[70] These jurisdictions combine an important civil law tradition of German influence with fundamental reforms of American origin.[71] There is no formal intercolonial transfer, but these countries were under the sphere of a civil law jurisdiction in the first stage of legal reform and, due to later political changes, came under the sphere of a common law jurisdiction.[72]

Israel provides another example of this approach.[73] The Ottoman influence explains the prevalence of German civil law in the region.[74] The British Mandate for Palestine established in the early 1920s brought the common law to this area of the world.[75] The coexistence of civil and common law was noticeable by the time Israel became independent in 1948.[76] Waves of immigration with lawyers who transferred from different legal origins reflected different experiences.[77] The intercolonial transfer was reinforced by a significant change of the composition of the population, in particular lawyers.[78]

ii *Merger of sovereignties* (mainly Scotland): the Act of Union of 1707 keeps strict separation between Scottish and English law.[79] Scottish private law is respected but the Union effectively merges public law and public institutions.[80] The new political and judicial institutions promoted the reception of English law, although it is debatable if the combination of legal traditions was already there before the Union due to trade, political and economic influence.[81]

The importance of precedent with binding effect even in areas of traditional civil law has been recognized as the main source to combine substantive civil law with a common law approach in Scotland.[82] However, some areas have been largely immune to legislative incursion from English law unless absolutely necessary (such as criminal or family law).[83] Legal scholars mention the Scottish examples as a unique voluntarily combination of civil and common law that struggles for legal consistency.[84]

The European Union can be discussed in the context of this model. Strictly speaking, the European Union created a new legal order independent of the Member-states.[85] However, the law of the European Union has to be enforced and applied by national courts subject to a complex institutional framework (including the principle of supremacy of European Union law).[86] Inevitably, these national courts reflect their own traditions and practices.[87] Therefore, European Union law combines elements of common law and civil law in response to the ongoing need of improving and balancing a new legal order.[88] The European Union is not, strictly speaking, a merger of sovereignties, but the institutional arrangement reflects a similar process due to the impeding incompleteness of a recent legal order that requires the cooperation of national courts.[89]

As noted by legal scholars, when coded, the incumbent civil law is likely to be more resistant to common law influence.[90] We can use the French or Spanish experiences when compared to the Dutch group to provide an illustration.[91]

In most cases of mixed legal systems around the world, there are significant common elements that have been identified by comparativists to explain the patterns of development of a mixed legal family.[92] The most immediate is language as we have already mentioned. Usually there is a linguistic factor that requires, at least in early stages, that the law be in a language different from English.[93]

A second aspect is the influence of Anglo-American law on legal institutions and procedure which is usually determined by the political power of the English-speaking community.[94] Examples include powerful courts, influential judges, some form of *stare decisis* where judicial decisions are accepted as a source of law (*de facto* or *de jure*) and bind inferior courts (in a much less flexible way than the Spanish *doctrina jurisprudencial* or the French *jurisprudence constante*), and assimilation of common law rules of civil procedure (although usually with no formal separation between common law and equity).[95]

A third element is the slow penetration of common law in the context of private law. According to legal scholars, the patterns of common law influence in private law are usually the following: some in torts, less so in contracts, even less in quasi-contracts and unjust enrichment, very little to none in property.[96] Commercial law tends to adhere to common law more easily, generally not by imposition but due to self-interested economic reasons and the inadequacy of the old civil law.[97]

As we discussed in the previous section, comparative law has identified general patterns of development of a mixed legal family. Civil law arrives first due to the initial colonization or political influence (in the case of Scotland).[98] Common law follows after some transfer of sovereignty.[99] Common law is not developed because the local community is unsatisfied with civil law, but due to political and military reasons.[100] Not surprisingly, common law dominates legal institutions, procedure and public law.[101] However, common law does not easily penetrate private law.[102]

Public law depends mostly on political or constitutional decisions.[103] Often a mixed system follows a common law pattern in criminal law, judicial proceedings, or administrative matters.[104] This is the case of mixed jurisdictions within a constitutional framework based on common law such as the American Southern states, Puerto Rico, Israel or Scotland.[105] The opposite tends to happen within the European Union, where the United Kingdom and Ireland are subject to legislative proceedings drafted according to the civilian tradition.[106]

Public law responds less immediately to individual incentives and decisions, but more to the political arrangements.[107] From this perspective, the imposition of common law structures has less to do with the evolution to efficiency resulting from the competition of different legal systems; it is more easily explained by the political influence of the legal tradition of the dominant power.[108]

The challenge comes from private law. We wonder why civil law survives when the legislature as well as the judiciary follow common law principles. According to the legal origins literature[109], transition to common law should follow mature economic growth.[110] In fact, the legal origins literature strongly recommends adopting common law principles in private law in order to enhance economic growth.[111] It seems that the mixed jurisdictions remain under civilian tradition for two possible reasons. One explanation is due to their current poor economic progress. Therefore, there is no pressure to change their legal system in the area of private law. A second reason is the limitations derived from their rigid civilian framework which precludes change. If the legal origins thesis is correct, mixed jurisdictions governed by common law principles should opt into the common law at a particular stage of economic growth.[112] Additionally, such mixed jurisdictions are embedded in a common law institutional framework, as a consequence of common law governing public institutions and their proceedings, and therefore are expected to recognize the importance of judicial precedent (unknown in pure civil law systems).[113]

An immediate explanation for the observed pattern could be mere path dependence. In other words, mixed legal families are still in a process of transformation.[114] Common law will eliminate civil law in some distant future much the same way it has happened in some American Southern states.[115] The reason for this delay would be the codification of civil law principles in many of those jurisdictions described in Table 8.1. Codification bolsters civil law and therefore reinforces path dependence.[116] The problem with this explanation is that legal scholars do not detect such a trend in those jurisdictions. Civil law seems to be there permanently.

Absent mere path dependence, if we take literally the legal origins movement, common law should replace civil law in the areas of private law.[117] Common law is more efficient. Common law is better for business interests and conducive to economic growth.[118] The persistence and survival of civil law is, therefore, puzzling. Why would a second-best legal tradition persist in private law when a first-best legal alternative is already available in public law?

A possible explanation is that mixed legal families are locked into an inefficient institutional arrangement and cannot move out. There is some market failure that inhibits the common law's ability to take over civil law in the areas of tort, contracts and property.[119] The costs of switching are so immensely large that mixed legal families cannot easily abandon the old civil law and adhere to common law.[120]

It is difficult to see what these significant costs could be. Legal economists have recognized that changing legal regimes has important disadvantages, but they do not seem to be as significant in this context as they are in the economic literature of transplants.[121]

Following the economic literature on the subject, the list of possible costs from replacing civil law by common law should include:

i   Direct cost from acquiring information, importing new rules and introducing new practices, interpreting and applying them.[122] These costs seem less significant when common law has prevailed already in public law and in procedure.

ii Rent-seeking or entrenchment costs from those who plausibly lose from changing legal rules (long-entrenched interests) and are willing to waste resources to avoid those changes (e.g., lawyers or the bar association).[123] These costs could have been relatively high in early stages when the jurisdiction was dominated by a non-Anglophonic community, but surely they must have been reduced as English influence expanded; lawyers are usually educated in both legal traditions, so there is no obvious reason to fear loss of rents to a competing or alternative legal profession.

iii Indirect costs due to the potential loss of legal coherence, consistency, network effects and potential development of contradictions and instability within the emergent law.[124] In this context, overall legal coherence increases since common law would dominate both public and private law.

iv Private legal order costs by limiting individual benefits from opting-out of the current legal order or developing third-party arrangements, that is, by imposing public adjustment of the law which is an imperfect substitute for private adjustment (assuming that existing arrangements allowed for such adjustment).[125] In our analysis, replacing civil law by common law presumably increases flexibility to accommodate private ordering given the alleged superiority of the common law in this respect. Alternatively, the introduction of common law would facilitate the malleability of the legal system given the general perception that case law is more flexible to local preferences.

v Lack of innovation costs since systems without local variations are less likely to innovate and adjust to dynamic preferences.[126] Comparing the current patterns of legal innovation in mixed legal families with the pure common and civil law jurisdictions, this lack of innovation cost does not seem very significant.

vi Subsequent costs of adjustment and administrative costs on the production of more law when transplants deviate from indigenous law.[127] Given that a mixed legal system is being replaced by a pure common law system, it is unclear how costs of future adjustments and more law can be significantly increased.

vii Potential costs due to coordination failure derived from the presence of strategic externalities or the public good nature of transplanting.[128] This could be a significant problem if the switch from civil law to common law is left to the market. However, in all these jurisdictions, there is a central government that was able to impose common law on areas of legal institutions, public law and procedure. Presumably the same central government could easily internalize these externalities, solve the public good under-provision of legal change, and consequently impose common law in the area of private law.

viii Transaction costs resulting from harmonization and legal unification.[129] Although these costs could be relevant given the entrenchment of civil law codification, they should be less significant than in a situation of legal transplanting from a different jurisdiction given the existing pluralism.

After reviewing all the possible costs from switching from civil law to common law, our conclusion can only be that it is unlikely that mixed legal families are merely locked into an inefficient arrangement that cannot easily change. We are not suggesting that these costs are non-existent or irrelevant. Nevertheless, we are not persuaded that these costs are so significant as to lock in mixed legal jurisdictions and justify their considerable loss of efficiency and economic growth.

As with the economic literature on transplants, the only reasonable explanation has to be related to preferences. Preferences (understood as legal culture, tradition and social inclination for a particular legal family) are the standard explanation for the prevalence of different legal systems.[130] In the legal transplant literature, the usual argument is that cultural, political and social preferences might explain why jurisdictions do not switch their legal regime.[131]

In order for the story about preferences to be consistent with the legal origins movement, it has to be the following. Even though the new legal regime (after transplant) is more conducive of economic growth, a particular jurisdiction could be willing to sacrifice (economic) effectiveness in order to maintain a legal regime more consistent with cultural preferences.[132] Therefore, in the absence of significant switching costs, different legal families persist because preferences undermine legal unification in an inefficient way.[133]

Sacrificing efficiency (in the sense of an economically better legal regime) due to cultural preferences seems unrealistic in the context of mixed legal families. Presumably initial preferences for a civil law model should be prevailing in private and in public law. Apparently they were not strong enough to deter change in public law, but they were powerful enough to undermine transformation in private law. Yet, several generations later, the same preferences are unchanged and uncontaminated by the observation of a superior legal order in public law.

It seems to us unlikely that the same preferences that support a more efficient legal regime in one area of the law do not support that same efficient legal regime in a different area of the law. Therefore, it seems that preferences are important, but not in the way the legal origins movement would suggest. Mixed legal families persist because, due to cultural preferences, switching legal regimes would be less conducive to economic growth and therefore less efficient. Our argument is that we cannot separate preferences that generate a particular demand for a legal system and the efficiency of that legal system. Under the cultural preferences that dominate a particular jurisdiction within a mixed legal system, civil law is likely to be more efficient than common law in the field of private law.[134] That is the only plausible explanation for why civil law has persisted and continues to persist in these jurisdictions.

The argument also sheds light on the Southern American states. The nature of the switching costs is not different between these jurisdictions and the ones described on Table 8.1. It is a matter of dynamic preferences. The sharp differences concerning legal preferences within the United States have faded away with time, therefore promoting the development of common law in the area of private law.[135] In those other jurisdictions, preferences have not developed in the same way. Most of these jurisdictions are sovereign states and they are not integrated into a federal arrangement that induces a particular cultural, political and social dynamics that favours the prevalence of the Anglo-American elements.[136] And when they are integrated, such as Quebec or Scotland, distinctive elements of the non-Anglophone community have survived by virtue of a different language and history.[137]

If our theory is correct, and in sharp contrast with the legal origins movement, forcing mixed legal families to abandon the civil law aspect in search of the efficiency of the common law would probably be detrimental for economic growth. In fact, our theory is closer to the so-called 'grafted transplants', that is, successful transplants embedded in the local context or fused with local norms.[138] Changing the context could have significant implications for legal reforms that are apparently based on (in our view, obviously misplaced) efficiency grounds.[139]

In summary, we reject path dependence as a convincing explanation given the political and institutional context. Obviously history is important. We also recognize that codification encroaches civil law in a nontrivial way. However, the institutional setup, including the importance of judicial precedent, is extremely favourable to the development of a common law approach to private law.[140] It seems unrealistic that a significantly inefficient form of law persists in an environment already dominated by the most efficient form of law merely because of some odd path dependency.

Preferences seem to be a better explanation. In order to be consistent with the legal origins story, it must be that social preferences are willing to sacrifice economic growth (induced by the common law) for the sake of some other goals (presumably better defended by civil law). However, this argument also seems problematic when those same preferences have already been sacrificed in the area of public law and legal institutions.

Our explanation does rely on preferences, but with a different insight. Under the cultural and social preferences that dominate a particular demand for a legal system, it could be that the mixed arrangement of civil and common law is more efficient. Therefore, if common law replaces civil law in the area of private law, it could be less conducive to economic growth. Unlike the legal origins theory, there is no single 'one-size-fits-all' solution. Mixed legal systems have survived because the complexities of the legal system illustrate that cultural preferences matter. To demonstrate this further, we are taking a closer look at the role and development of trusts in mixed legal jurisdictions.

Contrasting common and civil law: the role of trusts and mixed legal jurisdictions

Trusts are traditional common law devices, economically significant due to their role in the common law world: large sums of assets are carried and used through them all over the world. At this point they are chosen for a deeper analysis as such with the intent to use this particular economic relevant example to prove that the lack of this institution in civil law systems does not influence the efficiency of division of legal interest over the same assets in those jurisdictions.

Details in the regulation of trusts change among common law jurisdictions, but all of them recognize some kind of trust. Probably, one of the most wide and inclusive contemporary definition of the trust is that provided by the §2 of the Restatement (Third) of the Law: Trusts, published by the American Law Institute in 2003:

> A trust, as the term is used in this Restatement, when not qualified by the word 'resulting' or 'constructive', is a fiduciary relationship with respect to property, arising from a manifestation of intention to create that relationship and subjecting the person who holds title to the property to duties to deal with it for the benefit of charity or for one or more persons, at least one of whom is not the sole trustee.

The definition contains the main features of the trust. In its basic structure, the trust is based on a fiduciary relationship according to which one person (the trustee) holds legal title to certain assets for the benefit of another person (the beneficiary). Once the trust is settled, the settlor cannot be considered the owner of the assets put into the trust. The property becomes an autonomous set of assets, managed by the trustee in benefit of the beneficiaries of the trust. The assets constitute a separate fund and are not a part of the trustee's own estate. The trust lacks legal personality, though is entitled to act and to enter into legal relationships.

The Restatement also refers to the main kinds of trusts. Section 2 of the Restatement, quoted above, defines the so called 'express trust'. It is the trust agreed by the settlor, who nominates the trustee and designates the beneficiaries and the requirements under which they can get the benefits. The express trust has a contractual origin. Since the beneficiaries are not necessarily part in such a contract, express trusts have been usually presented as an exception of the doctrine of privity of contracts.[141]

'Resulting' and 'constructive' trusts are the two additional versions of the phenomenon. Both are ordered by statute or by court under different circumstances. The former can be a product of gifts made under some conditions or payments made for benefitting a third person. The latter resembles de civil law idea of the 'quasi contracts', and it is the answer to situations like those than the French Civil Code, among others civil law codifications, identify as 'paiement de l'indú'. Situations in which someone has been benefitted by mistake and becomes obliged to redress the situation or to give back what has unduly received. Resulting as well as constructive trusts are, in fact, remedies to situations in which a transfer has been made without a legal ground or in which the legal ground that justified legally the transfer is not valid anymore.[142]

The current research will focus on 'express' trusts. They are voluntary and their nature is more contractual than remedial. They can be established by an agreement between settlor and trustee, at least, in which the management rules as well as the third beneficiaries have to be duly specificied and identified. They are also a useful way to determine the 'mortis causa' transmission of some assets once the settlor deceases.[143]

Hence, they are good examples of ways for conveying wealth 'inter vivos' as well as 'mortis causa'. Trusts allow the settlor to transmit some assets to certain beneficiaries under a specific administration regime managed by the trustee. They are extensively used in common law jurisdictions, though with differences, more or less subtle, among them.

In the common law tradition, trusts have been used for dividing entitlements over the same property. It is a mechanism that has become very useful in for maximizing assets managements and portfolio strategies.[144] Trustees as well as beneficiaries hold different titles over the same assets. The former is a fiduciary holder of the assets. The latter have an interest in the trust. None of them can be deemed as owner of the assets that fund the trust, neither in whole nor in part. Hence they are not entitled to change the goals pursued by the settlor when he funded the trust. The division of the ownership entitlements that is familiar to the trust means the allocation of the burdens to the trustee and of the benefits to the beneficiaries, being the trust a separate set of assets. The peculiar relation between the trustee and the beneficiaries with the trusted funds is what distinguishes the trust from other ways of conveying wealth and what poses problems on its legal understanding.[145]

Once they have been established and funded, common law trusts become autonomous institutions. Although they are not considered as legal entities, trusts enter into legal relationships independently, at least from a formal point of view, from the trustee and the beneficiaries as well.

Civil law jurisdictions have developed institutions other than the trusts for dividing legal interests over the same assets and to fix them to specific goals. In the realm of contracts, fiduciary agreements allow one of the parties to take care of the other's assets. Usually, the fiduciary holds just a formal ownership over the asset that, according to the agreement between the parties, does not correspond with the real ownership. The fiduciary, in performing the fiducia, acts as the owner though in interest, and eventually on behalf, of the real holder of the assets. In the 'mortis causa' sphere, civil law jurisdictions use the 'fideicommissum' for linking inherited assets. According to the 'fideicommissum', the first heir receives the assets under the mandate of conveying them to a second heir already identified by the testator. The first heir is acting as a fiduciary. He holds the inherited assets with the obligation of passing them to the next heir.

Both institutions, fiducia as well as 'fideicommissum', resemble the trust. In fact, they allow the owner of some assets to establish a specific legal regime to them according to which they were either managed or passed in a specific way, benefiting specific persons or entities, and performing specific goals. Otherwise, differently from the trust, under fiduciary agreements and 'fideicommissum' the assets are always legally bound to either an individual or a legal person acting as the formal rightholder. Assets belong always to an identified rightholder, and they are never considered as autonomous, that is to say, the assets do not act legally independently of their rightholder, though he is just a fiduciary or temporary one. Although in civil law jurisdictions fiduciary agreements and 'fiseicommissum' achieve, at least in part, the goals pursued by the trust under common law jurisdictions, the mentioned institutions differ from the trust in the absence of autonomy granted to the assets.

It is usually stated that the trust is strange to civil law tradition. It is true. Civil law jurisdictions attach rights and duties to legal persons, and such category is formed by individuals and legal entities, being the later only those that have been previously designed and defined by statute. Under such a way of understanding the distribution of legal rights and duties, trusts do not fit in the traditional civil law pattern of potential rightholders. Generally speaking, civil law jurisdictions are reluctant to deal with sets of assets independently of their rightholder. Only legal persons, that is to say, either individuals or legal entities are deemed as capable to enter into legal relationships. Property, rights and legal duties are considered to depend always on legal persons.

The key difference between civil law and common Law approaches remains in the ability to contract. While in the civil law tradition such ability is linked to the owner, in the common law tradition the trustee, though does not held ownership is able to sell the trust's funds. The trustee becomes, in fact, an owner of another's assets, though he is only entitled to act in the benefit of the trust's beneficiaries or within the scope defined by the settlor. The trustee is then located somewhere between the pure owner and the agent. A position that is strange to the traditional civil law institutions.

According to the perspective adopted in the present research, the starting point relates with the presumption of efficiency of the common law. Just for summarize, according to the thesis that the present work tries to contradict, the common law, in whole, promotes more efficient results than civil law. The arguments used by the supporters of such a thesis have been already discussed in previous chapters. It is time now to check if the trust, being a unique common law legal institution, supports the thesis.

The globalization of the markets has generalized the trust. Financial markets, where common law trusts are usual, have promoted the presence of trusts in civil law jurisdictions. How to deal with trusts when they invade civil law traditions is one of the challenges that face civil law lawyers. Solutions differ, though civil law jurisdictions mostly tend to omit the autonomy of the trust and to consider either the trustee or the beneficiaries as the rightholders. Under civil law perspective, the trust is not a legal entity and then it is not entitled to act separately from the individuals or the legal persons underneath it.

The interaction of the trust with civil law jurisdictions is especially interesting when dealing with mixed jurisdictions. In such jurisdictions, as it is known, civil law and common law traditions interact. As it has been already showed in previous sections, mixed jurisdictions are a good laboratory to check the behaviour of legal institutions belonging exclusively to one of the legal families but applied by jurists and courts familiar with civil law as well as common law traditions. Being the trust one these legal institutions, it is worthy to check how it has been settled by mixed or hybrid jurisdictions and, in general, by civil law jurisdictions highly influenced by common law institutions.

If the trust, as a characteristic legal institution of the common law, would promote more efficient results than the civil law alternatives already mentioned, mixed jurisdictions as well as civil law jurisdictions strongly influenced by the common law tradition would have incorporated the common law trust instead of the traditional civil law fiduciary agreements or 'fideicommissa'. At the end, as it has been said, fiduciary agreements and 'fideicommissa' achieve in the civil law systems equivalent goals to those pursued by the trust in the common law tradition. Interaction between both legal families should result in the best legal institution prevailing over the worst legal institution. Being the trust a part of the common law, and therefore, more efficient than any other alternative coming from the civil law, trust should take the place of its alternatives in the civil law systems close to the common law or in the jurisdictions that have mixed both legal traditions.

However, an overview over those jurisdictions closer to the trust does not permit to conclude that they have adopted the trust instead of their traditional civil law institutions. As it will be next pointed out, all of them have allowed to some extent the existence of the trust, but only if the trust adopts some legal features familiar to the civil law tradition. It seems that the pressure derived from the vicinity of the common law has pushed the necessity of some kind of recognition of the trust in jurisdictions highly influenced by the common law or located in countries belonging to the common law tradition. The analysis shows that no-pure common law jurisdictions have been reluctant to adopt the trust as it has been defined and understood in the common law.

Specifically, they do not give autonomy to the trust as an independent and autonomous institution. The trust, though its existence, depends on either an individual or legal person, usually the trustee, that acts as the rightholder. The adopted-trust does not have in mixed, hybrid or highly influenced jurisdictions by the common law the autonomy granted to the trust in the pure common law jurisdictions. Coming back to the critique of the hypothesis on the common law efficiency, if the trust would be a more efficient institution than those already acknowledge to the civil law tradition, the jurisdictions at hand would had abandoned their civil law tradition, at least when referring to the trust and to the possibility of granting autonomy to some assets attached to specific purposes.

The most of the jurisdictions that do not belong to the common law tradition but that have to deal with the common law trust have developed ways for embedding the common law trust in the civil law structures. Specifically, all of them have used the fiduciary ownership already known in the civil law tradition as the best way of understanding the common law trust:

a   In the case of Scotland, the trust fund belongs to the trustee, who will act as its owner, though the fiduciary nature of the ownership promotes the separation of the trusted funds from the trustee's personal assets. The mechanism has been called by Scottish legal scholars as the 'dual patrimony theory'. The Scottish Law Commission explained such a theory as follows:

When a person becomes a trustee he acquires a second patrimony: he now has his private patrimony as before and a trust patrimony. The trust patrimony consists of the trust fund which is owned by the trustee and any obligations he has incurred in the proper administration of the trust. If as will usually be the case there are two or more trustees, the trust patrimony is owned by them jointly. Although owned by the same person the trustee's private patrimony is a separate legal entity from the trustee's trust patrimony.[146]

b   In Louisiana, the §9:1731 of the Louisiana Trust Code (2011) defines the trust as '[...] the relationship resulting from the transfer of title to property to a person to be administered by him as a fiduciary for the benefit of another'. Such a person will be named 'trustee' as sets forth the §9:1781[147].

c   In Puerto Rico, the 'Ley núm. 219, de Fideicomisos (2012)' have replaced the provisions contained in the Puerto Rican Civil Code on Trust and offers a complete regulation of the common law institution in the Puerto Rican legal system. According to the article 3 of the 'Ley de Fideicomisos', the owner of the assets subject to the Puerto Rican trust will be their fiduciary owner, who will administer them in interest of the beneficiary.

d   According to the article 6(1) of the Maltese Trust and Trustees Act, as enacted after the revision made in 2004, 'A trust exists where a person (called a trustee) holds, as owner or has vested in him property under an obligation to deal with that property for the benefit of persons (called the beneficiaries), whether or not yet ascertained or in existence, which is not for the benefit only of the trustee, or for a charitable purpose, or for both such benefit and purpose aforesaid.'

In all of the abovementioned examples, it seems clear the effort made by the mentioned jurisdictions to adopt the common law trust to their traditional civil law structures. The trustee is in charge of the trust, and performs a function closer to the mandate than to the management of some assets, autonomous and independent. Fiduciary duties are used to define the scope of the trustee's conduct, though it is the rightholder of the trust's assets. The trust does not seem to be granted with autonomy, since it has to act through the trustee. It is true that that the trust becomes a separate group separate from the trustee personal property. The trust's assets will be protected against the trustee's creditors, but the existence of the trust is intertwined with the trustee.

At the end, fiduciary duties accomplish a general function, in all legal families, that allow the real owner to vest someone else with a formal ownership in order to perform some purposes.[148] The difference does not consist in the existence of fiduciary duties, acknowledge by all legal systems, as stated, but in the way in which those duties are vested and performed. The mentioned jurisdictions have adopted the trust model to their own legal structures instead of changing them in order to make the common law trust fully workable.

Other mixed of hybrid jurisdictions have adopted the trust in a broader way, and have accepted the autonomy of the trust's funds, that do not have to be owned, though separately, by the trustee.

This is the case of Quebec whose Civil Code grants a wide range of autonomy to the trusts incorporated to the Quebec rules. According to the article 1261 of the Civil Code of Quebec, 'The trust patrimony, consisting of the property transferred in trust, constitutes a patrimony by appropriation, autonomous and distinct from that of the settlor, trustee or beneficiary and in which none of them has any real right.' In Quebec, the trust is not anymore a part, though separated, of the trustee's assets, but an autonomous fund in relation to which only a specific legal relationship, the 'appropriation' can exist. Article 1278 of the Quebec Civil Code defines the trustee as a pure administrator of the trust, hence limiting strongly his condition as rightholder of the administered assets:

> 'A trustee has the control and the exclusive administration of the trust patrimony, and the titles relating to the property of which it is composed are drawn up in his name; he has the exercise of all the rights pertaining to the patrimony and may take any proper measure to secure its appropriation. A trustee acts as the administrator of the property of others charged with full administration.

In South Africa, the Trust Property Control Act (1988) names the trustee as a pure administrator of alien assets, obliged to invest them to the purposes declared by the settlor. In the same vein, the Trustee Law (1955) of Cyprus refers the trustee as a personal representative of the settlor, managing assets in a way close to the general agent.

In conclusion, all mixed or hybrid jurisdictions at hand have embedded the trust within the fiduciary and agency structures. The trust itself is considered as a group of assets subject by the settlor to a specific management regime and the trustee is understood as an agent in charge of such assets. In those hybrid or mixed jurisdictions that have adopted the trust, it has become a special regime within the general category of administration of estate.

The process experienced by the hybrid or mixed jurisdictions that have been to adopt themselves in order to grant some recognition to the common law trust shows that they have implemented it according to their traditional civil law structures. Besides other possible explanations, the process allows to conclude that is not crystal clear that the trust could be always deemed as a more efficient institution that those regarding fiducia and agency already acknowledged by the civil la tradition.[149] The result also shows that in the contemporary world, legal transplants do not mean the adoption of foreign legal structures but the transformation of the own structures for pursuing specific goals.[150]

In order to facilitate the intervention of the trusts in civil law jurisdictions, the Hague Conference on Private International Law promoted the Convention on the Law Applicable to Trusts and on their Recognition, concluded on July 1, 1985 (the Convention, hereinafter). The Convention entered into force on 1 January

1992, and since then has been ratified or accepted by only twelve countries.[151] The Convention only applies to express trusts, created voluntarily and evidenced in writing (see Article 3).

The Convention deals with the recognition of the trust and with the law applicable to them. Then, allows to a settlor subject to a civil law jurisdiction to set a common law trust and to force national authorities to deal with the trust according to the law chosen by the settlor. Article 6 of the Convention sets forth that:

> A trust shall be governed by the law chosen by the settlor. The choice must be express or be implied in the terms of the instrument creating or the writing evidencing the trust, interpreted, if necessary, in the light of the circumstances of the case ...

Hence, the Convention grants a high freedom of choose to those subject to a civil law system interested in devoting some assets in trust to specific purposes. The Convention is a proper way of allowing the use of trust in civil law jurisdictions. If the trust would be a better solution that those already allowed by the civil law system, civil law jurisdictions would have ratified the Convention massively. However, this is not the case.

It is important to highlight that the list of countries that have ratified the Convention does not correspond with the traditional distinction between common Law and civil law. Some of the signatory countries belong to the common law tradition. This is the case of Australia, Canada, United Kingdom and the United States of America. They have probably signed the Convention to allow the recognition of foreign trusts, created in other common law jurisdictions in a way different to the proceedings required in other common law jurisdictions. For such countries, the Convention facilitates the recognition of foreign trusts, though within common law systems the trust itself could not be deemed as strange to their own legal tradition.

The most of the remaining signatory countries belong to the civil law tradition. They are the People's Republic of China, France, Italy, Monaco, Luxembourg, The Netherlands and Switzerland. Although they are important countries, in demographic as well as economic terms, they do not represent the majority of civil law countries in the world. Then, it is not possible to identify an international move to the recognition of the trust from the civil law systems. At the same time, the presence of countries like Switzerland, Monaco or Luxembourg leads to suppose that financial interests in attracting investments from common law trusts have been more relevant than the objective necessity of adopting the trust for granting nationals with a tool strange to their legal system.[152]

Cyprus and Malta are the only mixed or hybrid jurisdictions that have signed the Convention. In addition to the national changes introduced to allow the trust, to some extent, in their own legal systems, as it has been already seen, Cyprus and Malta have probably signed the Convention for promoting the presence of common law trusts within their borders. For sure, financial and banking interests supported the decision of entering into the Convention. In any case, what should be emphasized is that other mixed or hybrid jurisdictions have not felt the necessity of ratifying the Convention. If they would have considered the common law trust as the only way for pursuing some goals regarding the management of assets, they would have ratified the Convention. Instead of doing it they have adopted the trust using their traditional civil law structures.

Notes

1 Ugo A. Mattei, Teemu Ruskola and Antonio Gidi, *Schlesinger's Comparative Law* 7th ed. (New York: Thomson Reuters 2009) 223–247.
2 Daniel Berkowitz, Katharina Pistor and Jean-François Richard, 'Economic Development, Legality, and the Transplant Effect' (2003) 47 *European Economic Review* 165, 168–169.
3 Konrad Zweigert and Hein Kötz, *Introduction to Comparative Law* 3rd ed. (New York: Oxford University Press 1998) 374–319.
4 On Japan, see Hiroshi Oda, *Japanese Law* 3rd ed. (Oxford and New York: Oxford University Press 2009) 13–20. The Ottoman Empire slowly shifted to German civil law and adopted a civil code inspired by the Swiss model in 1926. See Ruth A. Miller, 'The Ottoman and Islamic Substratum of Turkey's Swiss Civil Code' (2000) 11 *Journal of Islamic Studies* 335, 335.
5 Oda (n4); Carl F. Goodman, *The Rule of Law in Japan: A Comparative Analysis* 2nd ed. (Alphen aan den Rijn and Frederick, MD: Wolters Kluwer Law & Business 2008) 20–23.
6 Berkowitz et al. (n2) 180.
7 See generally Philippa Levine, *The British Empire: Sunrise to Sunset* (Harlow and New York: Pearson Longman 2007).
8 Ibid. 43.
9 The British defeated the French at the Seven Years' War and the Treaty of Paris (1763) transferred most relevant parts of the French colonial empire to the British. The Portuguese and Spanish decline after the 1600s benefited primarily the British. The Dutch empire was largely contained by the British when William III became king (1688). Britain was the major winner of the Berlin Conference (1885), where Africa was partitioned among the European powers. The defeat of Germany, Austria and the Ottoman Empire in 1918 benefitted the British and the French.
10 Levine (n7).
11 Daniel Klerman et al. 'Legal Origin and Colonial History'. *Journal of Legal Analysis*, 2011.
12 Ibid 11.
13 Vernon Valentine Palmer, *Mixed Jurisdictions Worldwide: The Third Legal Family* (Cambridge and New York: Cambridge University Press 2001) 18–20.
14 Ibid.
15 Ibid. 19.
16 Ibid. 19–21.
17 Daniel Berkowitz and Karen Clay, 'American Civil Law Origins: Implications for State Constitutions' (2005) 62 *American Law and Economics Review* 62; Daniel Berkowitz and Karen Clay, 'The Effect of Judicial Independence on Courts: Evidence from the American States' (2006) 35 *Journal of Legal Studies* 399.
18 Palmer (n13) 18–20.
19 Ibid. 11.
20 Ibid. 21–22 (on the historical characterization of the common law stronger position).
21 Kensie Kim, 'Mixed Systems in Legal Origins' (2010) 83 *South California Law Review* 693.

22 Jacques Du Plessis, *Comparative Law and the Study of Mixed Legal Systems* in Mathias Reimann and Reinhard Zimmermann eds, *The Oxford Handbook of Comparative Law* (Oxford: Oxford University Press 2006) 478: 'Legal systems generally are "mixed" in the sense that they have been influenced by a variety of other systems. However, traditionally the term "mixed" is only used to describe a relatively small group of legal systems or jurisdictions which have been shaped so significantly by both the civil law and the common law traditions that they cannot be brought home comfortably under either. Thus, as far as their substantive law is concerned, key areas of the private law in many of these systems are predominantly civilian (in some it is even codified), whereas commercial law quite often strongly bears the imprint of the common law. And while public law in general has been strongly influenced by the common law, aspects of the criminal law, and more recently even constitutional law, at times display civilian features. Procedurally, these systems have in turn generally adopted a common law approach to adjudication: the judge is at the forefront of legal development, and precedent is generally regarded as binding and as more authoritative than academic writings.' Furthermore, see Esin Örücü, 'What is a Mixed Legal System: Exclusion or Expansion' (2008) 12 *Electronic Journal of Comparative Law* 1 (observing that current European legal systems are better seen as overlaps rather than pure common law or civil law since contamination exists and borrowing has been the practice of legal development).
23 Nuno Garoupa and Anthony Ogus. 'A Strategic Interpretation of Legal Transplants'. *Journal of Legal Studies*, vol. 35, 2006, p. 342.
24 Mattei (n1) 8–10; Andrew Harding, 'Global Doctrine and Local Knowledge: Law in South East Asia' (2002) 51 *International and Comparative Law Quarterly* 35, 49 (making the argument that the standard distinction common vs civil law is inappropriate to understand Asian legal systems); and Örücü (n22) (discussing alternative models of classification).
25 H. Patrick Glenn, *Quebec: Mixité and Monism* in Esin Örücü, Elspeth Attwooll, and Sean Coyle eds, *Studies in Legal Systems: Mixed and Mixing* (The Hague: Kluwer Law International 1996), 1.
26 Ibid.
27 Mattei (n1).
28 Glenn (n25).
29 Ibid. 2.
30 Ibid. 6.
31 Ibid. 13.
32 Ibid. 15.
33 Ibid.
34 Ibid.
35 Ibid.
36 Esin Örücü, *General Introduction: Mixed Legal Systems at New Frontiers* in *Mixed Legal Systems at New Frontiers* (London: Wildy, Simmonds & Hill 2010) 1.
37 Ibid. 4.
38 Ibid. 3–4.
39 Ibid. 2–4.
40 Ibid.
41 Palmer (n13) 19, 45–47.
42 Ibid,
43 Ibid,
44 Oda (n4) discussing the particular case of Japan.
45 Peter Wesley-Smith, 'The Content of the Common Law in Hong Kong' in Raymond Wacks ed., *The New Legal Order in Hong Kong* (Hong Kong: Hong Kong University Press 1999) 9, 10; Randall Peerenboom, *China's Long March Toward Rule of Law* (Cambridge: Cambridge University Press 2002) 7–8.

46 See generally Paul Craig and Gráine de Búrca, *EU Law: Text, Cases and Materials* 5th ed. (Oxford University Press 2011).

47 Palmer (n13).

48 Ibid.; Hein Kötz, 'The Value of Mixed Legal Systems' (2003) 78 *Tulane Law Review* 435.

49 Kötz (n48) 435; Palmer (n13) 4–6.

50 Palmer (n13) 7 (a general definition provided by Sir Thomas Smith in 1965 having the case of Scotland in mind).

51 Ibid. 4.

52 Ibid. 7–8.

53 Ibid.

54 Ibid. 9–10.

55 Ibid. 55.

56 Ibid. 19.

57 Ibid.

58 Ibid.

59 Ibid. 19–20.

60 Ibid. 21–22.

61 Ibid. 41–42.

62 Ibid. 42.

63 Ibid. Such constraint could explain why Spanish civil law faded away in Florida, Texas or California, Dutch civil law in New York and German (Japanese) civil law in the Mariana Islands, but not in South Africa, Louisiana, Quebec, Puerto Rico, Malta and the Philippines. See David Carey Miller, *South Africa: A Mixed System Subject to Transcending Forces* in Örücü, Attwooll and Coyle (n25) (discussing the case pertaining to South Africa).

64 Joseph M. Ganado, *Malta: A Microcosm of International Influences* in Örücü, Attwooll and Coyle (n25) 225.

65 Ibid. 229.

66 Ibid.

67 Ibid. 225.

68 Japan influenced legal reforms in Korea since the 1870s. Korea was formally annexed by Japan in 1910. Taiwan was ceded to Japan in 1895.

69 Oda (n4) 20–21; see also Yves Dezalay and Bryant G. Garth, *Asian Legal Revivals: Lawyers in the Shadow of Empire* (Chicago: University of Chicago Press 2010) 49–61, 102–104.

70 Tom Ginsburg, *Judicial Review in New Democracies: Constitutional Courts in Asian Cases* (Cambridge: Cambridge University Press 2003) 106-57.

71 Hideki Kanda and Curtis Milhaupt, *Reexamining Legal Transplants: The Director's Fiduciary Duty in Japanese Corporate Law* in Daniel H. Foote ed., *Law in Japan: A Turning Point* (Washington: University of Washington Press 2007) 437.

72 Ibid.

73 Yoram Shachar, 'History and Sources of Israeli Law' in Amos Shapira ed., *Introduction to the Law of Israel* (The Hague and Boston: Kluwer Law International 1995); see generally Menachem Mautner, *Law and Culture of Israel* (Oxford: Oxford University Press 2011).

74 Shachar, 'History and Sources of Israeli Law' 4.

75 Ibid. 5.

76 Ibid. 2.

77 Ibid.

78 Ibid.

79 Robin M. White and Ian D. Willock, *The Scottish Legal System* 4th ed. (Haywards Heath, UK: Tottel 2006) 26–28; Bryan Clark, *Scottish Legal System* 2nd ed. (Dundee: Dundee University Press 2009) 4–6.

80 Palmer (n13) 29.
81 Ibid.; Jan Smits, 'Introduction: Mixed Legal Systems and European Private Law' in *The Contribution of Mixed Legal Systems to European Private Law* (Antwerp: Intersentia 2001) 1, 5 (making the point that it is unclear if Scottish law is a consistent mix or a confusing interaction of common and civil law while, for example, South African law is more consistent. Furthermore, according to the author, it is unclear if Scottish courts improve the mix or dilute the internal structure of some areas of the law).
82 Elspeth Attwooll, *Scotland: A Multi-Dimensional Jigsaw* in Örücü, Attwooll and Coyle (n25).
83 Palmer (n13) 29.
84 Ibid.
85 Craig and De Búrca (n46).
86 Ibid.
87 Ibid.
88 Ibid.
89 Ibid.
90 Palmer (n13) 6.
91 Ibid.
92 Ibid.
93 Ibid. 41.
94 Ibid. 21–22.
95 Ibid; William A. Robinson, *Justice in Grey: A History of the Judicial System of the Confederate State of America* (Cambridge, MA: Harvard University Press 1941) 45, 80–81 (explaining that the distinction between common law and equity was eliminated in the Confederate States of America, in 1861, because it was considered unjustified given the civil law tradition of many Southern states).
96 Palmer (n13) 57–59.
97 Ibid. 66–67.
98 Ibid. 5.
99 Ibid. 18–19.
100 Ibid. 20–22.
101 Ibid. 62–67.
102 Ibid. 67.
103 Ibid. 9–10.
104 Ibid.
105 Ibid. 25–31.
106 Jan Smits, 'A European Private Law as Mixed Legal System' (1998) 5 *Maastricht Journal of European and Comparative Law* 328, 329; Mathias Reimann, 'Towards a European Civil Code: Why Continental Jurists Should Consult their Transatlantic Colleagues' (1999) 73 *Tulane Law Review* 1337.
107 Palmer (n13) 9–10.
108 Ibid. 20.
109 Rafael La Porta, Florencio Lopez-de-Sillanes and Andrei Shleifer. 'The Economic Consequences of Legal Origins' (2008) 46 *Journal of Economic Literature*, 285.
110 Ibid. 286.
111 Ibid. 286, 310, 321.
112 Ibid. 327.
113 Palmer (n13) 45–50.
114 Ibid.
115 Ibid.
116 Ibid.
117 La Porta et al. (n109) 286, 310.
118 Ibid.

119 Ibid.
120 Ibid.
121 Garoupa and Ogus (n23).
122 Ibid.
123 Ibid.; Anthony Ogus, 'Competition Between National Legal Systems: A Contribution of Economic Analysis to Comparative Law' (1999) 48 *International and Comparative Law Quarterly* 405, 411.
124 Garoupa and Ogus (n23); Anthony Ogus, 'The Economic Basis of Legal Culture: Networks and Monopolization' (2002) 22 *Oxford Journal of Legal Studies* 419, 420, 434.
125 Garoupa and Ogus (n23) 345.
126 Ibid. 346.
127 Peter Grajzl and Valentina Dimitrova-Grajzl, 'The Choice in the Lawmaking Process: Legal Transplants vs. Indigenous Law' (2009) 5 *Review of Law and Economics* 615, 617.
128 Garoupa and Ogus (n23); Emanuela Carbonara and Francesco Parisi, 'Choice of Law and Legal Evolution: Rethinking the Market for Legal Rules' (2009) 139 *Public Choice* 461, 462.
129 Garoupa and Ogus (n23) 339; Emanuela Carbonara and Francesco Parisi,' The Paradox of Legal Harmonization' (2007) 132 *Public Choice* 367.
130 Pierre Legrand, 'European Legal Systems Are Not Converging' (1996) 45 *International and Comparative Law Quarterly* 52, 55; Pierre Legrand, 'Against a European Civil Code' (1997) 60 *Modern Law Review* 44, 45–46; Pierre Legrand, *Fragments on Law-As-Culture* (Deventer: W.E.J. Tjeenk Willink 1999) 133–134; see also Smits n81). (citing Pierre Legrand's work against European codification and his interpretation that such debate reflects the arrogance of common law lawyers convinced of their superiority over continental lawyers).
131 Palmer (n13) 77.
132 Carbonara and Parisi (n129) 461 for a more detailed discussion.
133 Ibid.
134 Du Plessis (n22) 510 ('[...] as far as the quality of the mixture is concerned, there is no firm indication that the processes of borrowing in mixed jurisdictions have *generally* given rise to law which is particularly good or particularly bad. In assessing the quality of the mixture, care must be taken not to ascribe change to a single factor, such as foreign dominance.')
135 Palmer (n13) 21–22.
136 Ibid.
137 Ibid.
138 Kitty Calavita, *Invitations to Law and Society: An Introduction to the Study of Real Law* (Chicago: University of Chicago Press 2010); Smits (n81) suggesting mixed legal systems are an excellent example to inspire European private law.
139 Calavita (n138).
140 Ibid.
141 Edwin Peel, *Treitel on the Law of Contract* 12th ed. (London: Sweet & Maxwell 2007) 684ff.
142 Elias Clark et al., *Gratuitous Transfers: Wills, Intestate Succession, Trusts, Gifts, Future Interests, and Estate and Gift Taxation – Cases and Materials* 5th ed. (St Paul, MN: Thomson West 1999) 472–627.
143 John H. Langbein, 'The Contractarian Basis of the Law of Trusts' (1995) 105 *Yale Law Journal* 625.
144 John H. Langbein, 'The Secret Life of the Trust: The Trust as an Instrument of Commerce' (1997) 107 *Yale Law Journal* 165, showing that the trust is not limited to gratuitous transfers.

145 Avihay Dofman, 'On Trust and Transsubstantiation' in Andrew S. Gold and Paul B. Miller, *The Philosophical Foundations of Fiduciary Law* (Oxford: Oxford University Press 2014) 339–362.
146 Scottish Law Commission, Discussion Paper on the Nature and Constitution of Trusts, October 2006, Edinburgh www.scotlawcom.gov.uk/law-reform-projects/trusts/.
147 Louisiana Trust Code RS 9:1781. Trustee defined. A trustee is a person to whom title to the trust property is transferred to be administered by him as a fiduciary.
148 Robert Sitkoff, 'An Economic Theory of Fiduciary Law' in Gold and Miller eds, *Philosophical Foundations of Fiduciary Law* 197–208; Robert Sitkoff, 'The Economic Structure of Fiduciary Law' (2011) 91 *Boston University Law Review* 1039.
149 Henry Hansmann and Ugo Mattei, 'The Functions of Trust Law: A Comparative Legal and Economic Analysis' (1998) 73 *New York University Law Review* 434.
150 Holger Spamann, 'Contemporary Legal Transplants, Legal Families and the Diffusion of (Corporate) Law' (2010) 2009 *Brigham Young University Law Review* 1813.
151 At the present moment, they are: Australia, Canada, The People's Republic of China, Cyprus, France, Italy, Luxembourg, Malta, Monaco, The Netherlands, Switzerland, United Kingdom and the United States of America, besides two countries that, in spite of not being members of The Hague Convention, have ratified the Convention. They are Liechtenstein and San Marino.
152 Smits, *The Contribution of Mixed Legal Systems.*

Part III

Modern dilemmas in US and EU law as representatives of the two distinct legal families

In order for us to demonstrate our arguments further, the next two chapters took a different approach and are examining differences among the two economically strongest representatives of the common law and civil law systems that are also in direct competition with each other in the global market today. While chapter 9 examines the differences between the EU and US in the field of intellectual property law as the field of law currently carrying the most demanding task of following the modern fast-paced development of the area of intellectual property, chapter 10 concludes our work by examining the modern developments in the area of corporate law, bringing us back to the beginning where legal origins theory got its teeth, suggesting that the arguments inherent in the claims of legal origins commentators have been disproved by the sheer reality of recent theoretical and empirical research. Hence the book finishes essentially where the legal origins started and shows how the most important considerations inherent in the nature of corporate law have been simply disregarded and thereby causing the results found by the legal origins commentators unsustainable and inherently flawed.

9 Contrasting civil and common law
The area of intellectual property

The field of intellectual property law, the result of the influence of the frequent and vast changes in technology in the last two decades, is in need of modern makeover. But such a makeover has not been readily following the pace of the changes themselves in any of the jurisdictions. This not only questions the findings of the legal origins on the efficient and constantly improving nature of the common law, but at the same time poses additional questions concerning how is it possible that the solutions enacted by the civil law system seem to be very similar to the ones found in the intellectual property law of the common law world.[1]

The comparison of rules enacted in this field will be carried out on the US–EU level. Even though the EU legal system seems to belong to a mixed jurisdiction, the vast majority of its legal tradition is derived from civil law systems of its most influential member states and its approach to legislation seems to be largely prescriptive. Due to the fact that there is no such thing today as a pure common or civil law system, the duet compared should not influence heavily on the findings contained in this chapter, since the field of intellectual law in the EU has not been influenced by common law, but rather civil law notions on the field.[2]

Why intellectual property law?

Since both the US and the EU economies rely heavily on innovative and creative industries, the need to keep incentivizing innovation through intellectual property law institutes is more or less clear.[3] The numbers in this regard are impressive: in the US in 2010, the most intellectual property-intense industries directly employed 27.1 million people and indirectly another 12.9 million, together representing 27.7 per cent of all jobs in the economy. Those industries generated about US $5.06 trillion in value added, amounting to 34.8 per cent of the US's gross domestic product. Moreover, the merchandise exports of intellectual property industries from the US in that year amounted to 60.7 per cent of all US goods exports. On the other hand, observing the EU in the period from the year 2008–2010 shows that about half of EU industries are intellectual property intensive[4] and approximately 56.5 million or 26 per cent of all EU jobs were generated directly by these industries, with 20 million jobs being further added as an indirect employment. The added value of intellectual property intensive industries amounted to €4.7 trillion, or 39 per cent of EU GDP. It has been said that 88 per cent of EU imports and 90 per cent of EU exports were intellectual property intensive in the observed period.[5] All in all, as concerns the trade between the US and EU, in the year 2012 the royalties and licence fees based on intellectual property rights were among the top five services traded.[6]

Based on the data presented, intellectual property does matter for the state of economies in the common and civil law world, as seen from the realities facing the two strongest economies representing the two distinct legal families. Under the law and economics approach, Posner sees trademarks as an incentive to create information for the benefit of markets. Trademarks reduce the information costs and the transaction costs within a market, promoting the attainment of competitive equilibria.[7] Following the reasoning of the legal origins, through its superior legal mechanisms, common law should also have an advantage in this specific legal field. Reviewing the field in the light of this theory by scrutinizing closely the main institutes of intellectual property should shed a light on the alleged supremacy of the common law and answer the question if the theory could have some foundational flaws also outside the classic civil law fields?

On intellectual property

Intellectual property law is protecting the property of intellectual goods as intangible goods, whose economic value today many times surpasses the value of physical property.[8] Besides this 'special feature', when compared to the property of tangible goods, knowledge and information represent resources that are not scarce, so the intellectual property assets can and often are used simultaneously by different users, making it difficult to enable the exclusion of others without a clear and enforceable legal rule. This is one of the reasons behind the vast and detailed US legislation on the issue, quite untypical as a legislative approach of a common law country.[9] Intellectual property law is based on the principle of territoriality, which limits the scope of its protection to the territory of the granting state and additionally limits the rights in time and scope, differently from other property rights.

Another special feature of intellectual property law is the fact that it protects expressions of ideas, but not the ideas themselves, to ensure recognition for the moral and economic rights of creators over their creations and so provide incentives for innovation.[10] Economic analysis of intellectual property historically focused on achieving the right balance between the owner's rights and the interests of society in using those inventions, while modern questions shifted towards the length of protection of intellectual property, with rules allowing considerable copying of intellectual property without permission of its owner and rules governing derivative works.[11] For the purpose of our debate on the intellectual property law and legal origins, we will be examining the common and civil law institutions of the industrial property (patents, trademarks, designs) as well as of copyright (literary and artistic works and related rights), in the light of modern economic analysis questions, showing that the field of intellectual property is not more fruitful for confirming the legal origins theory than any other fields of law examined before in our book.

How are the US and the EU approaching the field?

Since intellectual property rights have been gradually included among the competences of the EU through the reviews of the Treaties, European Court of Justice case law and the harmonization of legislation and since at the same time the US legislation on the topic is enacted at the federal level,[12] comparing the legislation of these two large entities in the legal origins context seems appropriate. Although the US follows a national and the EU a regional exhaustion regime, due to the territoriality principle enshrined in the intellectual property law, this affects only the territorial scope of protection and not its substance, which is what will be examined in this particular chapter.

Looking at the EU, Article 118 TFEU provides it with an explicit competence to create European intellectual property rights throughout the Union. The US on the other hand determines intellectual property protection in Article I Section 8 of its Constitution, through Congress-passed laws[13] and case law, regulating intellectual property rights more extensively and in large detail when compared to EU and European countries. In this field, the US retained legislative power and somewhat secluded the courts from much law-making, suggesting that efficiency in this particular field does not stem from adaptability of law through case law, but rather from careful balancing of interests by the legislator himself. Here judge-made law steps aside and leaves way to civil law-like law-making. Legal origins proponents would need to admit that already without looking at the substance of the rules, their enactment and positioning suggests that the field is regulated in the spirit of the civil law approach.

In this chapter the comparison of trademark protection, protection of geographical origins and patent protection in common and civil law systems is carried out, applied on the US and the EU legal solutions. In the scope of the copyright, a closer look is taken of the common law 'fair use' doctrine and of the issue of the plausibility of its inclusion in a civil law system. The overall effect of law in these fields adds value to our elemental debate on efficiency and demonstrates how the legal origins theory lacks standing also in this particular field.

Efficiency of trademark protection in common and civil law systems

Although both the US and the EU are contracting parties to a multitude of international treaties on intellectual property protection,[14] these international documents do not regulate the complete substance of the intellectual property protection, but in turn determine minimal standards and simplified procedures of registration of those rights.[15] Those documents are not scrutinized further; the emphasis rather lies on the US and the EU legal sources, through which the substance of the mentioned treaties has been transposed into respective jurisdictions.[16]

The trademarks today serve primarily to give exclusive rights to its owner knowing that others cannot exploit the mark's reputation.[17] In the history of commerce, distinctive signs represented a way to communicate the origin of goods to the public and authorities. After the liberalization of the markets, such signs enabled the producers to address their customers from distance and in such way convey the message on the quality of goods to them.[18] Even though the trademark should originally simply serve to identify the origins of the goods, purchasers extract the information about the quality of the good from their own past experience or of that of others.[19] Trademarks are not protected on the ground of their originality but due to their capacity to convey information to customers efficiently. They are actually fostering and not restricting competition, since they also produce economic incentives of the trademark owner to maintain the quality of products sold under such a trademark.[20]

The definition of trademarks does not differ severely in the two jurisdictions. Under 15 USC § 1127 'A trademark is any word, name, symbol, or design, or any combination thereof, used in commerce to identify and distinguish the goods of one manufacturer or seller from those of another and to indicate the source of the goods.' while under Trademark Regulation '[T]rademark is any sign capable of being represented graphically, particularly words, including personal names, designs, letters, numerals, the shape of goods or their packaging, provided that such signs are capable of distinguishing the goods or services of one undertaking from those of other undertakings.'

In the regulation of trademarks, similarities and differences can be found between the US and the EU. In the EU, the Community Trademark system is formed by the Council Regulation EC No 207/2009 Trademark Regulation and the Directive 2008/95/EC on approximation of laws of Member States with regard to trademarks. To be protected in the EU, the trademark must be registered, and to be registered it must be clearly defined and distinctive.[21] Once registered, the Community Trademark can be renewed indefinitely every ten years. The EU trademark carries with it single application, single language, single fee and single administrative centre.[22] This system offers an attractive and simplified protection system for the European market with a minimum of costs for the applicant. While the EU employs 'first-to-file' approach for trademark protection, the US uses the 'first-to-use' approach. In the US registering a trademark is not required for its protection; the trademark must just be distinctive and used in commerce. Such unregistered trademarks are in practice often denotated by the symbol ™.[23] A Federal trademark registration under the Lanham Act of 1946 (as amended)[24] is possible, but not necessary.[25] The symbol used to denote a registered trademark is ®.[26]

Let us imagine a case where two companies in two US states are producing a similar product, an application, and selling it in their respective states under a very similar name. Not knowing about each other they are developing their product and start to sell it with success all over the US. A dispute on the trademark ownership is inevitable and since they are not aware of each other's efforts, the unsuccessful party to the dispute will lose not only money but the incentive to continue under a different name. Such an example is easily imaginable in today's globalized and technologically constantly developing world. Is therefore the solution of obligatory trademark application in the EU the more efficient one? The procedure before Office for Harmonization of Internal Market (hereafter: OHIM) in Spain guarantees the producer to know in the early stages of his inventions if the trademark he is investing in will bring him exclusive rights of use and if it is worthy investing in it. Changing the trademark at the beginning of the process is less costly and deterring for a producer than doing so in the later stages of the production or invention process, when your initial investment in the product quality is lost in the eyes of the customers for a while when your trademark needs to be changed.

Even though at the OHIM there is no ex officio review of 'relative' grounds for trademark refusal or cancellation,[27] and even though such procedure exists in the US, the trademark law in the EU cannot be claimed as being the less efficient one, according to International Trademark Association research from 2005.[28] The respondents to the research from absolute examination system welcomed the lower cost of obtaining registration, while there is no indication that there are more oppositions lodged in absolute than in relative system. Moreover, Denmark in 1999 switched from a relative examination system to an absolute one and has not seen a dramatic increase in opposition or cancellation proceedings.[29] It is therefore the EU legislation that puts the burden of protection of the trademark on its owner (economically more efficient and less costly), where the initial incentive for the protection of the right lies, and the US taking over the role of the authority to keep an eye of prior registrations. From the efficiency of law perspective it is therefore the US taking the less efficient approach. Another research from year 2015 suggests that more company's trademark budget is spent on enforcement in the US than in EU,[30] which can indicate that either litigation is more costly in the US or that actually there are less cases litigated in EU. In any case, under these numbers, the US trademark system seems not to be more efficient than the EU one.

Another difference among the US and EU system lies in what happens to a denied application for trademark protection at the supranational level. Since separate applications are necessary in the US, being denied protection at the federal level is the end of the procedure. Although similar system operates in the EU, the moment of application for the EU trademark protection counts as the moment of application also at the possible later application for a national trademark protection, in the case that protection at the EU level is denied.[31] In this case priority filing date of the unsuccessful application is retained. Although this fact may just be seen as a consequence of the inconvenient system of protection based on 'first-to-use', it seems to lessen even further the efficiency of the US trademark protection system. The unsuccessful applicant loses time and money and therefore incentives to seek federal protection of its trademarks and would maybe prefer to apply in specific states first, causing the market to lose altogether: customers a potentially strong federal market product and the producer the incentive to do business with that trademark on the federal level.

Today, a new demand for possibility of protecting colour, sound, scent, motion, shape or taste seems to be high among companies.[32] Although there is some debate at the EU level if under current legal regime all such signs are capable of being protected by the Community trademark,[33] and the US seems to be on paper more open to registering such trademarks, the research shows that in fact only 24 per cent of the survey respondents from the US already successfully registered such a trademark, while the number among EU respondents is higher: 40 per cent.[34] The market seems to be demanding the development of non-traditional trademarks and once again the US seems to be lagging behind. The presupposed rigid, non-efficient, slower evolving civil law system based EU law-making seems to have no trouble in following the market developments and providing the appropriate legal institutes.

Geographic indications

Seeing how the US trademark protection system is not necessarily more efficient than the EU one, it is even more interesting to note that the US protects the geographical indications under a trademark system and at the same time claims at the international level for this protection to be more efficient as the EU sui generis protection offered to such intellectual property rights.

As an intellectual property right on its own, geographic indications (GI) are not a new phenomenon,[35] but the attention given to them in the last decade is. In this field regulated by national, regional and international regulations,[36] a dispute arose between EU and US in the trade negotiations on the WTO level and ever since the GIs have been debated both at the academic and political level.[37] While the US has a more 'relaxed' attitude towards designation of geographical origin, protecting it only with traditional notions of trademark law,[38] the EU brings to the field sui generis protection of GI and recognizes them as an own category of intellectual property rights.[39]

At the international level, the GIs were first recognized as a separate branch of intellectual property rights[40] at the introduction of the Agreement on Trade Related Aspects of Intellectual Property Rights (TRIPS).[41] This agreement in Article 22(1) determines the GIs as

> [I]ndications which identify a good as originating in the territory of a Member, or a region or locality in that territory, where a given quality, reputation or other characteristics of the good is essentially attributable to its geographical indication.

Reducing transaction costs is the rationale behind trademarks as well as GIs, but they nonetheless differ fundamentally. While the trademark is informing customers about the source of a good or service from *particular company*, the GI identifies a good as originating from a *particular place*, allowing the consumer to associate the good with a particular quality, characteristics or reputation. The information function of GIs is of particular importance where the provenance of the goods bears a direct influence on the objective quality of the goods offered.[42] The trademarks can protect any goods or services, while the protection offered by GIs is limited: in the US to wine and spirits and in the EU to agricultural products as well as wine and spirits.[43] The known examples of GIs are Basmati rice, Cognac, Bordeaux wines, Roquefort cheese, Sherry, Parmigiano Reggiano, etc.

The economic rationale behind the GIs is simply the correction of a market failure caused by asymmetric information between sellers and buyers and the fact that GI is without any legal remedy a public good, causing the problem of free riding. In practice, most of the GIs are geographical names, administered by the state.[44] Attractiveness of the GIs lies first and foremost in protecting the economic interests of producers of well-known and largely exported regional products from imitation and usurpation. GIs facilitate development of origin-based reputation through the GIs quality standard and as such serve as territorial development initiatives.[45]

As mentioned, in the US the protection of GIs falls under general trademark law and the form of certification mark is the principle way in which US law provides such protection.[46] The Lanham Act defines this mark as 'any word, name, symbol or device, or any combination thereof ... used to certify regional or other origin, material, mode of manufacture, quality, accuracy, or other characteristics of ... goods ...' that alerts consumers as to the quality of a product or its origin.[47] These marks can be owned by a person, a state, the nation or any other public or private legal entity, but their owners are not permitted to use the mark. They only carry an obligation to ensure that the mark guarantees that the product on which it is used possesses certain qualities.[48] What that means in practice is that certification marks are owned by trade associations who certify the geographical origin of their member's products.

Although certification marks are the primary way of protecting GIs in the US, they are not the sole way. Collective marks are also used, owned by a group or an organization, and they indicate that an entity using the mark is a member of a group or organization. Owners of such a certification mark are allowed to use the marks themselves.[49]

Now in both cases, the US system is pretty self-regulating. Since the rationale behind GIs is protecting the value behind certain quality of ingredients and ways and means of production, this system calls for abuse. Rationale of companies, especially in the shareholder-value-maximization oriented company law in the US, is the maximization of profits. When applying that fact to the field of GIs and the issue of large self-regulation, the outcome does not seem to be efficient. If GIs are meant to protect the distinctiveness and quality (especially in the field of agricultural products), maximization of profits is not and cannot be the most efficient outcome. And that is exactly what the system in the US seems to be producing. Since there is not one sole company paying the price for misleading information (claiming quality of its certification mark, using the same name as the one used in the EU for a specific product, creating expectations with consumers of providing the same quality), free-riding is not dis-incentivized.

On the other hand, the EU with its Foodstuff Regulation[50] also distinguishes between two ways of GI protection (albeit in sui generis system): 'protected designation of origin' (PDO) and a 'protected geographical indication' (PGI).[51] While the registration of PDO allows producers in Member States an exclusive right to a name of particular agricultural good that is determined unique due to the fact that the production, processing or preparation takes place in a specific area by using local resources and expertise, the registration of PGI does not require such association of unique characteristics with a specific geographical area but grants protection based on their reputation.[52] The recognition of GIs here depends on an assessment of their intrinsic value through an arbitration process managed by the EU (or in the case of regional, national GI, by the Member State in question).

While there can be present, especially from the point of view of common law origin states, fear that the GIs can become a legal tool to serve particular objectives of public policies, the experience with the effects of its protection on the market is pointing more towards efficiency than in-efficiency of the system, based solely on the arguments of the US against the system. The US is against this strong protective system in the EU due to the fact, that some of the products used in the US now are named after places named in Europe[53] and many of those names such as 'Feta' or 'Parmesan' became generic names in the US, since after many years of production the link between the product's original territory and its name has expired.[54] Therefore, what seems to worry the US is not the fact that the EU sui generis GI system would be inefficient, but rather that the US producers are under such system forced to change the names of their products, which is costly and time consuming, and could cause consumer confusion and considerable administrative costs, that would ultimately translate in higher prices for consumers.[55]

Or could it be the other way around? What the US seems to be claiming here is that the EU legislation is harming the US producers, while it is the US producers that have been free-riding for decades on the reputation of goods produced in the territory from which they obtained their names. US legislation has been causing consumer confusion and not holding the producer accountable for the quality of their products.[56] Let us take as an example the famous French Cheese 'Brie'. In Europe, such cheese is traditionally made from raw milk under a specific procedure, giving it its creamy texture and specific taste. This cheese has also been registered in the US in the 1970s as a trademark. Now the US 'Brie' does not taste the same as the French 'Brie', as noticed by its consumers, who do not know that in the US such cheese is not produced from raw milk, since that is in fact prohibited in the US by law. Consumers are often deceived by 'Brie' denomination in the US and the GI protection would prevent such deceit. In this specific case, the US legislation on the matter seems not to be efficient in correcting the market asymmetry but it actually creates it.[57]

By its permissive approach to the GI regulation, the US does not provide any particular assessment of criteria related to the methods of production, biological resources and no mechanism of state arbitration amongst producers. As far as the 'generic names' argument goes, the EU law provides with straightforward possibilities for cancellation procedures: a reasoned request can be made to the EU by any natural or legal person having a legitimate interest in connection with a specific product.[58] This approach seems to be more efficient than just claiming that a package of GIs has become generic and so dis-incentivizing a whole package of traditional producers of products protected by such GIs. The EU prescriptive approach to GIs links their legal protection to a very detailed and narrow definition of the products concerned in relation to specific concepts developed within the framework of public policies and it is based on a legal process of registration. Under this system a name accentuates tradition, a place, a way of life and the quality of a product. It allows a country to preserve their traditional culinary culture by preventing the destruction of recognized tradition. The EU is so aiming for quantity to quality based exports by providing a means for consumers to identify products of quality originating from the territory connected with those quality traits. The long term economic benefits of GIs might far outweigh the costs incurred by the few producers who may be required to re-label due to their previous free-riding.[59]

Not just the US but also other common law countries rely solely on trademark law to protect GIs and in the spirit of the efficiency some authors claim that this system should become an international model.[60] While searching for convincing arguments to support that statement, we only found strong counter-arguments, from efficiency perspective as well as others. Same authors supporting the US system of protection of GIs admit that today GI protection is essential, because without it confusion may arise amongst consumers as to the origin or quality of a product.[61] The trademark system of protection of GIs allows names such as 'Californian Champagne', which in fact allows deception of consumers which will, by buying such product, expect the luxurious wine of same quality as original French 'Champagne', while the production methods and ingredients of the former are by no means the same as the ones of the latter. The GIs as a separate intellectual property right prevent such free-riding, they frustrate registration of the indication as a trademark by a third party and limit the risk of the GI becoming a generic term. At the same time, GIs serve as an inexpensive and particularly for small businesses the only possibility to efficiently protect their intellectual property rights.[62]

Today the US sees the EU GI protection, seeking to preserve the traditional ways and means of production, processing and preparation of local specialties,[63] as inefficient and protectionist, but only in connection with agricultural products. In the field of wine and spirits the US welcomes such protection. At this level, the reasoning is already weak. How can in the view of this common law country the protection of GIs be efficient in one field and not in another? This arbitrary differentiating stirs curiosity, even more so since research found that the differentiating of any product with GIs can be a way of enhancing economic results.[64] Moreover, the US itself used to be a proponent of such separate GI protection, but not in relation to historically stronger EU countries in the field of agriculture, but towards its southern countries. In 1929, the US protected GIs in its Inter-American Convention, whose Article 23 applied to all goods.[65] Now that could be viewed also as an inefficient relict of US legal system, but when contrasted with today's US arguments against sui-generis GI protection, it seems not to be the case. The US is fighting against comparative advantages in agriculture of European countries with long agricultural traditions, and not against inefficiency of the sui generis protection system of GIs. Moreover, as the efficiency of common law hypothesis would suggest, such sui generis civil law protection systems should be too stiff and rigid to adapt to the market realities. In the EU legal systems, such worries seem to be mitigated by the legal frame that facilitates change; the codes of practices for PDO and PDI are the result of a collective and continuous process and the policies are changing under the changing circumstances of producers of protected GIs.

The US suggestion that the trademark system is a better means of GI protection, since it leaves the quality to the market, takes away all the rationale on which the GI protection is based on the first place. The incentives of self-regulating producers go towards higher profits and not higher quality. Claiming higher quality for obtaining higher profit is a likely outcome under such system, deceiving consumers and producing inefficiencies on the markets. The supremacy in terms of efficiency of US legal system here is therefore highly disputable.

Patent protection in the US and EU

Another important part of the intellectual property rights protection lies in the protection provided by patents. The economists have recognized that the development and spread of economic innovations are the most powerful factors affecting how fast an economy grows.[66] The granting of patents was historically meant to spur innovative attributes to promote technical progress. They were used from the industrial age on, providing the country competitiveness in new technology by rewarding inventors with exclusive market protection for a limited number of years. Since the term 'patent' derives from the Latin word '*patere*' (lying open), the obligatory disclosure of such patent is its inherent characteristic, ensuring that this new technical knowledge becomes publicly available.[67]

As an intellectual property right, government grants with patent exclusive rights to the inventor for a limited period of time to produce, sell and use an invention deemed novel, inventive and useful. Patents are meant to reward innovators by creating strong incentives to invest in new ideas and promoting additional progress by publicly disclosing the details of original innovation to any potential rival.[68]

The law on patents has overall not changed significantly for more than a century[69], but its role and impact in the society has changed immensely due also to fast modern technological development.[70] Today many patents may apply to a single product, entailing high transaction costs. The efficiency of the patent system today lies in its ability to deal effectively with the increasing number of inventions, to maximize the innovation process itself and also to maximize the flow of this new technology to the public.[71] Needless to say that even in this field the legal regimes applicable in the US and Europe differed historically and also today.

In last two decades the patent regimes have changed importantly in the direction of strengthening patent rights.[72] The exclusive rights conferred to patent holders have been reinforced and their coverage has been expanded, with the belief that such developments are beneficial for innovation. Since in reality such exclusive rights may distort competition and the efficient allocation of resources and represent an obstacle to follow on innovation, the patent policy needs to determine an appropriate balance between creating incentives for innovation and enabling the diffusion of knowledge to stimulate further research even in new, changed circumstances of fast technological development.[73]

The EU and US are trying to achieve such balance in different ways. Since we are interested in the substantive rules on the patents to determine if the common law legal family truly found the more efficient answers to the modern issues in the field, the structural aspects will here not be taken into account, in any case not more than just through a brief overview of the current situation.

The reality is that there is no European patent automatically valid throughout the EU.[74] The EU patent system is based on European Patent Convention 1973 (EPC),[75] an international convention established outside the EU legal frame, not signed by all of the EU Member States.[76] This system only creates bundle of national legal patents and not sui generis EU patent, thus trying to lower the administrative burden on inventors trying to obtain patents in several European countries.[77] In the given circumstances, this system has been a success story in terms of the continual increase in the number of patent applications received and patents granted, as well as by an ever increasing number of Contracting States.[78] Due to the high costs that this system still entails, new arrangements are being born from the desire to ensure an expeditious, reliable and cost effective patent granting system at the EU level.[79] With the fast developing field of the patent protection such changes are indeed needed. In the system as it stands today in Europe, the applicant needs to designate small number of the most important EPC Contracting States in which he seeks protection, and the patent protection is valid in those states only after the designation fees have been paid and the translation of the specification has been filed with the respective national office.[80] Although this system managed to reinforce the rights of patent holders in some European countries by introducing examination and opposition proceedings where only registration system previously existed,[81] it is still too burdensome and expensive, and it does not serve to ensure high level of efficiency and legal security as it is structured. Looking at the substance of the system though could give us different answers.

On the other hand, in the US the patent is automatically valid for the whole territory of the US,[82] following united federal legislation that is based on previously mentioned Article I, Section 8 of the US Constitution, which determines that the Congress can grant exclusive rights to inventors in order '[t]o promote the progress of Science and useful Arts'.[83] In 2011, the latest reform of patents in the US has been embodied in the so-called 'America Invents Act' (AIA), signed into law on 16 September 2011. This act is the result of repeated attempts in the US, since 2000, to improve and harmonize patent law in the US (Patent Reform Acts of 2005, 2007 and 2009), where several modifications were considered necessary in the light of the granting of questionable business-methods patents, the scope and impact of granted software patents, the increasing and expensive patent litigation and the lack of harmonization at the international level.[84] The bottom line is that the AIA has been necessary to introduce efficiency into the US patent law, a trait that many how found as profoundly missing and for which this common law jurisdiction did not find the most efficient remedy through its judge-made law. Already the fact that the US incorporated in its system the solutions found in the civil law systems, clashes violently with some notions of the legal origins theory and the notions on the efficiency of the common law suggested by Judge Posner and others. Moreover, the whole renewed system of US patent law, enacted in AIA, seems to base all the changes made after more than 200 years of following previous patent law system on the civil law solutions in the field of patent law. Therefore the whole vast field of the patent law seems to disagree with the findings of the efficiency of common law theory, as will be shown on some brief examples in this part of the book.

In this part the substance of the US and European patent laws is taken a look at and focus taken off the negative and/or positive consequences of the institutional differences between the systems, since they do not influence the dichotomy of content of the common law or civil law based institutes. We will start by examining the small but influential differences between the patent law institutions in the two jurisdictions, only to build up to the most influential and basic differences, deciding on the overall efficiency of the system and on trying whether in this field the US as the common law system representative found the most efficient solutions for today's patent-related issues. Since the AIA entails big changes to the traditional US patent law system, the comparison between the systems will be made in terms of the 'old' US system and the system in Europe as established by the EPC.

US re-examination v. European opposition procedure

Too many patent applications and too many patent grants diminish their value and quality.[85] As some studies have shown, valuable patents are generally more likely to be challenged in the US as well as in Europe, but the rate of the opposition at the European Patent Office (EPO) is 30 times higher that re-examination at the US Patent and Trademark Office (USPTO). Moreover, the opposition lead to a revocation of the patent in 35 per cent of the cases and to a restriction of the patent right in another 33 per cent of the cases. On the other hand, the re-examination resulted in a cancellation of the patent right in only 10 per cent of all cases.[86] Not only that the US patent examination system did not impose a sufficiently rigorous review of patent and non-patent prior rights, resulting in the issues of patents of low quality, but also the demands for patent application in the US law were lower than in EPC. While some authors applauded the fact that the typical US re-examination procedure lasted 'only two years',[87] others warned that the US re-examination system did not provide a real alternative to expensive litigation, since it was not adversarial and limited to issues based on prior art patents or printed publication.[88] It seemed to allow patents of low quality to go unchallenged, which could discourage innovation by leaving other innovators uncertain about their scope. While the EPO opposition proceedings (post-grant adversarial administrative proceedings) allow the challenger to bring in expert witnesses, submit briefs and new experimental data as well as request an extension to deadlines, no such third-party inclusion was possible in the US re-examination system.[89] And last but not least, the EPO opposition proceedings are less expensive than the US re-examination proceedings, since Europe enacted strict regulation of attorney fees in EPO proceedings.[90] The US solution seems not to be the more efficient here and there is no bigger authority to agree with our findings than the US itself, which in the AIA enacted the opposition system next to the previous re-examination procedure.[91]

Demands of the patent applications, their publishing and the patent protection term

While in Europe under Article 54 EPC the invention needs to fulfil the requirement of absolute novelty,[92] the US generously offers to the inventors a so-called grace period of one year[93] starting from the first barring moment (first offer for sale, a first offer for public use, publication of the invention).[94] This is a clear expression of the different patent policies inherent to the two legal systems; while in the US patent policy requires rapid disclosure of inventions to the public (and only the inventor giving the public the benefit of the knowledge of his innovation is entitled to a patent), the Europe sees its patent policy as a means to stimulate invention.[95] Under Article 54 EPC, the invention that becomes publicly available in any way before the application was filed, is not susceptible to be protected by a patent. From the efficiency perspective, the US argument that such period gives time and opportunity to the inventor to build on the invention undisturbed in order to market it later on in its best form seemed not to work in practice. What actually happened was that the inventors were modifying slightly their inventions and each modification counted as a starting point for the grace period. This fact in combination with the US patent term of seventeen years from the date that patent is issued produced unstable market for patents, legal uncertainty and overall inefficiency.[96] Such legal construct promoted delay in the presentation of the patent application by the inventor and actually encouraged him to file patent applications on speculative inventions of little immediate value to delay the start of the patent term.[97] Since the patentee's period of exclusive use is seen as an inventive incentive, the solution found in the civil law system and enacted in 1977 by the UK as another common law jurisdiction, seems to offer a more efficient outcome. It offers twenty years of protection from the day the application is filed and so encourages the applicant to process his application as quickly as possible.[98] Adhesion of the US to the TRIPS Agreement in 1995 changed the US system and enacted the international solution of twenty years,[99] signalling the agreement of the US that this is the more efficient solution. Once again, the legal origins theory does not seem to offer any explanation for such development.

There were some serious concerns expressed also in connection with the publishing of patents and patent applications in the US in this era of global business community when obtaining patent protection in multiple jurisdictions became increasingly common.[100] Until the year 2000, patent applications to the USPTO were not published until they were granted.[101] Under this system, finding any type of patents in the US has been problematic for domestic as well as foreign investors. Therefore the US system after the year 2000 adopted a variation of the EPO system rule and patent applications are now published after eighteen months unless the applicant has sworn not to file a patent application in any other jurisdiction.[102] The problem with this 'improvement' is that it does not eliminate the initial problems: the system still entails high legal uncertainty and disincentivizes foreign inventors to apply for an US patent. Under EPC, the patent application is published with the search report eighteen months after the date of filing. The citations contained in EPC patents also tend to be more consistent and objective compared to the USPO, since they were assigned by a single team of patent examiners,[103] minimizing the number of citations per patent.[104] Both facts combined insert more legal certainty in the European patent system, bringing more stability and more efficient outcomes than in the US.

First-to-file principle as superior to the first-to-invent principle

Until AIA the US used the first-to-invent principle, under which the patent belongs to the first inventor, while the European countries historically used the first-to-file principle and granted patent to the person with the earliest effective filing date.[105] AIA changed the US approach that has been in place for more than 200 years.[106] Under the old approach, only the 'first inventor' who made the invention can obtain the patent. An invention under this system occurs when a 'conception' and a 'reduction to practice' have taken place. Conception is the formation in the mind of the inventor of a definite and permanent idea of the complete and operative invention, while the reduction to practise can be actual or constructive (finalized or advanced-stage product).[107] The legal uncertainty behind this approach seems to be self-evident; presenting evidence and proving ownership of the invention in patent application under this system is close to art. The UK as another common law country enacted in its Patent Act the opposite system as early as in 1977.[108] The first-to-file system eliminates uncertainties and delays and expense incurred when two or more investors contest priority on the basis of the date of conception of the invention. It speeds up the identification and the filing of the investor and expedites disclosure of inventions to the public.[109] It enabled two distinct system failures in the US that persist even in the newly established US patent system: the problem of so-called 'patent trolls' and inefficient case law that has even been codified in the AIA.

'Patent trolls' is the name given to the practice of US patent holders, who possessing a patent covering a key element of the non-substitutable technology needed demand exorbitant sums as license fees and/or are filing excessive damage claims for its infringement. They used flaws in the US patent system to shake down honest businesses, attacking investors and hindering innovation; exactly the opposite of what the patent system should enable them to do. The first-to-invent system allowed for such unreasonable patent infringement actions due to its broad and undefined system of granting patents, combined with previously mentioned non-publication, protection period and inefficient doctrines developed in the field of patent law.

The US Doctrine of Inequitable Conduct is one of such inefficient relicts, at the end actually enacted in the AIA. Under this doctrine, 'any patent secured by "unclean hands" by omitting or manipulating critical information, is unenforceable'. One act of inequitable conduct in one aspect of a long and complex patent application can render the patent as a whole non-enforceable.[110] The legal uncertainty inherent in this concept is immense, imposing harmful effects on the efficiency and the quality of the overall patent system.[111]

Today, AIA brought to the US the so-called 'first-inventor-to-file' system as a hybrid system[112] between the first-to-invent and first-to-file approach, bringing more legal certainty and replacing the obsolete inefficient system.[113] It still entails the one-year grace period under the 35 USC §102(b)(1), but the move has most certainly been made in the direction of international and at the same time historically European solution, which increased the overall efficiency of the US patent system.

The technologies covered by the patents

Even though the US with its new legislation recognized the inherent efficiencies of the European patent system, the differences between the US and Europe as well as between the US and other common law countries persist, and they do not necessarily point towards the supremacy of the US patent law system. Even though patents have originally been granted for new machines and other mechanical inventions, now they have expanded also to chemical processes, products, biotechnological inventions, business methods and software,[114] a development accompanied with much scepticism in the academic community. Traditional notions of patents protecting advancements in technology, specifically encompassing only 'manufactures and machines', opposes such developments.[115] Furthermore, the software and business method patents proved to be on average of poor quality and were applied for merely to build portfolios rather than for protecting of real inventions.[116] Although the US federal patent system was influenced by England's Statute of Monopolies, the scope of the patentable subject matter in the US evolved beyond mere technological innovation, so to say away from the traditional common law notions, which has also been affirmed in the decisions of the US Court of Appeals for the Federal Circuit (CAFC), embracing the patentability of methods of doing business.[117] Even though the proponents of the efficiency of the common law hypothesis seemed to be clearly against the French system specialized courts and claiming their inefficiency, one such court has been created in the US in 1982 (CAFC), having jurisdiction over appeals of patent cases at US federal circuits. The invalidity rate of patents declined severely after its establishment from 63.7 per cent in years 1975–1976 to 25 per cent in years 1994–1995,[118] actually pointing to its efficiency. Although at this point this is not one of our principal arguments, inconsistencies with the legal origins theory can be seen also at this level.

In reality, patents for business methods are not justifiable under any existing policy and they can actually be economically detrimental. Patents should follow the traditional notions and should only be granted in areas where there is little or no incentive to create without a resulting proprietary right,[119] which is not the case with the business method. The incentive for improving such methods lies in the companies themselves, bringing them more efficiency, productivity and profit, without the need for additional protection of such methods. Moreover, since non-compete and confidentiality clauses are available and widely used in majority of the companies, additional protection is not needed nor wanted and it seems to serve exclusively for building portfolios, which should be seen as an abuse of patent law and not as its expression. Intrusion of patent protection into such competitive market system may serve only to disrupt the competitive process.[120] For example in Europe, such business methods (as well as computer programs) may be patentable only if they are incorporated as a part of an invention producing a technical effect,[121] following the traditional rationale of the patent protection law.

In general the US offers much broader scope of patentable inventions than Europe and the academics are sceptical about such development. Too broad of a definition of patentable material diminishes the value of such protection and distorts the underlying policy. With that in mind, the chapter finishes with a brief comparison of developments in three different common law jurisdictions in two specific fields to portray the inability of the US system to find the most efficient answers to patent dilemmas even when compared to other common law systems.

New Zealand takes a step forward in the field of software patents; UK seems to balance incentives of employees and employers

As a brief illustration in the field of patentability of software, New Zealand serves as a good common law example. A software patent is a patent for an invention involving software and USPTO has a long-established practice of granting such patents.[122] While the US system protects software developers against competitor creating an equivalent solution, it at the say time hinders the research and innovation by allowing monopolies where they are not necessary. Patent fees can allow powerful companies to exclude others from the market.[123] Furthermore, patent processes are slow and software patents represent a great burden for software developers, e.g. a smartphone developer in the US is theoretically burdened by 250,000 restrictions on his design.[124] The European approach of patenting software only when imbedded in technical innovation therefore seems more rational and much more efficient, which has been recognized also by the New Zealand legislator.

In New Zealand, the Patents Act 1953 allowed computer programs to be patented in New Zealand if they produced a commercially useful effect.[125] But by 2013 New Zealand abandoned the US approach and with Patent Bill 2013 embraced the European one, prohibiting the software 'as such' to be patented. In this way some software patent protection is retained, like in Europe, and the inventors retain the incentives to innovate and create new material, since others cannot free ride on that investment.

Another example of different development of patent law in distinct common law jurisdictions is the treatment of employer–employee inventions. While the US statutory patent law contains no provisions allocating patent rights to an invention between the employer and employee, the common law doctrine distinguishes between three situations: one where the employer is hired to invent or is assigned the task of developing a specific device or process, second when the employee has not been hired to invent and he made an invention during his own time without employer's resources and third when the employee is not hired to invent but uses the employer's facilities and resources to make an invention (the so-called 'shop right' doctrine).[126] In the first case, the inventor needs to assign his invention to the employer; in the second case the inventor should keep the invention and pay for the patent and in the third, the invention belongs to the inventor, but the employer obtains a non-exclusive, non-transferable royalty-free license to make and use the invention.[127] In theory, the system seems efficient and fair, keeping the right balance of incentives. In reality, due to the imbalances in the negotiating power, this doctrine is often superseded by contracts, diminishing research and development, which on their own determine the ownership of the inventions. Even though the common law courts do have the power to strike down such clauses, in reality they rarely do,[128] keeping the inefficient developments in the system.

The UK, as another common law jurisdiction, took another road. Before Patents Act 1977 the UK had no statutory provisions governing employee inventions, but the British Parliament decided to remedy this lack and to balance the employer and employee patent rights. In its Section 39, a simple determination is made: only in two circumstances the invention belongs to the employer (when it is in the scope of employee's normal duties or where an employee has special contractual obligation 'to further the employer's business interest'), in all other cases the invention belongs to the employee.[129] Furthermore, Section 40 determines a monetary award scheme under which outstanding benefit of the employer due to the employee's invention needs to be shared with the employee.[130] And last but not least, the inherent uneven bargaining position between the employee and employer is remedied by Sections 40 and 42, which prohibit employers from varying employee compensation rights by pre-invention contract.[131] This common law country did not fail to strike a balance between the incentives of the inventor and employer to innovate. Once again, the US solutions seem not to be the most efficient ones.

All in all, with these brief examples one can see that the arguments of the legal origins theory proponents cannot be held up in the field of patent law. Not only that the institutes used and created in the US proved to be insufficient and faulted, but also the US changed significantly its view on the matter by the AIA. It would be interested to see how the arguments of the mentioned theory could deal with the problems presented in this part. In any case, in the field of intellectual property law in general, the US did not advance the legal institutes that would solve the modern issues and more often than not it just followed the solutions found either at the European or at international level, negating the findings of the efficiency of common law hypothesis as well as the legal origins theory.

The efficiency of the 'fair use' doctrine under the conditions of two distinct copyright law systems

Copyright protects original works in the field of literature and the arts, but in last years it started to expand its protective domain also to computer programs and databases. The specificity thus intellectual property right is that copyright in all legal systems comes to existence without any formalities. Its term is limited in the US as well as in the EU to the life of the author plus 70 years.[132] Moreover, the US and EU share the same historical origin of their copyright systems in feudal laws licensing printers to publish books as a derogation from the as a principle needed concession of the royal authority.[133] This presumption has been reversed with the industrial revolution. Today as a rule publication is legitimate and any limitations upon publication are exceptions from this general principle. With the appearance of national law systems and legal codifications the different regimes of intellectual property law became now clearly different and divergent.[134]

Today the EU and the US views on copyright broadly diverge. In the US, the perspective on copyright is utilitarian and economic. Under such view, the copyright is granted because it encourages authors and inventors by rewarding them for their acts of creation. The inherent logic of such policy is to maximize social wealth, therefore the protection granted to copyright is less extensive than in Europe.[135] While under this policy the US copyright law contains only limited rights of authors to the integrity of their person as expressed in the work (the so-called 'moral rights') and subjects them to the §107 US Copyright Act's Fair Use exception, in Europe the whole copyright is considered from a perspective of the author's moral right.[136] The focus of the EU is on the integrity of a person, a view shared also by international treaties concerning the matter.[137]

The differences between the US and the EU in the field of copyright caught our attention especially in the field of limitation of such rights, largely debated among the academics in the last decade, especially due to the US Fair Use doctrine. The balance between information production and diffusion in copyright law is difficult to determine and even in the international field the US claims that their Fair Use doctrine is the tool needed for delivering efficiency also to the EU copyright law, if transposed into its legal system.[138] They claim, in the spirit of the legal origins theory, that this doctrine represents the superior legal institute able to achieve the appropriate balance in any legal system.[139]

Although there exists a widespread worldwide consent for the need for more openness in copyright law in today's information society of dynamic and unpredictable change and copyright law lost much of its flexibility in the past century, simply transposing an institute inherent to US copyright law, already criticized on its own merit for its openness and lack of legal certainty, does not seem to offer the best solution.[140]

In this part, a closer look is taken at the Fair Use doctrine as it stands in the US and comment on its efficiency and the possibility of its use in the civil law systems. Even in this limited field of copyright exceptions the solutions found in the US common law system do not a priori seem to be the most efficient ones and the EU law offers copyright flexibilities capable of assuring the same benefits without the legal uncertainty inherent in the US Fair Use doctrine.

The fair use doctrine

The Fair Use doctrine is a legal doctrine of US copyright law providing for the licit, non-licenced citation or incorporation of copyrighted material in another author's work under certain specifiable conditions.[141] It dates back to the nineteenth century and has been codified since 1976 in the US Copyright Act. Its statutory framework is set in Section 107 of the US Copyright Act, identifying also certain types of uses as examples of activities that might qualify as fair use, such as criticism, comment, news reporting, teaching, scholarship and research.[142] In evaluating whether something can be considered as fair use, four factors need to be taken into account: the purpose and character of the use, the nature of the copyrighted work, the amount and substantiality of the portion used in relation to the copyrighted work as a whole and effect of the use upon the potential market for or value of the copyrighted work. The court is not limited by this provision; by weighing a fair use, the court can decide upon circumstances given, taking into account other non-statutory factors.[143] The interpretation of fair use therefore depends on the judge's personal perspective, on the relative copyright expertise of the court and on the personal value system of individual judges.[144] Without going into unnecessary details, a non-commercial nature of the use or use for non-profit educational purposes as well as transformative works are more likely to be considered as fair use. At the same time, using a factual work is more likely to be considered fair use than using a more creative or imaginative work.[145] Moreover, only 'repeated and exploitative copying' of copyrighted works may already constitute a commercial use.[146] Also, there is no fair use if the work has not yet been published; US grants authors the right to control the first public appearance of their expressions.[147] For the amount of copied material, not only the quantity but also the quality and importance of the copied material counts.[148]

What deserves to be noted at this point is that the fair use is not a right in itself but a defence against copyright infringement claims. Its question appears only before courts, which evaluate fair use claims on a case by case basis, making the outcome of any given case dependent on a fact-specific inquiry.[149] As a plastic example: you will only come across this doctrine if you have used a part of someone else's work and the author of this work now claims before court that you have infringed his copyright. The circumstantial nature of the Fair Use doctrine created a number of ambiguities and divisions in how the mentioned factors are interpreted and applied in case law, which made this doctrine controversial. Despite its gradual marginalization, this doctrine still continues to stand as 'the oldest, broadest, and most important' limitation on the rights of copyright holders.[150] Due to the recognized need for flexibility of copyright limitations in today's world of rapid and unpredictable technological development and the need for creating technologically neutral copyright norms,[151] the inherent flexibility of the Fair Use doctrine in balancing the desired effect of copyright law in specific circumstances became appealing also to the academic community in civil law countries, which in turn opened a debate on the feasibility of its use in European copyright laws. At the same time, the academics in the US kept opening the debate on the inefficiency and legal uncertainty that the Fair Use doctrine has been causing on the American soil. Before we take a look at how efficiency could be reached in Europe, let us explore how the US has been struggling with the consequences of the Fair Use doctrine.

The purpose behind the Fair Use doctrine has traditionally been fostering the development of new ideas and means of expression, serving as an expression of social desirability of permitting others to build upon copyrighted works, but it has always been an elusive concept.[152] It has been built as a means of maintaining flexibility in copyright law, allowing courts to adjust in accordance with the circumstances as they arise; a tool for maintaining a proper balance between the copyright goal of rewarding creators with exclusive rights and the First Amendment goal of protecting freedom of expression.[153] Under the economic analysis of law, the Fair Use doctrine should be used in two specific categories of cases only: when the transaction costs of negotiating with the copyright owner for permission to use exceed the private value of the use to the would-be user and when the individual use generates some positive externality and the net social value of the use exceeds the value to the copyright owner of preventing the use.[154] While in theory, the Fair Use doctrine is an indispensable tool to achieve the right balance, the practice showed that its outcome is far from efficient. Evidence suggests that the public is often deterred from engaging in conduct that would likely fall within the ambit of this doctrine due to concerns over incurring attorney fees and the uncertainty and unpredictability of the doctrine itself.[155] The balance of private costs and benefits under the Fair Use doctrine as it stands causes users to forego legitimate fair use, while at the same time incentivizes the copyright owners to use systematic copyright over-enforcement,[156] which further dis-incentivizes the potential information users. Moreover, when fair use rests upon the positive externalities justification, it relies on individuals to further the public interest in the production of those externalities without providing them with a sufficient incentive to do so.[157] Instead of remedying the market failure, in its current form the fair use actually worsens it by further compromising the author's right in already virtually costless dissemination of information and at the same time deterring risk averse information users to serve themselves of the offered fair use.[158]

The absence of consistent, principled application of this doctrine of this US has been commented upon from many different aspects. It has been debated in the Judiciary Committee of the US House of Representatives,[159] several 'official' and formal guidelines have been issued in the attempt to define the scope of fair use for specific fields (education, research, library services),[160] comments have been made how in the current system only popular litigants tend to win in fair use cases,[161] comments have also been made on how the Congress failed to clarify the doctrine's ambiguities upon codification in the US Copyright Act, which has just aggravated the said problems,[162] the findings have been published that the consequence of this doctrine is very long and expensive litigation entailing significant costs to the potential beneficiary of the fair use user,[163] in 2000 federal court cases on fair use have been analysed and it was found that there was no correlation between the four factors from the Section 107 US Copyright Act and the court's ultimate ruling on fair use,[164] and last but not least, the Fair Use doctrine does not entail the respect of moral right of author as it does not comply with the Berne Convention and the TRIPS Agreement, making it unacceptable in Europe.[165]

What seems to be clear is that a more definitive copyright law in the US would be beneficial for both copyright holders and producers of derivative works; it would encourage such works by enabling greater certainty and generating less dispute over what constitutes infringing conduct, while at the same time allowing the public the benefit of this increased activity.[166] The inherent flexibility of this doctrine needs to provide more legal certainty if it wishes to provide the incentives for which it has been created in the first place. That being said, under the legal origins theory and the efficiency of common law hypothesis, the European copyright law should be even less efficient and provide even less flexibility than the given US copyright law exception and limitation system. Does it?

In search of flexibilities in Europe

Europe has historically held a closed list of copyright exceptions and maintaining it became increasingly difficult in today's world of rapid technological change.[167] Throughout the Europe, national and supranational initiatives appeared for introducing more flexibilities in the existing systems, UK being one of them. One might expect that a common law country would not find it difficult to implement an institute coming from another common law country and thereby ensuring the wanted flexibility, but the reality is that the US legal system institutes turned out not to be superior.[168]

Under UK copyright law the copyright is limited by provisions in the Copyright, Designs and Patent Act 1988 (CDPA), allowing limited use of copyrighted material without requiring permission from the rights holder,[169] in order to strike the balance between the exclusive rights if a copyright owner and the public's need for access to his work. The so-called 'doctrine of fair dealing' is contained in Sections 29 and 30 of CDPA, representing the most significant defences to copyright infringement. Under this doctrine, a person is not liable for copyright infringement if its act amounts to fair dealing for the purposes of non-commercial research or private study,[170] criticism or review[171] or reporting current events.[172] While this doctrine seems to be offering insufficient flexibility in today's legal environment, the propositions did not go in the direction of Fair Use doctrine but only to introducing more numerous exceptions.[173]

As to why the US doctrine does not seem to be the appropriate solution, two reasons have been voiced, next to the already mentioned problem of the legal uncertainty: the fact that this doctrine is not compatible with international obligations of the UK, the US and the EU as well as with the EU law on the matter. Concerning international obligations, Article 9(2) of Berne Convention introduced the so-called 'three-step test', determining three conditions for exceptions to the reproduction right to be introduced into national legislation; an obligation further extended to any TRIPS Agreement exclusive right in 1994.[174] Under this test, all limitations and exceptions must be confined to certain special cases, they must not conflict with a normal exploitation of the work and must not unreasonably prejudice the legitimate interest of the author.[175] The first and third conditions are not complied with by the Fair Use doctrine as it stands today. The US doctrine is furthermore not in compliance with EU law, which in Article 5 of the Directive 2001/29/EC provides besides this 'three-step test' also an exhaustive list of exceptions from which Member States cannot derogate.[176]

A fortiori, if the Fair Use doctrine is not appropriate solution for the UK copyright law, it is even less so for the EU copyright law. But the propositions to insert the Fair Use doctrine in the EU law nonetheless occurred, coming from companies whose business activities usually involve the internet.[177] Those companies were not persuaded by claims that the application of the Fair Use doctrine carries with it high level of legal uncertainties and that European copyright system with its current exceptions fulfils the same needs within a defined framework.[178] In Europe it is the national and supranational legislators that in a precise manner determine the balance contained in the legal provisions on copyright, and not judges in specific cases. In this civil law influenced world, the compromise between legal security and fairness is achieved by codifying relatively abstract and open legal provisions that spell out the general rules without impeding civil courts to apply general normative principles such as 'reasonableness and fairness' to arrive at fair judgments. Here the statutory limitations accommodate the variety of cultural, social, informational, economic and political needs and purposes.[179] Although based on what has been said one might expect that the codification is more precise and extensive in the civil law world, that is actually not true. While, for example, the Dutch Copyright Act contains only about 75 provisions laid down in 20 pages, the US Copyright Act exceeds 200 pages.[180] Therefore, the fact that the Fair Use doctrine still seems to be unpredictable and unclear, combined with the fact that the copyright provisions in the US are so detailed and numerous, already seems to suggest that the solution found in the US is not leading to efficient outcomes.

Although it is true that the civil law copyright codifications lost much of their flexibility in the course of the twentieth century due to the frequent updates of copyright laws accommodating the needs of a changing society and implementing the EU harmonization measures,[181] they still follow a logic that is different from the one of the US copyright system. In Europe, we are not protecting the author's right as a matter of economic benefits pertaining to him, but rather as a matter of fairness, to which limitations must remain 'exceptions'.[182] In accordance with that, the European courts have been interpreting such restrictions restrictively and the Fair Use doctrine is not compatible with such view. Due to the inherent vice pertaining to the Fair Use doctrine, the academic propositions for changes in copyright laws in Europe lean in the direction of a statutory system of limitations and exceptions that guarantees both a level of legal security and fairness, by combining relatively precise norms with sufficient flexibility to allow a fair outcome in unpredictable cases.[183] Since Directive 2001/29/EC, the so-called Information Society Directive (ISD) in its Article 5 sets forth a closed list of exceptions and limitations to the harmonized rights of reproduction and communication to the public[184] and gives the freedom to the Member States to offer optional exceptions contained therein[185] (under the conditions of the 'three-step test' from Berne Convention), the most flexible implementation of these exceptions can be achieved by including all of them in national law of EU Member States.[186] Such implementation could lead to semi-open norm, coming close to open-ended defences such as fair use, without the undesired legal uncertainty.

The same effect, wished for by creating the Fair Use doctrine in the US, can therefore be achieved in the civil law system, as it stands today, without the unnecessary negative consequences. To reiterate once again, we do not claim that the EU copyright system is superior to the US one, we are simply portraying that the solutions found in the US are not the most efficient ones and have been repeatedly commented on and criticized in academic circles all over the world. If the proponents of the legal origins theory and the efficiency of common law theory were right, the Fair Use would be the most efficient and superior legal institute to be followed by jurisdictions all around the world in the field of copyright. And that today is simply not the reality.

Notes

1 Report from European Parliament on Overcoming Transatlantic differences on intellectual property. IPR and the TTIP negotiations. Online at www.europarl.europa.eu/RegData/bibliotheque/briefing/2014/140760/LDM_BRI(2014)140760_REV1_EN.pdf (accessed 6 October 2015).
2 Annette Kur and Thomas Dreier, *Intellectual Property Law: Text, Cases and Materials* (Cheltenham: Edward Elgar 2013) 338–360.
3 At this point, we are not entertaining the economic analysis of law debate on what balance is appropriate for the optimal protection of rights of owners of intellectual property and universal access of society to new inventions; we limit ourselves only to looking at the systems as they are in place today. For more on the topic see Richard A. Posner, 'Intellectual Property: The Law and Economics Approach' (2005) 19 *Journal of Economic Perspectives* 57.
4 The US and EU definitions of intellectual property intensive industries differ amongst each other; while former counts in patent, trademark and copyright, the latter adds to the mix also geographical indication. The differentiation caused fundamental disagreements between the two; European Parliament (n1).
5 Ibid 13.
6 Ibid. 15.
7 Giovanni Battista Ramello, 'What's in a Sign? Trademark Law and Economic Theory' (2006) 73 POLIS Working Paper 7–8.
8 European Parliament (n1) 5.
9 Ibid. 15 on the legislation applicable in the US on the topic.
10 Ibid. 8.
11 Posner (n3) 57.
12 European Parliament (n1) 15.
13 Multiplicity of federal intellectual property laws shows the need for positive regulation of the issue; codifying some case law but not exclusively made out of it; suggests that the adaptability of judge-made law here does not suffice and does not offer sufficient

legal certainty; debated further in the chapter. Example: The American Invents Act of 16 September 2011, Lanham Act from 1946, US Copyright Act from 1976 (amended by 1998 Digital Millenium Copyright Act), Uniform Trade Secrets Act from 1985, Economic Espionage Act from 1996, etc.

14 E.g. in the field of trademarks one such document is the Protocol Relating to the Madrid Agreement Concerning the International Registration of Marks (as amended on November 12, 2007) under the auspices of WIPO.
15 European Parliament (n1) 7.
16 E.g. the Lanham Act 1946 in the US at the end contains provisions on the Madrid Protocol on trademarks, signed under the auspices of WIPO.
17 Guy Tritton and Richard Davis, *Intellectual Property in Europe* 3rd ed. (London: Sweet & Maxwell 2008) 225.
18 Kur and Dreier (n2) 157–158.
19 Ramello (n7) 3.
20 Tritton and Davis (n17) 225.
21 Ibid. 18.
22 US Commercial Service at the US Mission to the European Union (2010) *United States Mission to the European Union's Toolkit on Intellectual Property Rights*, 13
23 Ramello (n7) 5.
24 The Lanham Act, 15 USC §§ 1051 et seq.
25 European Parliament (n1) 18.
26 Ramello (n7) 5.
27 Annette Kur, 'The EU Trademark Reform Package: (Too) Bold a Step Ahead or Back to Status Quo?' (2015) 19(1) *Marquette Intellectual Property Law Review* 14.
28 Report of International Trademark Association, *Relative Examination Systems vs. Absolute Examination Systems: Whether INTA should endorse one system or the other* (2005). Online at www.inta.org/Advocacy/Documents/INTARelativeAbsolute Examination2005.pdf (accessed 6 October 2015).
29 Ibid. 7.
30 E.g. 38 per cent in Europe against 43 per cent in the USA; see *Global Trademark Management Benchmarking Report 2015* (Hoghan Lovells 2015). Online at http://limegreenip.hoganlovells.com/resources (accessed 6 October 2015).
31 The EU trademark law carries with it the 'all-or-nothing' principle; the EU trademark is denied if there are grounds for refusal in any of the EU Member States. See US Commercial Service (n22) 13.
32 Seventy per cent of the survey respondents expressed their interest in non-traditional trademarks. See *Global Trademark Management Benchmarking Report 2015* (n30).
33 Kur (n27) 25 (the debate is on whether 'graphical representation' contained in the Community Trademark Regulation can cover all possible non-traditional trademarks).
34 *Global Trademark Management Benchmarking Report 2015* (n30).
35 France has been protecting them since 1909; Christine Haight Farley, 'The Protection of Geographical Indications in the Inter-American Convention' (2014) 6 *WIPO Journal* 68, 71.
36 Kur and Dreier (n2) 341.
37 For a brief overview see Congressional Research Service, *Geographical Indications in US–EU Trade Negotiations* (2014). Online at http://nationalaglawcenter.org/wp-content/uploads/assets/In%20Focus/IF00016.pdf (accessed 6 October 2015).
38 Farley (n35) 70.
39 Ibid.
40 Although they were awarded limited protection already with Paris Convention for the Protection of Industrial Property 1883, The Madrid Agreement 1891 and the Lisbon Agreement 1958. see more in Tory Westbrook, 'The Proper Standard of Protection to be Afforded to Geographical Indications: A Discussion of the International Debate Surrounding GIs'. Online at www.academia.edu/8975605/The-proper-standard-

of-protection-to-be-afforded-to-geographical-indications-tory-westbrook (accessed 6 October 2015).
41 TRIPS: Agreement on Trade-Related Aspects of Intellectual Property Rights 1994, Marrakesh Agreement Establishing the World Trade Organization, Annex 1C.
42 Kur and Dreier (n2) 338.
43 EU Member States can determine further products; ibid. 338–345.
44 Swiss Federal Institute of Intellectual Property (2011) *The Effects of Protecting Geographical Indications: Ways and Means of their Evaluation* (Publikation 7) 1.
45 Ibid. 4.
46 Westbrook (n40) 14–15.
47 Ibid. 15–16.
48 Ibid. 16.
49 Ibid.
50 Council Regulation 2081/92/EEC of 14 July 1992 on the protection of geographical indications and designations of origin for agricultural products and foodstuffs [1992] OJ L 208.
51 Westbrook (n40) 17.
52 Kur and Dreier (n2) 341.
53 Since European immigrants brought with them geographic names from their countries, connected to reputable products, and used those names to advance their own products; Westbrook (n40) 22.
54 Ibid.
55 Ibid. 23.
56 Ibid. 20.
57 Jack Ewing, 'When Taste Is a Trade Issue'. *New York Times* (24 June 2015). Online at http://nyti.ms/1SJoo3q (accessed 6 October 2015).
58 Kur and Dreier (n2) 345.
59 Westbrook (n40) 24–27.
60 Ibid. 4.
61 Ibid. 6.
62 Since they are collective, they are protected and controlled by the state, certification agencies or producer collectives; see more in Kur and Dreier (n2) 338–343.
63 Ibid. 338.
64 Swiss Federal Institute of Intellectual Property (n44).
65 Farley (n35) 5.
66 Robert J. Shapiro and Aparna Mathur, 'The Economic Implications of Patent Reform. The Deficiencies and Costs of Proposals Regarding the Apportionment of Damages, Post-Grant Opposition, and Inequitable Conduct' (2008). Online at www.bio.org/sites/default/files/Patent_Reform_Study.pdf (accessed 6 October 2015).
67 Kur and Dreier (n2) 84.
68 Shapiro and Mathur (n66) 5.
69 To the exclusion of last twenty years.
70 Kur and Dreier (n2) 85.
71 Terje Gudmestad, 'Patent Law of United States and the United Kingdom: A Comparison' (1982) 5 *Loyola of Los Angeles International and Comparative Law Review* 173.
72 Catalina Martinez and Dominique Guellec, 'Overview of Recent Changes and Comparison of Patent Regimes in the United States, Japan and Europe: Patents, Innovation and Economic Performance' (2007) OECD Conference Proceedings 127–162.
73 Ibid. 131.
74 Patentanwälte Reihard Skuhra Weise and Partner (2002) *Information for Intellectual Property Users*, 1.

75 Convention on the Grant of European Patents (European Patent Convention) of 5 October 1973 as revised by the Act revising Article 63 EPC of 17 December 1991 and the Act revising the EPC of 29 November 2000.

76 Joseph Straus, 'The Present State of the Patent System in the European Union. As Compared with the Situation in the United States of America and Japan' (European Commission 1997) 10.

77 The European Court of Justice emphasized at several occasions, a European patent is no more than a bundle of national patent pursuant to a single application at this point; see ECJ decisions in Case C-539/03 *Roche Nederland BV v Frederick Primus et Milton Goldenberg* [2006] I-06535 and Case C-4/03 *GAT v LUK* [2006] ECR-I 06509.

78 Not only EU Member States, today the number is 38; see more in Straus (n76).

79 The so-called European patent to be created following the example of the Community Trademark System; but still not in place today.

80 Patentanwälte Reihard Skuhra Weise and Partner (n74) 1.

81 Martinez and Guellec (n72) 134.

82 Patentanwälte Reihard Skuhra Weise and Partner (n74) 1.

83 Jay A. Erstling, Amy M. Salmela and Justin N. Woo, 'Usefulness Varies by Country: The Utility Requirement of Patent Law in the United States, Europe and Canada' (2012) 3 *Cybaris Intellectual Property Law Review* 2.

84 Shuba Haaldodderi Krishnamurthy, 'U.S. Patent Reform Act of 2011 ("America Invents Act"): The Transition from First-to-Invent to First-to-File Principle' (2014) 5 *Journal of Intellectual Property, Information Technology and E-Commerce Law*.

85 Kur and Dreier (n2) 85.

86 Stuart J. Graham et al., 'Post-Issue Patent ""Quality Control": A Comparative Study of US Patent Re-examinations and European Patent Oppositions' (2002) NBER Working Paper No. w8807, 1.

87 As opposed to three to five years under the EPO opposition proceedings; Robert J. Shapiro and Aparna Mathur, 'The Economic Implications of Patent Reform: The Deficiencies and Costs of Proposals Regarding the Apportionment of Damages, Post-Grant Opposition and Inequitable Conduct' in C. Sri Krishna ed., *Patent Reforms: Policy Approaches* (Hyderabad: ICFAI University Press 2008).

88 Ibid. 8.

89 Ibid. See also Bronwyn H. Hall, Grid Thoma and Salvatore Torrisi, 'The Market Value of Patents and R&D: Evidence from European Firms' (2007) NBER Working Paper Series No.13426.

90 EPO opposition proceedings at €15,000–25,000 each, US re-examination proceedings $10,000–100,000 each; see more in Shapiro and Mathur (n87).

91 Ibid.

92 E.g. not forming a part of the state of the art; everything made available to the public by written or oral description or in any other way before the priority date of the EP application; *see more in* Patentanwälte Reihard Skuhra Weise and Partner (n74) 1.

93 35 USC §102(b)(1): the inventor can freely publish his invention without losing its patent right; AIA effectively limited this grace period to publications by the investor himself or someone who directly obtained the information from the inventor, so that today a third party publication would destroy the novelty of the invention

94 Patentanwälte Reihard Skuhra Weise and Partner (n74) 1.

95 Gudmestad (n71) 174.

96 With AIA, this term has been harmonized with the international community and now counts twenty yearsfrom the date of the patent grant; see more in Gudmestad (n71) 195–196.

97 Ibid. 196.

98 Ibid. 195.

99 Martinez and Guellec (n72) 151.

100 Erstling et al. (n83) 3.

101 Hall et al. (n89) 3.
102 Ibid.
103 EPO grant procedure comprises of a priori art search ex officio and continues with substantive examination, while the USPTO leaves that to the applicant; EPSO also offers an accelerated examination without any additional cost which is very efficient; see more in Erstling et al. (n83).
104 Ibid. 17.
105 Patentanwälte Reihard Skuhra Weise and Partner (n74) 1.
106 This switch has been proposed already in the year 2005; see Krishnamurthy (n84).
107 Gudmestad (n71) 187.
108 Ibid. 189.
109 Which at its basis is exactly what the US patent policy aims for; see Gudmestad (n71) 187–190.
110 Shapiro and Mathur (n87) 16.
111 Ibid.
112 Krishnamurthy (n84).
113 The old system has been kept on Constitution arguments, keeping in place the inefficiencies; ibid.
114 Last two especially in the US with the rest of the world not being in accordance to broaden the scope of patents in such a way; Kur and Dreier (n2) 86.
115 Brian P. Biddinger, 'Limiting the Business Method Patent: A Comparison and Proposed Alignment of European, Japanese and United States Patent Law' (2001) 69(6) *Fordham Law Review* 2523, 2524.
116 Hall et al. (n89) 1.
117 The opposition to patents for conceptual inventions began to fade with the acceptance of claims for computer programs in 1994, which made CAFC decide to extend this treatment to methods of doing business; *see* more in Biddinger (n115) 2524–2533.
118 Martinez and Guellec (n81) 136.
119 Biddinger (n115) 2525–2528.
120 Ibid. 2545.
121 Ibid. 2537.
122 Daniel Dimov, 'Software Patent Law: EU, New Zealand, and the US Compared'. In *Management, Compliance and Auditing* 2013. Online at http://resources. infosecinstitute.com/software-patent-law-eu-new-zealand-and-the-us-compared/ (access date)
123 Such fees are approximately $18,000; average patent litigation may cost around $3,000,000 and subsequent appeal procedure $2,000,000; see more in Dimov (n122).
124 Also covering trivial inventions; see more in Dimov (n122).
125 Ibid.
126 Gudmestad (n71) 181.
127 Ibid.
128 Ibid. 181–183.
129 Ibid. 184.
130 Ibid. 185.
131 Ibid.
132 Kur and Dreier (n2) 241.
133 Eric Allen Engle, 'When is Fair Use Fair? A Comparison of E.U. and U.S. Intellectual Property Law' (2002) 15 *The Transnational Lawyer* 187.
134 Ibid. 198.
135 Ibid. 199.
136 Ibid. 199–201.
137 Among which the two most influential are the 1883 Berne Convention and the previously mentioned 1994 TRIPS Agreement, to both of which the US and the EU are signatories; see more in US Commercial Service (n22).

138 In reality, even authors that seem to argument for the same solution admit, that such transposition would need adaptation and changes before it could truly be efficient and beneficial also for other legal systems; see more in Engle (n113) 187.

139 Ibid. 194.

140 Bernt P. Hugenholtz and Martin R. F. Senftleben, 'Fair Use in Europe: In Search of Flexibilities' (2011) *IVIR*, 2.

141 Rehana Gubin, 'Borrowing Privileges: How Does (or Should) Copyright Law define a Derivative Work? Patents, Innovation and Economic Performance' in Briefing Book Signal/Noise 2k5. *Harvard Journal of Law and Technology*, 9.

142 Due to the inherent legal uncertainty of the doctrine, the US Copyright Office set up an internet page to guide to the Fair Use practice; see more at http://copyright.gov/ fair-use (accessed 6 October 2015).

143 Ibid.

144 Martin Brenncke, 'Is "Fair Use" an option for UK legislation?' (2007) 71 *Wirtschaftsrecht* 13.

145 See more at http://copyright.gov/fair-use (accessed 6 October 2015).

146 Christina Olson, 'A Practical Guide to the Fair Use Doctrine in American Copyright Law' (2005) in Briefing Book Signal/Noise 2k5, *Harvard Journal of Law and Technology* 4.

147 Ibid. 6.

148 Ibid.

149 Ibid. 3.

150 Ibid. 2.

151 Hugenholtz and Senftleben (n140) 4.

152 Manal Z. Khalil, 'The Applicability of the Fair Use Defense to Commercial Advertising: Eliminating Unfounded Limitations' (1992) 61(3) *Fordham Law Review* 661.

153 Ibid. 662.

154 Thomas F. Cotter, 'Fair Use and Copyright Overenforcement' (2008) 93 *Iowa Law Review* 1271.

155 Ibid.

156 Ibid. 1272.

157 Ibid. 1274.

158 Federation of European Publishers (2011) 'FEP Position Paper on a Transposition of Fair Use at EU Level', 4.

159 The most prominent one has been held on 28 January 2011, but no large moves from the existing system have been envisaged; see more in Cotter (n154) 1271–1320.

160 They do not have the force of law, actually they interfere with the actual understanding of the law and erode the confidence in the law as created by Congress and the courts; none of the principal fair use cases is actually within the scope of these guidelines; see more in Kenneth D. Crews, 'The Law of Fair Use and the Illusion of Fair-Use Guidelines' (2001) 62(2) *Ohio State Law Journal*.

161 The claim that the richer and more known authors of copyrighted works tend to have the upper hand in the courts; see more in Andrew Gilden and Timothy Greene 'Fair Use for the Rich and Fabulous?' (2013) 80 *The University of Chicago Law Review Dialogue*.

162 Khalil (n152) 662.

163 Federation of European Publishers (n158) 2.

164 Ibid.

165 Ibid. 6.

166 Gubin (n141) 9.

167 Hugenholtz and Senftleben (n140) 4.

168 Hargreans Review in the UK in 2011 found that importing the Fair Use doctrine is unlikely to be legally feasible in Europe and that copyright exceptions already existing

with some adaptation could achieve the flexibilities without sacrificing the legal certainty; see more in Hugenholtz and Senftleben (n140).

169 Brenncke (n144) 6.
170 CDPA ss 29(1) and 29(1)(c).
171 CDPA s 30(1).
172 CDPA s 30(2).
173 Brenncke (n144) 6.
174 Ibid. 14.
175 Ibid. 15.
176 Ibid. 18.
177 Federation of European Publishers (n158) 1.
178 Ibid. 2.
179 Hugenholtz and Senftleben (n140) 6.
180 Ibid.
181 Ibid. 7.
182 Ibid.
183 Ibid. 9.
184 Directive 2001/29/EC of the European Parliament and of the Council of May 2001 on the harmonization of certain aspects of copyright and related rights in the information society [2001] OJ L 167, Art. 5(1).
185 Ibid Art. 5(2) and Art. 5(3).
186 Hugenholtz and Senftleben (n140) 17.

10 Contrasting common and civil law

Corporate law in the US and EU

To finish our line of thought, this final chapter deals with the field of law where the legal origins theory has been the most successful and influential: in the field of corporate law.[1] Although its original version from 1996 has been named 'Law and Finance',[2] it was essentially dealing with the investors' rights, law enforcement and concentration of ownership across the different jurisdictions classified as belonging to civil or common law legal family.[3] Even though its initially strong claims, such as the claim that highly concentrated ownership is an adaptive response to poor investor protection in a corporate governance system,[4] have been somewhat watered-down in subsequent research,[5] its conclusions remained firm and all-encompassing, continuing to claim the supremacy of the common law legal family and the positive influence of the solutions inherent therein on the economic environment and growth.[6]

Thus we are finishing where the legal origins theory started, in the field of corporate law, by applying our arguments developed throughout this book to this particular field of law, while at the same time using academically and practically relevant dichotomy among the US and EU as two distinct legal systems meeting each other with similar force on the today's global market. In this finishing chapter, we aim to portray the inherent flaws in the research made by the legal origins scholars as well as applying their findings to specific institutes as they stand in modern corporate laws of the US and EU. This chapter will therefore not be merely descriptive, but it will actively challenge the findings of the theory in its most prominent field, the corporate law, on the basis of the dichotomy between the EU and US corporate laws as the centre of interest to modern comparative law scholarship.[7]

Inherent flaws of the legal origins in researching the field of corporate law: the taxonomy of countries

While one might expect the comparative lawyers to be the loudest critics of the legal origins theory in the corporate law field, the most prominent responses to the legal origins theory actually originate from the sphere of economics. So before any additional factors are suggested as influencing the economic growth more than the legal frame itself, a closer look will be taken at the so-called 'Leximetric approach',[8] which has actually started with the legal origins theory and has built further upon its 'beginnings'. And the doubts that this approach expressed regarding the conduct of the research of the legal origins serve as our starting point in this final chapter.

The taxonomy of countries as belonging to the civil or the common law legal family has spurred quite some criticism among economists and legal scholars. It has been found that the legal origins categorization of most countries is to a large extent arbitrary,[9] since it is disregarding not only the societal, political and cultural context of law, but also the law beyond mere formal rules.[10] Such partial research based on randomly picked legal rules can lead to absurd results as shown by a research that found a legal order influenced by the French civilian tradition to correlate with World Cup success in a statistically significant way.[11] This clearly points to a further problem of legal origins in the corporate sphere: correlation does not equal causation and the fact is that regression as a method can be misleading. Classification itself has actually been seen by some scholars as the biggest issue of the legal origins theory[12] and further research confirmed that in 80 per cent of the 129 countries examined the categorization according to the legal origins was far from unambiguous.[13] Even more interesting results stem from studies of particular countries, of their legal system with its cultural and societal underpinnings, coupled with historical research and with a view beyond formal legal rules.

One of such studies revealed that although under the legal origins theory Brazil has been (without much explanation) labelled as of a French-style civil law jurisdiction,[14] the way in which the corporate law has actually been transplanted and received in Brazil seemed to be the most important factor in predicting the effectiveness of the resulting legal system,[15] causing Brazil not to simply follow the French civil law tradition but further adapt the law to local circumstances. Such adaptation actually produced superior results to simple blind copying of unknown legal orders.[16] Brazil had a taste of such 'blind' copying of Anglo-American law in the twentieth century in the case of the use of non-voting preferred shares, which at the end actually resulted in minority shareholder expropriation[17] and confirmed that such approach to rule transplantation across countries can be harmful.

Canada can serve as another remarkable example of wrongly determining the legal origins of a country contrary to its actual taxonomy in world financial markets. Classified as of a common law legal origin, Canada actually entails both common and civil law traditions.[18] While its federal government and twelve of thirteen provinces and territories operate under the common law system, Quebec in its province actually operates a civil law system.[19] Canada's capital markets differ from the US or UK capital markets, with cost of capital in Canada approximately twenty-five basic points higher than in the US,[20] and further differences could be observed in the reactions to recent credit and financial crisis, where the Canadian banking system managed to maintain a level of profitability, liquidity and financial stability not seen in other jurisdictions.[21] The case of Canada so serves as another example of the fact that context matters when looking at the countries' corporate laws.

The fact that common history is reflected in legal rules, culture and practice can also be seen by the way the legal origins classified China as belonging to the German legal origin.[22] Codified Chinese company law is to a large extent a mixture of various legal influences and not simply of German legal origin.[23] China can at the same time serve also as an example of the inappropriateness of simply transplanting legal instruments from other legal systems on the basis of its unsuccessful implementation of Organization for Economic Co-operation and Development (hereafter OECD) Principles of Corporate Governance 1999 in the year 2001,[24] where by following the logic of the legal origins China used this 'move' to create a signalling effect to international capital markets to attract their monetary attention – a move which ultimately failed.[25]

Besides these particular examples of classification of countries according to their legal origins, it is even more surprising that the legal origins scholars in their taxonomy make no distinction between the developed and developing countries.[26] When new research was conducted under the same definition of the crucial substantive rules as contained in the legal origins but differentiating between developed and developing countries, the results showed that the poorest one third of the countries examined has better substantive law than the richest third.[27] Another study provided additional empirical proof that when the countries are categorized by their stage of development, developed countries performed better than developing countries regardless their underpinning corporate legal rules.[28] Due to the oversimplification and coding of particular third world countries as countries of French civil law origin in the legal origins theory database[29] the findings of this theory in the field of corporate law are questionable at its best.

Even if we for the purpose of a more thorough research neglect all the findings in this subchapter and in that spirit agree with the legal origins on their taxonomy of countries, one fact cannot escape our scrutiny as being inconsistent with the real picture in modern legal systems: there actually is large variance in corporate legal systems within the countries belonging to the same legal family, and this variance should be taken into account. In the sphere of corporate law, innovation is needed to answer efficiently to developments in the markets[30] and therefore the capacity of legal systems to innovate in this field is also important next to the level of protection the legal system affords to particular stakeholders at any point in time.[31] Examining the countries on the basis of the 'innovative' point of view it showed that the origin countries are more innovative in their corporate law than transplant countries.[32] Moreover, since in the field of corporate law the claimed general positive characteristics of the legal origins theory under the 'adaptability' and the 'political channel' cannot be applied, due to the fact that in all jurisdictions corporate law is largely statutory law[33] and judiciary is highly active in all legal families,[34] it is interesting to note that at the time of enactment of the first of corporate statutes in England as the origin country of common law legal family only a few of the indicators of high level of minority shareholder protection as measured by the legal origins were present.[35] Moreover, pre-emptive rights did not even exist in England before it joined EU[36] and we cannot overlook the fact that even though England is a social democracy it coexists alongside a strong securities market,[37] contrary to what the legal origins theory predicts. On the basis of corporate law's innovative function, little evidence has been found that the dichotomy civil law – common law provides explanations for differences in corporate legal innovation.[38] In fact, most of the business law innovations, even in the nineteenth century, were in fact statutory.[39]

Even when comparing the US and England as two common law countries, substantial differences can be found between their corporate laws. British institutional investors tend to be more interventionist than their American counterparts and the British boards possess a balanced mix of inside and outside members, while in the US it is common that the CEO is the only full time manager on the board.[40] Moreover, in some respects the British system is more shareholder friendly than that of the US.[41] Also their reaction to the recent credit and financial crisis has been fundamentally different: while the US opted for compulsory approach (more in line with the civil law approach) with SOX and the rules of Security Exchange Commission (SEC) as well as the creation of the Public Company Accounting Oversight Board (PCAOB) for regulation of the accounting profession, Britain as the origin country built on the principle of voluntary compliance with non-statutory codes of conduct and their concept of 'comply or explain' for listed companies.[42] Besides the fact that the Continental Europe followed the British example,[43] so did the international community in the OECD Principles of Corporate Governance 1999,[44] but the US law produced no single phenomenon comparable to this common law approach. In many respects the US corporate law actually represents a deliberate rejection of common law principles and prefers more affirmative ideas clearly and directly taken over from civil law sources.[45] Not accounting for such distinctions inherent in the legal families themselves casts doubts on the results produced through such analysis.

All in all, as we have seen, the taxonomy of countries under the legal origins is already flawed and it did not account for cultural, political and other factors that might influence the way law is implemented in a particular country and the effects that such law has in practice. Neither did it account for the actual differences between countries of the same legal origin. But if we disregard completely these facts and continue with the analysis of the legal origins theory in the field of corporate law, we touch upon additional issues that are worth mentioning as influencing its final results.

Inherent flaws of the legal origins in researching the field of corporate law: coding errors

For an index to be a meaningful representation of the effects of legal rules across different jurisdictions it must contain coding that is transparently accurate and consistent, but in the case of the legal origins theory a systematic re-coding of the anti-director right index[46] brought about results differing from the initial ones.[47] The anti-director index has been criticized on the basis of the selection of variables as having a common law bias,[48] on the basis of the binary weighting that it entails,[49] on the basis of it not taking into account the comparative law principle of functional equivalents[50] and on the basis of the fact that it is entirely based on cross-sectional data,[51] especially in a fast developing field of law such as corporate law. Besides purely theoretical criticisms, numerous new empirical studies emerged, showing that once these errors are accounted for and corrected, the results of the legal origins-like analysis are entirely different.[52]

What is fascinating from our point of view is the fact that not only the selection of shareholder rights has been made from a US point of view, carrying so-called 'home-bias', but it has also been at the same time coupled with a complete ignorance of the comparative law principle of functional equivalents.[53] This fact alone makes the legal origins theory unsustainable and diminishes its scholarly value. If one only takes a look at the formal law (or the so-called 'law in books') without actually paying attention how law is used and interpreted in practice ('law in action'), the results are bound to be biased. When the bias has been switched and legal origins rights of 'shares not blocked' and the 'oppressed minority mechanism' have been replaced by 'minority protection regarding authorized capital' and by 'minority protection regarding share repurchases' respectively, the index showed that civil law countries and especially France performed better than common law countries.[54] Furthermore, as the rights under the scrutiny of legal origins theory have been critically re-investigated in Delaware, Belgian and French law, France came out as the winner.[55] When the interrelation among different rules and their importance in comparative law has been taken into account, coupled with the case law in those three countries, US had worse 'actual' shareholder protection than France and have offered the same shareholder protection as Belgium.[56] Indeed, the problems emphasized by the legal origins theory are not necessarily the same problems that are most pressing in all legal systems and the evaluation of different legal solutions alone requires value judgments,[57] which are absent from the original legal origins theory.

Historically the common law and civil law countries did not have the same corporate ownership structure[58] and there has also been evidence of reverse causation, showing that the development of financial markets influences the development of shareholder rights in a particular country.[59] Consistent with these findings is also the fact that neither US neither England determined the shareholder rights at the time of the development of their capital markets.[60] Since the corporate law is context-dependent and develops in accordance with cultural, political and ideological environment, it should be examined as such and functional equivalents across legal families and across individual countries need to be taken into account. The finding after taking these factors into account is that although there is proof of functional convergence in the field of corporate law across the legal families, the complementarities across institutions do matter and they limit the scope for the successful transplantation of particular institutions in other legal systems, even if they functioned perfectly in the origin country.[61]

It therefore seems that the legal origins theory in the field of corporate law suffers from the same tendencies as functionalist comparative legal analysis; it assumes that different societies face similar problems and it implies the ability to make objective claims as to which legal solutions to those problems are superior.[62]

Once this fact is accounted for, the results of analysis do not speak in favour of the common law system anymore. Connected with this issue is also the issue of binary weighing of variables in the legal origins theory. The variables are assigned either value 0 or value 1, no nuance in between is allowed for. Although this issue is a part of the 'lack of functional equivalents' bundle, once graduated variables have been used to capture more detail on legal variation, the results again do not support the findings of the legal origins theory. While one research found a significant positive impact of shareholder protection on stock market capitalization in developing countries and in countries with a common law legal origin, no such impact has been found for civil law countries.[63] No significant positive relationship between the various stock market development indicators and the shareholder protection index has been found[64] and the higher the degree of shareholder protection, the lower was the number of listed companies per million of population.[65]

When on the basis of these facts empirical research has been carried out, unsurprisingly the results differed significantly from the results of the legal origins theory. Especially when the cross-sectional data have been replaced with longitudinal data, a different picture emerged. Since change is rapid in corporate law and the socioeconomic and technological change challenge persistently the legal system,[66] analysing corporate law through a longitudinal set of data is a necessity. Research has shown that countries with more enabling corporate laws are the leaders in developing new types of law-making and law enforcement institutions, while the dichotomy common law – civil law seems not to matter.[67] The longitudinal point of view brought the discovery that Germany offers a higher level of protection to the shareholders than the US[68] and that external finance constituted a lower proportion of corporate growth in common law countries than in civil law countries, contrary to findings of the legal origins scholars.[69] Moreover, when the whole period from 1820 to 1998 was taken under scrutiny, France outpaced Britain in the rate of per capita growth.[70] In observing the development of shareholder protection in twenty countries in the period from year 1995 to year 2005 through ten variables, another scholar noticed improvement in shareholder protection in most countries, while in general developed countries protected shareholders better than the developing countries.[71] Once again, no clear division between legal families has been found.[72] Furthermore, under this index both France and the US scored 7.25 out of 10, but here the author acknowledged that that does not mean that the shareholder protection laws of the two are identical.[73] Reasons for similarities in the common law systems were found as the consequence of the similarities in culture and history as well as sharing English as a common legal language, which enables easy transmittal of ideas between these countries.[74]

The coding of the legal origins theory has indeed not been flawless and the developments in the recent financial and economic crisis in the world add additional question marks to the equation. Although based on the ideas of legal origins, legal convergence would be expected and the responses to the crisis should follow the common law legal tradition as more suitable and adaptable to new developments in economic environment, the fact of the matter is that it was the US who opted for civil law-style compulsion after the crisis. It enacted the Sarbanes-Oxley Act, the SEC rules and improved listing standards at the New York Stock Exchange.[75] The UK at the same time built upon its principle of voluntary compliance with its non-statutory codes of conduct and the Continental Europe followed its example,[76] inserting flexibility in the corporate law. The division between legal origins is therefore neither static, neither all-encompassing, like the legal origins scholars would like to believe.

The inherent dangers of the persisting influence of legal origins theory on the international level

The sensitive field of corporate law and the unclear relationship between the corporate law environment and economic development proved to be an uncertain ground for creating all-encompassing corporate policy recommendations at the international level. Yet the recommendations built upon this theory still persist in the international community, even though the original findings of legal origins date almost twenty years back and were found faulty and misleading. The fact is that the legal origins theory is a standard reference in comparative corporate and financial law[77] and that its initial findings are still extremely influential: their index is being relied upon extensively as a quantitative measure of investor protection and it has been used in regression to establish the correlation between the investor protection and broad and deep capital markets, higher dividend payouts, higher corporate valuation, better access to external finance, more efficient capital allocation and the extent of the exchange rate depreciation and stock market collapse during a crisis.[78]

The biggest issue with this international dissemination of faulty ideas is that its effects will not be felt in developed countries but rather in developing and transitional countries, which are the ones heavily influenced by the policy prescriptions of aid agencies and international financial institutions.[79] The freedom of these countries to draft and implement their own measures to cope with their economic and financial challenges has been reduced in the recent years due to the direct pressure of adopting specific policy measures due to their international legal obligations and indirect pressure in the form of the power of ideas and the professional trainings received by policy experts.[80] The faulty conclusions of the legal origins theory form a sturdy basis for this indirect pressure. In fact, the involvement of the IMF, the EU and the US in the World Bank's *Doing Business* project, the legal origins influences the most important single statement by any development institution on the relationship between corporate law and business development.[81] And even though the advanced legal origins theory defines the legal origins as '... a style of social control of economic life ...' where '... common law stands for the strategy of social control that seeks to support private market outcomes whereas civil law seeks to replace such outcomes with state-desired allocations',[82] the conclusions of the legal origins theory that are used in the *Doing Business* reports stem from the original research.[83] Moreover, even though the legal origins scholars presented their conclusions as descriptive, the

Doing Business reports use them as hard facts[84] and emphasize the ease of doing business at the expense of other policy considerations, which entails the risk of the so-called 'race to the bottom'.[85] Other international organizations have recently realized the inherent dangers of such approach and changed their research agenda to analysing specific thematic topics in more detail from a comparative perspective, such as takeovers, derivative suits and self-dealing.[86]

The well-known fact is that legal change is often outpaced by economic change,[87] and that this should not be overlooked by international policy advisors and institutions. The fact that the association between minority shareholder protection and liquidity exists but in reverse cause and effect sequence follows from this reasoning,[88] therefore approaching the problem the other way around harms the countries that are struggling to find new solutions in their corporate laws.

Measuring the quality of corporate laws around the world with reduction of variables to a few shareholder rights that represent a measure of the quality of corporate law from a biased common law perspective cannot be the right way of creating modern, progressive corporate laws. Due to the systemic influence of historical, sociological, lingual and other reasons on national corporate law systems, there cannot be a 'one-size-fits-all' solution. In this context we see the legal origins theory as simply portraying the strong international need of reforming and re-establishing the corporate legal policy that would answer to the modern issues of global business-making and formulate new corporate law strategy on that basis. There is no international consensus on the role of corporate law today and there are even struggles of obtaining such consensus inside a particular legal family. The following paragraphs will attempt to show how complicated and inter-related the modern corporate law dilemmas are and that the solutions found for them in the US are not necessarily superior to the solutions found in the EU corporate law. With a few practical examples we will prove that even if we blindly trusted the findings of the legal origins theory, the practical institutes inherent in corporate law systems of the two biggest representatives of the two distinct legal families would cause us to find the theory faulty and misleading.

The US and EU: legal origins and individual institutes in US and EU corporate laws

Based on the findings of the legal origins theory, the body of US corporate law as a whole should prove to be more efficient than the solutions developed under the EU corporate law, which derives its corporate institutes almost exclusively from civil law legal families.[89] But there is global lacunae in the company law developments which became obvious especially by the repeating financial crises in the twenty-first century and neither the US neither the EU seemed to find the appropriate solutions for the consequences of these developments. Moreover, it was repeatedly stated that the US shareholder-oriented corporate governance created the enabling environment in the current economic sphere for the development of questionable business practices, focused on short-term gains, that can at best be called efficient in short term and unsustainable in long term. In line with the legal origins theory findings, the efficiency and competitiveness increasingly became the explicit goals of corporate law reforms, based more on economic than legal arguments, taking away the progressive role of company law that should be present in building renewed company law systems suitable to deal with new developments.[90] Short term efficiency proved to be secondary to the balancing of interests in the field of company law and the law should try to implement sustainable solutions through fairness; solutions that proved to be efficient in long term.[91] As a matter of fact, the emphasis on sustainable growth and 'better regulation' shies away from the traditional view that more growth, no matter its substance, is better for the economy in the long term, and that is precisely what the legal origins theory neglects in its research.

This part of our final chapter therefore shows the inherent conflicts of the US corporate law doctrine, the comparison between the relevant corporate law institutes in the EU and the US and portrays a picture of how even if the legal origins theory would not be inherently flawed in its basis, its findings are not in line with the real-life developments and the state of corporate legislation in the two observed jurisdictions.

Inherent conflicts of the US corporate law doctrine: the corporation as a nexus-of-contracts as incompatible with the shareholder primacy orientation

It is undeniable that company law in the US follows the shareholder maximization value maxim.[92] At the same time, theories developed in the common law world that see the company not as a separate entity bearing rights and obligations, but rather as a nexus-of-contracts, implying that the company is there only to minimize the costs of individual contracting for entities connected through the business.[93] Already at this point it is interesting to note that these two notions are essentially incompatible, and yet, together, they form the basis of modern US company law. The shareholders are deemed to be the owners of the company, since they contribute the capital and hire the management,[94] which serves as a justification for the shareholder supremacy, yet the nexus-of-contracts theory argues that the corporation is contractual in nature and the corporate structure in essence reflects what the participants have freely chosen.[95] There are no owners involved; the parties are equal and are deemed to contract freely with each other; the corporation serves just as a connecting factor among them. Essentially, neither of the two concepts is indisputable, and taken together the system is unsustainable. While it can be easily argued, especially in an economic system with dispersed ownership structure, such as in the US, that the shareholders are not the only ones providing the company with essential and specialized inputs and that a similar case can be made in favour of bondholders, suppliers and workers,[96] it can also be argued that the bargaining position for contracting differs essentially among workers, shareholders and suppliers, which at the end contract burdened with unequal bargaining strengths. This is even more so when the nexus-of-contracts theory is coupled with shareholder primacy, giving shareholders unparalleled power when compared to other stakeholders of the company.[97]

These US notions brought about real-life developments that seem not to be in line with the efficiency of common law hypothesis, neither with the legal origins theory findings. Can we claim that a legal framework that brings about corporate scandals of global size is truly efficient? If we rephrase it: the loose legal framework demanded from the side of the companies advocating minimum regulation spurred the economic and financial crisis of 2000 and 2007, particularly due to the pursuit of short-term shareholder-oriented goals,[98] and then the same companies demanded bail-outs from the government when they found themselves on the verge of bankruptcy.[99] At this point, the companies wanted regulatory assistance, after they have shown that the regulatory framework in which they were operating is not sufficient for sustaining modern businesses. All in all, nobody can claim that market failure is an efficient development. And it is fairly undeniable that the shareholder primacy, in today's environment of global financial markets and disinterested shareholders of block of shares, was one of the causes for such developments.[100]

Shareholder value maximization v. stakeholder value orientation as corporate law policies

As we are discussing the efficient outcomes under US and EU corporate laws, the underlying issue is one of immense importance: today there is no consensus on what efficient corporate law is. The claim is not that the EU company law stakeholder-orientation,[101] based on the consideration of non-utilitarian values, is by itself more efficient than the US company law shareholder-orientation,[102] but rather that the latter seems not to provide for the most efficient solutions in modern economic framework. In these following subchapters, to make sure we eliminate the 'home' bias as much as possible, we used US as well as EU literature on the topic of corporate laws in the two jurisdictions.

The issues with shareholder value maximization dogma are numerous and they are theoretical as well as practical. If the claims of the legal origins theory were true, the US corporate laws should prove to be the most efficient; it should respond quickly to changes in the markets and the new developments should readily follow from common law case law and not from positive legislation. According to the developments following the financial crises, none of it proved to be true.[103] Even valuating the shareholder value maximization out of the context of the crises, it does not seem to readily fit in today's economic environment as the most efficient guiding corporate policy principle. Originating in US case law at the beginning of the twentieth century[104], the laissez-faire conception of the market found its way into corporate governance[105] and got its ultimate expression in the principle shareholder primacy, which has prospered in the US corporate law policy almost unquestioned ever since. The fact that free market is a creation of law and not of nature has been overlooked at that time,[106] and further reasoning as to why the shareholders are the only residual claimants also readily looked over the fact that for more than a century, in the US the corporations were accepted as institutions with public obligations created to serve the public interest in exchange for receiving the special benefits of incorporation.[107] As the idea that corporations were a 'natural' mode of business organization came to being in 1889, the notion of corporation being a creation of the state fell into oblivion.[108] Since then, the utilitarian view prevails in the US corporate policy without strong theoretical underpinnings and despite real-life market events that point to its inefficiency.[109]

As one of the most common justifications for the shareholder primacy in corporate law serves the argument that the shareholders are the owners of the corporation since they contribute the capital. While it is true that limited liability opens a window for opportunistic behaviour against 'financiers', in the current environment the 'ownership' of the company changes so often that the shareholders cannot remain the main protected target of corporate laws. While the shareholder supremacy might have been seen as the easiest and the most rational solution to be found through the rules of corporate law in the twentieth century, now modern shareholders in companies change by the minute in liquid and dispersed US markets[110] and this diminishes the inherent benefits of this theory as a simple coherent framework for addressing a variety of policy areas in line with the general trend of neo-liberalism. While shareholder primacy works rather well in the factual framework of the UK interested active institutional shareholders[111] as another example of a common law country, it does not seem to readily fit the US reality. For shareholder primacy to serve the long term interests of companies as well as the interests of other stakeholders, shareholders should act like owners and cooperate in company's life and participate in its decision-making as an interested party. The US reality of the twenty-first century is that most investors are short-term and passive and that the average holding period of stocks by institutions has fallen below one year.[112] This hardly allows the benefits of the shareholder primacy to manifest and brings about the issues related to short-termism and consequential global financial and economic crisis.[113]

For example, the underlying claim of the shareholder primacy that since there is a vast amount of public and private information available to millions of investors through the stock market, the share price correctly reflects the long-term prospects of the company[114] felt short. Orienting the operation of the company towards share price as the best measure of company value is not the optimal corporate governance solution. The share price proved to correlate only weakly with company performance; it is actually highly correlated with the general movement of the stock market which reflects the mass psychology of investors and not the actual value of the company.[115] Moreover, this price does not reflect many societal and environmental costs,[116] which may at the end also be paid by the shareholders in their other societal roles. The gatekeepers that have a role of conveying the information of true value to the market on the value of the company[117] and whose role is indispensable for the functioning of the shareholder value orientation failed; not only that they have conflicting interests in the companies they monitor, they were also impaired by the modern US corporate governance policy, which does not acknowledge their limited capacity to monitor the company as independent directors and demands from them supernatural qualities.[118]

The short-term orientation of different stakeholders became self-reinforcing in the 'nurturing' environment of shareholder primacy. It was caused by shortening of time horizons through the interaction between shareholders and managers and further amplified by the actions of gatekeepers in mediating those relationships.[119] Short-termism represents preference of stakeholders for strategies that add less value and earlier pay-off relative to long-term strategies with more value but later pay-off.[120] In corporate governance, short-termism proved to be the disease of management: to 'serve' the shareholders (and due to the perverse incentives created by the shareholder primacy product of 'incentive-based compensation'), they were oriented to stock prices and inflated current earnings at the expense of the company's long-term interest and/or its intrinsic value[121] and prone to moral hazard of pursuing investments with faster pay-off due to insufficient long-term incentives[122] and sufficient short-term encouragements in the form of shares, options and other kind of profit-related remuneration schemes.[123] Stock-options help managers to internalize the short-term focus of shareholders and quarterly earnings statements by managers help shareholders to focus on short-term targets.[124] Self-reinforcing circle is therefore concluded and the US did not enact legislation to remedy it, although the problem became obvious as early as in the year 2000; France on the other hand reacted with providing incentives for shareholders in the form of receiving double voting rights after holding their shares in excess of two years,[125] contrary to what the legal origins theory predicted.

The solution to the problems created by the shareholder primacy could be taking into account the fact that besides shareholders, other stakeholders also provide essential specialized inputs into public companies; inputs that are essential to the success of the company.[126] The reduction of 'agency costs' under shareholder primacy between managers and the shareholders[127] brought about additional agency costs, that could be minimized through a newly developed stakeholder approach to corporate law. Although the US academics see such an approach as an invasion in the free market, the reality still is that the corporate law is the result of political agreement and that the change of its orientation is highly political and less economic and legal.[128]

The residual nature of the claim of shareholders in current highly liquid and dispersed global ownership markets seems to matter less than the workers'. The workers actually seem to have the highest explicit and implicit claims towards their company and theoretically and factually seem to be better placed as risk-averse stakeholders to take decisions that will maximize long-run profits of the company than the shareholders currently are.[129] In this context of efficiency as a fundamental assumption of US corporate law doctrine (making decisions based on maximizing utilitarian value, measured by willingness to pay),[130] not including concerns for non-utilitarian values actually means losing efficiency in the long term. By the shareholder primacy evolving to the point where the company's obligation to obey the law is subservient to the obligations to make money,[131] the shareholders are suffering long-term harm due to the adverse reputational effects and the loss in the firm's market value,[132] the creditors are directly affected by the illegal behaviour of the company since they can be deprived of their payment,[133] and all stakeholders in general (including the shareholders) bear the cost of illegality in other roles they play in the society, depending on the violation of law in question, thus externalizing the cost of the company's illegal behaviour. This scenario seems hardly to be efficient.

Furthermore, this US laissez-faire approach has brought about so-called 'jurisdictional competition', where Delaware came out as a winner. Even though this state has a population of one third of a per cent of the US, it is the state of incorporation of over 50 per cent of US public companies and 60 per cent of the Fortune 500.[134] The fact is that this was not a competition for an efficient shareholder-oriented governance framework but rather a competition among states for a legal regime that benefits managers to the expense of the shareholders.[135] This perverse produce of the shareholder value orientation gives Delaware the ability to define the rules of corporate governance, according to the so-called 'internal affairs doctrine', even when the corporation is only incorporated under its law, which is democratically illegitimate and economically inefficient.[136] If a company is doing business for instance exclusively in New York and has no real ties with Delaware, how can Delaware effectively regulate the matters of such company? How can its corporate law solutions fit the legal and economic realities of such company? And last but not least, how can Delaware observe and regulate the behaviour of such company which has no real ties with its place of incorporation? Under current legal corporate frame in the US, the managers are the absolute winners and the uninformed and mislead shareholders turn to their 'exit' right sooner than before.

Despite all of these well-documented and empirically proven issues with the shareholder primacy, the US stands firm in its use, contrary to the predictions of the legal origins theory. The reactions of the US corporate law frame to such pitfalls in the environment offered by current legal rules are nearly non-existent and reactionary at its best, while it is the Continental Europe in the frame of EU that is acknowledging the insufficiency of the shareholder value frame and that is developing new solutions for the modern corporate demands. As progressive corporate law developments are crucial for the efficiency of corporate law frame,[137] the EU law seems to take the more efficient road of developing new corporate law paradigms and switching from 'old Continental European stakeholder approach' towards US shareholder value maximization and now to the so-called 'sustainable company', which is essentially a renewed EU stakeholder orientation.[138] No such sustainability goals seem to be present in the US corporate doctrine. Under the so-called stakeholder theory, the company is seen as a social organization, dependent upon the contributions of different groups to the production of goods and services,[139] and is as such foreign to the US corporate law policy. Although at a certain point the EU corporate policy followed more shareholder oriented corporate policy, the reason behind this was not the supremacy of the US corporate law policy but rather the political inability of the EU as a supranational organization to set more than minimum standards in this field.[140] But by the year 2006 the implementation of shareholder value maxim has reached the limits of political space within the EU[141] and the debate on corporate governance shifted towards determining the institutional conditions for companies to promote long-term profitability and employment prospects; defining mechanisms for preventing mismanagement and guaranteeing transparency and accountability with regard to investments and their returns.[142] Before the recent financial and economic crisis, the EU saw the potential danger in the shareholder orientation, while the US was only working on finding the factual and theoretical support for an obviously malfunctioning corporate law policy. The so-called 'triple crisis' (financial crisis, climate change and social inequality) that can be currently observed in the society has been largely caused by this shareholder value maximization policy: companies are responsible for a great portion of the increasing pollution and subsequent global warming, and at the same time carry the role of determining the labour income, the policies on the debt and dividend levels. With these decisions they influence the shape and stability of corporate sectors and their general ability to invest in research and development projects which shape the future innovations.[143] Especially in the US, the corporations enjoy all the benefits of limited liability and they purportedly serve maximally to the interests of shareholders, while at the same time they bear little or none of the responsibility for their influence outside the corporate sphere or for any negative externalities they cause with such orientation. The awareness of this imbalance seems to be higher in the EU than the US, hence the progressive role that the legal origins theory reserved for the US as the common law country in the field of corporate law policy actually belongs to the EU.

The new EU approach of the so-called 'sustainable company' has been also called the new stakeholder approach and it is building on new corporate policy paradigm that seems to be more in line with modern markets. Sustainable goals and stakeholder value are crucial to this approach; it envisages a set of sustainability goals being determined at the level of corporate law and a detailed strategy to achieve them; it also envisages involvement of stakeholders in companies' decision-making and verifiable reporting system on financial and non-financial performance[144] as well as tying a portion of executive remuneration to sustainability goals and lost but not least, with the underlying policy it tries to achieve that long-term responsible investors would form the ownership base of the company.[145] Understanding at the EU level of the need for binding legislation in this field is the progressive development in comparison with the US; even though sustainability is in the enlightened self-interest of companies, it is impossible under the shareholder value maxim, since it will be punished by the market instead of praised by it.[146] Creating an enabling frame for sustainable solutions in corporate functioning is essential; a clear statement is needed in company law that company is a social entity obliged to pay attention to the interest of and increase the welfare of a broad range of stakeholder groups as well as a legislative mandate on companies to extend their reporting beyond financial matters.[147]

All in all, it is the shareholder value maxim as followed in the US that caused the financial crises, in particular to its inherent failures and weaknesses in corporate governance arrangements.[148] The recent financial crisis has been directly triggered by the failure of the US investment bank Lehmann Brothers and was rooted in the spread of the shareholder value maxim and the rise of unregulated high-risk financial investors and products.[149] There is a widespread consensus that the rise of directors' remuneration contributed greatly to the extent of the crisis and yet again it was not the US, bearing the largest increase in this kind of remuneration that legislated in this field to prevent similar events, but rather Germany,[150] a child of the civil law legal family. In the light of the presented facts, the US corporate law policy is not deemed the most efficient neither under the legal origins theory neither under alternative theories explaining the differences between jurisdictions and their corporate laws. The US seems to be the one stubbornly holding on to a paradigm that is theoretically unsustainable and clearly factually flawed.

Insider trading in the US as compared to the EU

In order to form a full circle with our topical debate, a specific institute of the narrower field of corporate law will serve us as the ultimate cherry-picked issue to be contrasted against the findings of the legal origins theory. Although technically insider trading is an issue belonging to the sphere of capital market law, it corresponds perfectly to the scope of the research done by the legal origins scholars as it touches upon the actions of public limited liability companies only. For the developments in the field of insider trading law to readily follow the findings of the legal origins theory in the US–EU comparison, the EU should lag behind the US and should accordingly enact less efficient legal frame than the US. But as we will demonstrate, even in this highly topical field the reality does not seem to readily follow what the legal origins scholars would expect.

Insider trading is in layperson's terms nothing else than the illegal use of undisclosed material information for profit, seen as harmful due its inherent unfairness towards other investors without access to the same information as the 'insider' of the company.[151] Although there are some fierce academic debates present, especially in the US, as to whether insider trading should be legally regulated at all,[152] the fact remains that all the major common and civil law jurisdictions prohibit insider trading as harmful for the market, but their legal approach to the question differs significantly. Before we take under scrutiny the historical developments in the field and the current issues, it is interesting to note that the law and economics approach actually opposes regulation in the field of insider trading on the basis of its economic efficiency.[153] According to this view, insider trading has a stabilizing effect on the market[154] and stringent regulation of this phenomenon would therefore be inefficient. The claim is that insider trading is less costly than traditional disclosure.[155] It is interesting to note that these law and economics claims suffer from the same disease as the legal origins theory: the 'efficiency' is not defined;[156] the claims are insufficiently grounded in empirical evidence[157] and the existing empirical literature on insider trading has been suffering from American bias.[158] Indeed, as soon as the empirical research has been carried out on the basis of comparative data, its findings showed that more stringent insider trading laws are generally associated with more dispersed equity ownership, greater stock price accuracy and greater stock market liquidity.[159] The law and economics approach was therefore mistaken; regulation in this field is indeed wished for. This claim can be further supported by the finding that in the wake of the recent economic and financial crisis, increased enforcement of insider trading violations around the world was noticed, serving as a sign of a shared perception by market regulators of diverse jurisdictions that there is a need to restore market confidence.[160] Empirical research further showed that enforcement of insider trading regulations leads to a decrease in the cost of capital, which in turn leads to economic growth therefore strengthening the insider trading legislation promotes economic growth.[161] Rules on insider trading are proven to adding value to our capital markets.

While the US was the pioneer in creating and enforcing the legal rules on illegal insider trading,[162] the EU seems to have been more successful in creating a consistent, transparent and certain legal frame for its treatment in today's modern information society. Under the US law no statute codifies the insider trading prohibition; the principal actors in this field are the SEC and the federal courts.[163] Even though in 1942 SEC enactment of Rule 10b-5 under Exchange Act section 10(b) did not explicitly address insider trading but merely contained broad and general anti-fraud provision, the Commission used this rule in 1960s to prosecute insider trading on impersonal markets in an administrative procedure.[164] It introduced the concept of 'disclose or abstain' based on the principle of equal access to information, according to which trading on the basis of material, non-public information was fraudulent under Rule 10b-5,[165] which was upheld soon after by the Second Circuit in *S.E.C. v. Texas Gulf Sulphur.*[166] The 'equal access to information' basis was soon abandoned in the fear of a broad approach resulting in unfair results that might hinder the development of active markets[167] and in 1970 the *Chiarella* case[168] brought about the narrowing pre-condition for the existence of illegal insider trading: the existence of a fiduciary duty owed by the insider to the investors with which he traded.[169] This was the critical move that overly complicated insider trading in the US; it hindered enforcement actions and later led to the enactment of additional regulations to cover conducts conflicting with the rationale of prohibiting insider trading[170] as the SEC sought to minimize restrictive Supreme Court Law.[171] Such are SEC rule 14e-3 under section 14(e) of the Williams Act (in the sphere of tender offers prohibiting insider of the bidder and target to tip confidential information on a tender offer) which is applicable independently from any violation of fiduciary duties[172] or the Commission rule 10b5-2 clarifying which relationships might be considered to determine if the fiduciary misappropriated the information belonging to the source (the so-called 'misappropriation theory')[173] or in the field of computer science the SEC *Dorozhko* decision[174] that found fraudulent access to inside information enough for illegal insider trading.[175] In the same spirit, Regulation FD was adopted by the SEC with the aim of terminating the practice by companies of selectively disclosing material non-public information to market professionals and favoured shareholders.[176]

The court-added condition of the existence of fiduciary duty is not the only condition complicating the application of insider trading rules. For illegal insider trading to exist in the US, the information in question needs to be material, which means that it 'must be substantially likely to be important to the reasonable investor in making an investment decision' or 'substantially likely, in the eyes of the reasonable investor, to significantly alter the total mix of information available in the market'.[177] The terms 'reasonable investor' and substantially likely' are typically common-law vague and in clear need of interpretation by the US courts, which further complicates the equation. It is also not clear what kind of state of mind is required from the defendant; it is more than negligence but less than intent.[178] The SEC tried to mitigate the situation by determining that an awareness standard is envisaged here under which insiders are liable if they are aware that their conduct would be important in investors' decision to trade, and that they are relying on non-public, material information.[179] And last but not least, it under the US jurisprudence, it was also unclear whether mere possession of inside information suffices for the finding of illegal insider trading or is its use needed. While the Second Circuit in 1993 adopted the 'possession theory',[180] inconsistent with the awareness standard of section 10(b), SEC tried to partially resolve the situation in 2000 with the adoption of Rule 10b5-1, under which a person is liable when trades while 'aware' of inside information and installed in the US legal order the presumption that someone who trades in possession of inside information has in fact used the information.[181]

Besides this overly complex development of a legal rule that was in first place not meant for covering the issue of illegal insider trading, there was as early as in 1934 provision explicitly addressing insider trading: section 16(b) of the Exchange Act.[182] This section is also not free from ambiguity. It mandates disgorgement of all profits made buying and selling, or selling and buying, equity securities for insiders on the basis of inside information within a six-month period,[183] but it says nothing on the computation of profits and in practice brought about punitive damages in excess of actual damages contrary to Section 28(a) of the Exchange Act.[184] All in all, this overly-complex legal frame on illegal insider trading coupled with the absence of an EU-style general duty to disclose material, non-public information diminishes the value of otherwise efficient and aggressive enforcement of rules on insider trading.[185] Academics are often reiterating the fact that the 'parity-of-information' theory, which forms the foundation against insider trading in the EU and has been originally adopted also in the US in 1960, should be brought back also in the US.[186] Here the common law system regulation by itself seems to be the cause of such fragmented and contradictory system in which the plaintiff must generally be able to establish the existence of fiduciary duty and the fact that it has been breached,[187] creating cost-ineffectiveness.[188] This heavy burden of proof is diminishing the value of otherwise strong and efficient private enforcement mechanisms in the US and it is an issue that seems to be lingering on the Congress agenda for a while now.[189] The substance of insider trading law in the EU seems to produce a more coherent set of rules and when coupled with the fact that for example there is no staggering difference in the level of public and private enforcement of insider trading violations between the EU and the US (when accounted for the dimensions of the different national markets),[190] the winner in terms of efficiency seems not to be the US but rather the continental-style EU.

Even though in the EU insider trading has been regulated much more recently than in the US[191] due to its structure of corporate ownership which did not entail as much insider trading abuse,[192] and despite some claims that it merely copied the already developed US system, the EU seems to have produced a more simple, elegant and effective regulation[193] that substantially differs from the current US insider trading legal framework.

The EU insider trading law simply provides that anyone who obtains inside information due to his professional activity or by virtue of a criminal activity, should abstain from dealing in securities to which the information relates using inside information, from disclosing inside information to third parties unless the disclosure is made in the normal course of employment, profession or duties and from recommending or inducing other persons, on the basis of inside information, to trade.[194] In the EU, the crucial concern behind the regulation of insider trading is market egalitarianism.[195] The default rule in EU is that inside information should be promptly disclosed to the market, but it comes with exceptions.[196] Notice the way legal clarity and certainty stems from the EU legal framework despite the fact that the EU does not have a federal, but supra-national power over its Member States. This points to the fact that all EU Member States agree on the necessity of a clear and precise insider trading legal framework and that they do not see the US legal framework as suitable for dealing with the issue.[197]

By taking a closer look at the substance of this Market Abuse Regulation, we notice that contrary to the US legislation on the issue, this EU instrument entails definition of inside information,[198] persons subject to the prohibition of insider trading,[199] extension of the prohibition to third persons as well as specific exemptions[200] that allow trading in possession of inside information when appropriate. The efficiency of such approach when compared to the US legal regulation of insider trading is clear. Even the ambiguity on the 'possession or use' condition did not last long; most EU national legislatures and regulators agreed that insider trading demands trade using and not merely possessing the inside information[201] and the Court of Justice of European Union introduced a rebuttable presumption of use on the basis of mere possession of inside information in the case when the insider deals in securities.[202] Since here only use that conflicts with the purposes of the Market Abuse Regulation of equal access to information is prohibited, this represents more clear and efficient approach.[203] What is more, even though the legal origins theory argued that the civil law legal family law-making is more prone to be influenced by interest groups and therefore inefficient rules are enacted, this proved to be true in the case of insider trading for the US law-making. While the US has used eighty years to develop overly-complex and inefficient framework for illegal insider trading, the EU managed to progress from its minimum standards setting in Directive 89/592[204] through more defined intermediary form of Market Abuse Directive[205] to arrive to the final product of Market Abuse Regulation, accompanied by the Directive on criminal sanctions for market abuse[206] and encompassing also multilateral and organized trading facilities to keep pace with market developments and avoid regulatory arbitrage among trading venues.[207] Such developments at least at first glance seem to be less influenced by interest groups than the overly complicated US legal framework changes. These developments are contrary to the findings of legal origins theory on the US being the more efficient legal system, especially when we add to the equation the fact that the EU's role in enacting regulations in the environment predominated by twenty-eight different nations and accompanying twenty-four different languages is difficult to say the least. But it somehow still managed to produce a clear, unambiguous legal framework on insider trading for all of its Member States.

All in all, even when taken a closer look at the specific institute of insider trading that is important in ensuring investors trust in today's capital markets, the US seems not to thrive. This final thought or reasoning on a specific cherry-picked institute serves as our last tiny contribution to the arguments on the un-persuasiveness of the arguments of the legal origins theory. When seen in the light of the insider trading legal framework, its conclusions are inherently and unambiguously flawed.

Notes

1   In their research from the year 1996 until 2000 they have been studying the impact of legal origins on the rules in the corporate sphere and tried to connect these rules to the economic growth of a specific country belonging to either the civil law family or common law family.

2   Rafael La Porta, Florencio Lopez-de-Sillanes and Andrei Shleifer. 'The Economic Consequences of Legal Origins' (2008) 46 *Journal of Economic Literature.*

3   As we will show later in this chapter, besides other criticisms of the legal origins theory, the criticism about the taxonomy of jurisdictions as belonging to one or another jurisdiction has been also heavily criticized and disputed. See more in Kenneth V. Dam, 'Legal Institutions, Legal Origins, and Governance' (2006) University of Chicago Law and Economics, Olin Working Paper 3, 18; Mathias M. Siems, 'Legal Origins: Reconciling Law and Finance and Comparative Law' (2007) 52(1) *McGill Law Journal* 57, 62; Ralf Michaels, 'Comparative Law by Numbers? Legal Origins Thesis, *Doing Business* Reports and the Silence of Traditional Comparative Law' (2009) 57 *American Journal of Comparative Law* 780; Sean Cooney, Peter G. Gahan and Richard Mitchell, 'Legal Origins, Labour Law and the Regulation of Employment Relations' (2009) 12 SSRN Electronic Journal; Poonam Puri, 'Legal Origins, Investor Protection, and Canada' (2010) CLPE Research Paper No. 03/2010; Mariana Pargendler, 'Politics in the Origins: The Making of Corporate Law in Nineteenth-Century Brazil' (2012) 60(3) *American Journal of Comparative Law* 805, 812; David Cabrelli and Mathias M. Siems, 'Convergence, Legal Origins, and Transplants in Comparative Corporate Law: A Case-Based and Quantitative Analysis' (2015) 63 *American Journal of Comparative Law* 109, 152.

4   La Porta et al. (n2) 41.

5   For example, in their research on corporate ownership from the year 1998 on the basis of data on ownership of large corporations in twenty-seven wealthy economies they already take into account that their results might not be the consequence of the legal origins and subsequent legal rules in a specific economy, but rather due to the more general structure of financial systems or some other specific aspects of the corporate governance system. See more in Rafael La Porta, Florencio Lopez-de-Silanes and Andrei Shleifer, 'Corporate Ownership Around the World' (1999) 54(2) *Journal of Finance* 471.

6   The claim that the legal families shape the legal rules which in turn influence financial markets and that the common law family seems to produce better results still stays in their later research; even though they consider other factors they do not perceive them

as relevant. See more in Rafael La Porta et al., 'Investor Protection and Corporate Governance' (2000) 58(1–2) *Journal of Financial Economics* 3.

7 As previously discussed, many comparative corporate lawyers do not perceive the dichotomy between the civil and common law legal family as existent today; rather, they speak of the fact that all legal systems are to a certain point mixed jurisdictions and that the dichotomy today lies in the US–EU legal systems. See more in Sofie Cools, 'The Real Difference in Corporate Law Between the United States and Continental Europe: Distribution of Powers' (2005) 30 *Delaware Journal of Corporate Law* 697.

8 Mathias M. Siems, 'Shareholder Protection Around the World ("Leximetric II")' (2008) 33 *Delaware Journal of Corporate Law* 111.

9 Ibid. 69.

10 Ibid. 62.

11 Mark West, 'Legal Determinants of World Cup Success' Discussion Paper No. 009, University of Michigan John M. Olin Center for Law and Economics, 2002, online: University of Michigan Law School <www.law.umich.edu/CENTERSANDPRO GRAMS/OLIN/abstracts/discussionpapers/ 2002/west02-009.pdf>.

12 Siems (n8) 65.

13 Simeon Djankov, Caralee McLiesh and Andrei Shleifer, 'Private Credit in 129 Countries' (2007) 12(2) *Journal of Financial Economics* 77.

14 Pargendler (n3) 810.

15 Ibid. 812.

16 Ibid. 813.

17 Ibid. 849.

18 Puri (n3) 1671.

19 Ibid. 1672.

20 Ibid. 1673.

21 Ibid. 1682.

22 Siems (n8) 66.

23 Ibid.

24 Cally Jordan, 'Cadbury Twenty Years On' (2012) Faculty Papers and Publications Paper 4, 16, online http://scholarship.law.georgetown.edu/ctls_papers/4 (access date).

25 Ibid. 18.

26 Dam (n3) 14.

27 Ibid.

28 Siems (n8) 123; John Armour, Simon Deakin, Prabirjit Sarkar and Ajit Singh, 'Shareholder Protection and Stock Market Development: An Empirical Test of the Legal Origins Hypothesis'. *Journal of Empirical Legal Studies*, vol. 6, 2009, 362.

29 Seeing that France is according to legal origins theory in the same group of with Angola and Egypt and that their scores simply add up under this theory and are then compared to common law legal family is already questionable on its own. See more in Dam (n3) 18.

30 Katharina Pistor et al., 'Innovation in Corporate Law' (2003) 31 *Journal of Comparative Economics* 676, 676.

31 Ibid. 679.

32 Ibid.

33 And subsequently the role of judiciary is virtually the same in the civil and common law legal family; another major flaw of the legal origins theory in the field of corporate law is neglecting this fact. *See more in* Pistor et al. (n30) 680: "…[s]ince the early nineteenth century … given the importance of statutory corporate law in all jurisdictions, the simple distinction between case law and statutory law is unlikely to capture major differences across legal families…"; see also Armour et al. (n28) 347, Cooney et al. (n3) 10.

34 Dam (n3) 12; it has also been argued that the common law judges have limited room for manoeuvre in interpreting statutes while judges in civil law legal family have inherent

powers to develop the law using 'general clauses' such as good faith, through which they ameliorate the rigidity of the codes in corporate law. *See more in* Armour et al. (n28) 348.

35 Pistor et al. (n30) 678.
36 Ibid. 688; although pre-emptive rights have not been included in the 1996 'Law and Finance' paper, they have been included into the subsequent research made by legal origins scholars.
37 Joseph McCahery and Luc Renneboog, 'Introduction: Recent Developments in Corporate Governance' in Joseph McCahery et al., *Corporate Governance Regimes. Convergence and Diversity* (Oxford: Oxford University Press 2002) 6.
38 Pistor et al. (n30).
39 Cooney et al. (n3) 10.
40 Tom Kirchmaier, Geoffrey Owen and Jeremy Grant, 'Corporate Governance in the US and Europe: Where Are We Now?' (2005), available online http://ssrn.com/abstract=708461 7–8 (access date).
41 Ibid. 8; the author names as examples the ability of the shareholders to call an extraordinary general shareholders' meeting with 10 per cent of the share capital and the fact that the shareholders can remove the board with a plurality of the votes.
42 Ibid. 13.
43 Ibid.
44 Jordan (n24) 8.
45 H. Patrick Glenn, *Legal Traditions of the World: Sustainable Diversity in Law* 4th ed. (Oxford: Oxford University Press 2010) 248, 251.
46 Index developed in La Porta et al. (n2).
47 Armour et al. (n28) 350.
48 Cools (n7) 701; Armour et al. (n28) 350; John Ohnesorge, 'Legal Origins and the Tasks of Corporate Law in Economic Development: A Preliminary Exploration' (2009) 2009(6) *Brigham Young University Review* 1619, 1628; Siems (n8) 68.
49 Armour et al. (n28) 352.
50 Ibid. 351; Siems (n8) 67; Michaels (n3) 777; Christopher A. Whytock, 'Legal Origins, Functionalism, and the Future of Comparative Law' (2009) 2009(6) *Brigham Young University Law Review* 1879, 1880; see also a study on that matter in David E. Andersson et al., 'Corporate Governance Structures, Legal Origin and Firm Performance' (2010) Ratio Working Paper No. 246.
51 Armour et al. (n28) 343, 350–352; Siems (n8) 111; Michaels (n3) 783.
52 Cools (n7) analysing the legal origins theory through functionalist approach by taking into account actual legal frame of Belgium, France and the US and shows that by doing so the comparative advantage of common law legal family disappears; Armour et al. (n28) on the basis of new data on shareholder protection investigate the legal origins hypothesis and disprove the findings of the legal origins scholars; Siems (n8) does similar with taking into account longitudinal data on shareholder protection across jurisdictions; Cabrelli and Siems (n3) show that due to more concentrated ownership structures the civil law countries of Continental Europe actually provide stronger protection for minority shareholders against the majority than the US or the UK.
53 Cools (n7) 701; Ohnesorge (n48) talking about blending of scholarship with political preference; Siems (n8) 69; Armour et al. (n28) 350.
54 Markus Berndt, *Global Differences in Corporate Governance Systems: Theory and Implications for Reforms* (Wiesbaden: Deutscher Universitäts-Verlag 2002) 18.
55 Cools (n7) 734.
56 Ibid. 704.
57 Whyttock (n50) 1887.
58 The First and Second World War made the difference between the ownership of listed companies in the UK and Germany; before the First World War the ownership of listed

companies was similar in both countries. See more in Kirchmaier, Owen and Grant (n40).

59 In the case of a developing country, on which the legal origins theory had its most prominent impact through World Bank Reports, see Simon Deakin et al., 'An End to Consensus? The Selective Impact of Corporate Law Reform on Financial Development' (2011) ECGI – Law Working Paper 182/2011.

60 Ibid. 8.

61 Ibid. 9, 10 and 21.

62 Whytock (n50) 1892.

63 Deakin et al. (n59) 20.

64 Armour et al. (n28) 366.

65 Ibid. 368.

66 As an example, the financial accounting frauds in the US have been mentioned by the author; see more in Pistor et al. (n30) 680.

67 Ibid. 693.

68 Sonja Fagernäs, Prabirjit Sarkar and Ajit Singh, 'Legal Origin, Shareholder Protection and the Stock Market: New Challenges from Time Series Analysis' (2007) Centre for Business Research, University of Cambridge Working Paper 3, 20.

69 Armour et al. (n28) 369.

70 Dam (n3) 14.

71 Siems (n8) 111.

72 Ibid. 123.

73 Ibid. 125.

74 Ibid. 138.

75 Kirchmaier, Owen and Grant (n40) 13.

76 Ibid. 14.

77 Cools (n7) 700.

78 Ibid.

79 Ohnesorge (n48) 1620.

80 Ibid. 1621.

81 Ibid. 1624.

82 Michaels (n3) 771.

83 Ibid. 783; Deakin et al. (n59) 2.

84 Ibid.

85 Ibid. 784.

86 For example, the OECD launched a review of its 2004 Principles of Corporate Governance to consider 'recent developments in the corporate sector and capital markets'; see more in Siems (n8) 112–113, Jordan (n24) 24.

87 McCahery et al. (n37) 6.

88 John C. Coffee Jr., *Convergence and its Critics: What are the Preconditions to the Separation of Ownership and Control?* In McCahery et al. (n37) 85.

89 Detailed debate on this issue surpasses the scope of our debate; it suffices to say that since the exact substance of EU company law is determined also by the national legal texts that transposed the directives in national legal systems of EU Member States, and that in four out of twenty-eight EU Member States derive their law from common law legal family (Cyprus, Malta, Ireland and the UK), in the spirit of path dependency such transposition followed the civil law family approach in vast majority of the Member States; see generally Mads Tønnesson Andenæs and Frank Wooldridge, *European Comparative Company Law* (Cambridge University Press 2012).

90 Sigurd Vitols and Norbert Kluge eds, *The Sustainable Company: A New Approach to Corporate Governance*. Brussels: ETUI aisbl 2011; William W. Bratton and Joseph A. McCahery, 'Comparative Corporate Governance and Barriers to Global Cross Reference' in McCahery et al. (n37) 23.

91 Common law systems have also been striving to achieve 'fairness' next to efficiency, first and foremost through the institute of fiduciary duties; see more in Christopher Shun, *An Empirical Investigation of the Role of the Legal Origin on the Performance of Property Stocks Within the Context of a Tactical Asset Allocation Strategy* (Universal-Publishers 2006), 28–31.

92 Kent Greenfield, *The Failure of Corporate Law: Fundamental Flaws and Progressive Possibilities* (Chigaco: University of Chicago Press 2006), 1–28.

93 Ibid. 59.

94 Ibid. 43.

95 Hayden M. Grant and Matthew T. Bodie, 'The Uncorporation and the Unraveling of "Nexus of Contracts" Theory' (2011) 109(6) *Michigan Law Review* 1127.

96 Greenfield (n92) 46.

97 See more in ibid. 66.

98 Even before the crisis, academics have been warning about the deficiency of the dogma on shareholder primacy. See more in C. K. Prahalad, 'Corporate Governance or Corporate Value Added? Rethinking the Primacy of Shareholder Value' (1994) 6(4) *Journal of Applied Corporate Finance* 40.

99 Greenfield (n92) 1–28.

100 Ibid.

101 As discussed earlier, the EU corporate law reflects more the corporate laws of civil law family than the common law family; therefore it is contrasted for the purpose of this chapter as a whole against the US corporate law as deriving its solutions from the common law family.

102 Greenfield (n92) 36.

103 Can M. Alpaslan, Sandy E. Green and Ian I. Mitroff, 'Corporate Governance in the Context of Crises: Towards a Stakeholder Theory of Crisis Management' (2009) 17(1) *Journal of Contingencies and Crisis Management* 38.

104 *Lochner v. New York* 198 US 45 (1905), where the labour contract was deemed as a product of private negotiations between the employer and the employee; no state interference was allowed and a free market has been relied upon. This decision spurred the so-called 'Lochner era' with less and less state interference being allowed in the creation and functioning of companies, resulting in the 'laissez-faire' approach also in corporate law. See more in Greenfield (n92) 33–35.

105 Ibid. 34.

106 Ibid.

107 Ibid. 35, 36.

108 Ibid.

109 Ibid. 38.

110 Sigurt Vitols, 'What is the Sustainable Company?' Vitols and Kluge eds (n90) 15,17.

111 Research has shown that British institutional investors promote research and development, engage in monitoring or improve the market value of companies with good future prospects but low current profitability and hence and shying away from short-termism; see more in Gregory Jackson and Anastasia Petraki, 'How Does Corporate Governance Lead to Short-Termism?' in Vitols and Kluge eds (n90) 206.

112 Vitols and Kluge eds (n90) 19.

113 Sigurd Vitols and Norbert Kluge, 'Introduction' in Vitols and Kluge eds (n90) 7.

114 Vitols and Kluge eds (n90) 16.

115 Ibid. 18.

116 Ibid.

117 Ibid. 19.

118 Jackson and Petraki (n111) 209.

119 Ibid. 199.

120 Ibid. 200.

121 Ibid. 204.

122 Ibid. 205.
123 Ibid. These share-based incentives at the same time created massive incentives for fraud; see more in Vitols and Kluge eds (n90) 18.
124 Jackson and Petraki (n111) 217.
125 Ibid. 218.
126 Greenfield (n92) 46.
127 Ibid. 48.
128 Laura Horn, *How Did We End Up Here? The Risse of Shareholder Value in EU Corporate Governance Regulation* in Vitols and Kluge eds (n90) 39.
129 Ibid. 55–59.
130 Ibid. 66.
131 Ibid. 74.
132 Ibid. 84.
133 Ibid. 90.
134 Ibid. 107.
135 Ibid.
136 Ibid.
137 Pistor et al. (n30).
138 Traditional stakeholder orientation coupled with the issue of sustainability that requires a much higher level of transparency; see more in Vitols and Kluge eds (n90).
139 Ibid. 15.
140 Demands of liberalized capital markets have also helped with this minimum standards settings; see more in Horn (n128) 39.
141 Ibid. 49.
142 Ibid. 50.
143 Vitols and Kluge eds (n90) 23.
144 Directive 2014/95/EU of the European Parliament and of the Council of 22 October 2014 amending Directive 2013/34/EU as regards disclosure of non-financial and diversity information by certain large undertakings and groups [2014] OJ L 330.
145 Vitols and Kluge eds (n90) 24.
146 As Greenfield (n92) reiterated throughout his work, being 'sustainable' in the current corporate law environment in the US is punished at the stock markets as the investors perceive this orientation as 'losing assets' by not enlarging the profits for the benefit of the shareholders but rather using it for other goals; it diminishes the wish for the companies themselves to be proactive and it disables them from being the reforming force behind the renewed corporate law policy agenda. This serves also as a practical argument against the findings of the legal origins theory: progressive possibilities are needed in this field but the lock-in effect disables the reactions and demands of market participants and thus progressive developments that would long-term also be more economically efficient.
147 Vitols and Kluge eds (n90) 31.
148 OECD (2009) 'The Corporate Governance Lessons from the Financial Crisis' *Financial Market Trends* 01/2009.
149 Vitols and Kluge eds (n90) 19.
150 Chapter 7.
151 The legal definition of insider trading differs from jurisdiction to jurisdiction, but the rationale behind the illegality of the act is extremely similar across jurisdictions, as well as the specific act itself.
152 It is argued that the insider trading's efficiency effects are larger than its harmful effects, therefore it should not be legally regulated at all; this argument has been brought about in the US but one must understand that the US does not know the obligation of full disclosure similar to the one inherent in the EU law on insider trading; see more in Richard A. Booth, 'Insider Trading: There Oughta Be a Law – or Not' (2015), available online http://object.cato.org/sites/cato.org/files/serials/files/

regulation/2015/9/regulation-v38n3-2.pdf (access date); Stephen M. Bainbridge, *An Overview of Insider Trading Law and Policy* (Cheltenham: Edward Elgar 2013); Kimberly D. Krawiec, 'Fairness, Efficiency, and Insider Trading: Deconstructing the Coin of the Realm on the Information Age' (2001) 95(2) *Northwestern University Law Review* 443.

153 Henry Manne, *Insider Trading and the Stock Market* (New York: The Free Press 1996).

154 Ibid. 77–91; this happens as changes in the price of a share of stock at the market will occur more rapidly when insider trading is prohibited than when it is permitted. An item of inside information has value, and the change in the stable price of a share of stock due to disclosure of the information may be computed by dividing the dollar value of the information by the number of shares of stock outstanding; disclosure of the information will ultimately result in a shift-in the market price of the stock from the price reflecting its value without the information to the price which reflects its value in light of the information; if absolutely no trading in the market is permitted until the information is completely public and completely understood, the price rise (or fall) will occur in literally no time once trading is resumed; if insiders alone must suspend trading until disclosure is complete or until the price change is complete, those outsiders who have the capability of quickly gathering, evaluating, and acting upon valuable information will enter the market and cause a rapid (though not immediate) price change; but if insiders are free to exploit on the market or otherwise the information they have, the price change will occur more slowly, since an initially small but increasing number of people wil receive the information and begin acting upon it over a longer period of time. Note though that there is no (full) disclosure present in the US market, neither is the author talking about the true value of stock at any point of this reasoning.

155 Laura Nyantung Berry, 'Insider Trading Laws and Stock Markets Around the World: An Empirical Contribution to the Theoretical Law and Economics Debate' (2007) 32(2) *Journal of Corporate Law* 237, 247.

156 Whether we are discussing efficiency of insider trading at the firm level or its effects on stock market; see more in ibid. 239.

157 Ibid. 240.

158 Ibid.

159 Ibid. 279; it is interesting to note that the author carried out this empirical research also on the basis of the findings of the legal origins theory and came to these results opposing the findings of the law and economics approach in the field of insider trading.

160 Christopher P. Montagano, 'The Global Crackdown on Insider Trading: A Silver Lining to the "Great Recession"' (2012) 19(2) *Indiana Journal of Global Legal Studies* 575.

161 Ibid. 597.

162 Marco Ventoruzzo, 'Comparing Insider Trading in the United States and in the European Union: History and Recent Developments' (2014) ECGI Law Working Paper No.257/2014, 5; Montagano (n160) 586.

163 Marc I. Steinberg, 'Insider Trading – A Comparative Perspective' (2002) available online https://www.imf.org/external/np/leg/sem/2002/cdmfl/eng/steinb.pdf> (access date).

164 Ventoruzzo (n162) 7.

165 The so-called 'parity of information theory'; Steinberg (n163) 5; Ventoruzzo (n162) 7.

166 401 F. 2nd 833 (2nd Cir. 1968)

167 Ventoruzzo (n162) 8; Steinberg (n163) 6.

168 *Chiarella v. US* 445 US 222 (1980)

169 Ventoruzzo (n162) 9.

170 Ibid. 5.

171 Steinberg (n163) 10.
172 Only applicable to the tender offer setting and leaving out mergers, which is problematic from the point of view of the similarity of the two situations; see more in Steinberg (n163) 9.
173 Ventoruzzo (n162) 10–12.
174 *SEC v. Dorozhko*, 574 F.3d 42 (2009).
175 Since there has not been any specific violation of fiduciary duty, absent such decision no illegal insider trading could be found; see more in Ventoruzzo (n162) 15.
176 Steinberg (n163) 11.
177 Ventoruzzo (n162) 15.
178 Ibid. 16.
179 Ibid.
180 *United States v. Teicher* (1993) 987 F.2d 112, 120 (2nd Circ. 1993)
181 Ventoruzzo (n162) 17.
182 Ibid. 21.
183 Ibid. 22.
184 Ibid.
185 Ibid. 5.
186 Ibid.
187 Ibid. 37; Steinberg (n163) 21.
188 Steinberg (n163) 21.
189 Booth (n152).
190 Ventoruzzo (n162) 39.
191 Ibid. 1.
192 Montagano (n160) 588.
193 Ventoruzzo (n162) 5.
194 Regulation (EU) No 596/2014 of the European Parliament and of the Council of 16 April 2014 on market abuse (market abuse regulation) and repealing Directive 2003/6/EC of the European Parliament and of the Council and Commission Directives 2003/124/EC, 2003/125/EC and 2004/72/EC [2014] OJ L 173, 1-61, Art. 14 in connection with Arts 7 and 8.
195 Ventoruzzo (n162) 23.
196 Ibid. 30.
197 Survey of the securities laws of developed markets on insider trading regulation revealed that these countries have rejected the US approach and they adhere to an insider trading prescription premised on participant equal access to inside information such as in EU; see more in Steinberg (n163).
198 Article 7 Market Abuse Regulation.
199 Article 3 Market Abuse Regulation.
200 Articles 5 and 6 Market Abuse Regulation.
201 For example, in UK Section 118(2) of the Financial Services and Markets Act as well as in Germany Article 14(1) of the Wertpapierhandelsgesetz; see more in Ventoruzzo (n162) 27.
202 Case C-45/08 *Spector Photo Group NV* [2009] I-12073
203 Ventoruzzo (n162) 28.
204 Council Directive 89/592/EEC of 13 November 1989 coordinating regulations on insider dealing [1989] OJ L 334.
205 Directive 2003/6/EC of the European Parliament and of the Council of 28 January 2003 on insider dealing and market manipulation (market abuse) [2003] OJ L 96.
206 Directive 2014/57/EU of the European Parliament and of the Council of 16 April 2014 on criminal sanctions for market abuse (market abuse directive) [2014] OJ L 173.
207 With the same aim and in the same spirit, definition of market manipulation has been extended to include transactions in related spot markets and attempts at market manipulation have been prohibited; see more in Ventoruzzo (n162) 31.

Bibliography

Abraham, Kenneth S. *The Forms and Functions of Tort Law* 3rd ed. New York: Foundation Press, 2007 (*Concepts and Insights* series).

Acemoglu, Daron, Cantoni, Davide, Johnson, Simon and Robinson, James A. 'The Consequences of Radical Reform: The French Revolution'. National Bureau of Economic Research Working Paper 14831, 2009.

Acemoglu, Daron and Johnson, Simon. 'Unbundling Institutions'. *Journal of Political Economy*, vol. 113, 2005, p. 949.

Acemoglu, Daron and Johnson, Simon. 'Disease and Development: The Effect of Life Expectancy on Economic Growth'. *Journal of Political Economy*, vol. 115, 2007, p. 925.

Acemoglu, Daron, Johnson, Simon and Robinson, James A. 'Colonial Origins of Comparative Development: An Empirical Investigation'. *American Economic Review*, vol. 91, 2001, p. 1369.

Aguilera, Ruth V. and Williams, Cynthia A. '"Law and Finance": Inaccurate, Incomplete, and Important'. *Brigham Young University Law Review*, vol. 2009, 2009, no. 6, p. 1413.

Ahlering, Beth and Deakin Simon. 'Labor Regulation, Corporate Governance and Legal Origin: A Case of Institutional Complementarity?' *Law and Society Review*, vol. 41, 2007, p. 865.

Aldashev, Gani. 'Legal Institutions, Political Economy, and Development'. *Oxford Review of Economic Policy*, vol. 25, 2009, p. 257.

Allan, James. 'You Don't Always Get What You Pay For: No Bill of Rights for Australia'. *New Zealand Universities Law Review*, vol. 24, 2010, p. 179.

Allison, J. W. F. *A Continental Distinction in the Common Law: A Historical and Comparative Perspective on English Public Law* rev. ed. Oxford and New York: Oxford University Press, 2000.

Allmendinger, Christoph. 'Company Law in the European Union and the United States: A Comparative Analysis of the Impact of the EU Freedoms of Establishment and Capital and the U.S. Interstate Commerce Clause'. *William & Mary Business Law Review*, vol. 4, 2013, no. 1, pp. 67–109.

Alpa, Guido and Zeno-Zencovich, Vincenzo. *Italian Private Law*. London and New York: Routledge-Cavendish, 2007 (*University of Texas at Austin Studies in Foreign and Transnational Law* series).

Andenæs, Mads Tønnesson and Wooldridge, Frank. *European Comparative Company Law*. Cambridge: Cambridge University Press, 2012.

Anderlini, Luca, Felli, Leonard and Riboni Alessandro. 'Why State Decisis?' CEPR Discussion Paper, 2011.

Andersson, David E., Andersson, Martin, Bjuggren, Per-Olo and Högberg, Andreas. 'Corporate Governance Structures, Legal Origin and Firm Performance'. Ration Working Paper No. 246, 2010.

Armour, John, Deakin, Simon, Lele, Priya and Siems, Mathias (2009) 'How Do Legal Rules Evolve? Evidence from Cross-Country Comparison of Shareholder, Creditor and Worker Protection'. *American Journal of Comparative Law*, vol. 57, 2009, p. 579.

Armour, John, Deakin, Simon, Mollica, Viviana and Siems, Mathias M. 'Law and Financial Development: What We are Learning from Time-Series Evidence'. *Brigham Young University Law Review*, 2009, no. 1435.

Armour, John, Deakin, Simon, Sarkar, Prabirjit and Singh, Ajit. 'Shareholder Protection and Stock Market Development: An Empirical Test of the Legal Origins Hypothesis'. *Journal of Empirical Legal Studies*, vol. 6, 2009, p. 343.

Arruñada, Benito. 'Property Enforcement as Organized Consent'. *Journal of Law, Economics and Organisation*, vol. 19, 2003, p. 401.

Arruñada, Benito. 'Pitfalls to Avoid When Measuring the Institutional Environment: Is *Doing Business* Damaging Business?' *Journal of Comparative Economics*, vol. 35, 2007, p. 729.

Arruñada, Benito. 'Property Titling and Conveyancing'. In *Research Handbook on the Economics of Property Law*, Harry Smith and Ken Ayotte eds. Cheltenham: Edward Elgar, 2010, pp. 237–256.

Arruñada, Benito and Andonova, Veneta. 'Common Law and Civil Law as Pro-Market Adaptations'. *Washington University Journal of Law and Policy*, vol. 26, 2008, p. 81.

Arruñada, Benito and Andonova, Veneta. 'Judges' Cognition and Market Order'. *Review of Law and Economics*, vol. 4, 2008, p. 665.

Arruñada, Benito and Garoupa, Nuno. 'The Choice of Titling System in Land'. *Journal of Law and Economics*, vol. 48, 2005, p. 709.

Atiyah, Peter S. *Essays on Contract*. Oxford: Oxford University Press, 1986.

Bainbridge, Stephen M. 'An Overview of Insider Trading Law and Policy'. In *Research Handbook on Insider Trading*, Stephen M. Bainbridge ed. Cheltenham: Edward Elgar, 2013, ch. 1.

Baker, J. H. 'The Law Merchant and the Common Law Before 1700'. *Cambridge Law Journal*, vol. 38, 1979, p. 295.

Bar-Gill, Oren and Hamdani, Assaf. 'Optimal Liability for Libel'. *B.E. Journal of Economic Analysis and Policy*, 2003, p. 1.

Barnet, Todd. 'The Uniform Registered State Land and Adverse Possession Reform Act, a Proposal for Reform of the United States Real Property Law'. *Buffalo Environmental Law Journal*, vol. 12, 2004, p. 1.

Barzel, Yoram. 'Dispute and its Resolution: Delineating the Economic Role of the Common Law'. *American Law and Economics Review*, vol. 2, 2000, p. 238.

Baum, Ido, Feess, Eberhard and Wohlschlegel, Ansgar. 'Reporter's Privilege and Incentives to Leak'. *Review of Law and Economics*, vol. 5, 2009, n701.

Beatson, Jack. 'Restitution and Contract: Non-Cumul?' *Theoretical Inquiries in Law*, vol. 1, 2002, p. 83.

Bebchuck, Lucian Arye. 'Litigation and Settlement Under Imperfect Information'. *RAND Journal of Economics*, vol. 15, 1984, p. 404.

Bebchuck, Lucian Arye and Chang, Howard F. 'An Analysis of Fee Shifting Based on the Margin of Victory: On Frivolous Suits, Meritorious Suits, and the Role of Rule'. *Journal of Legal Studies*, vol. 25, 1996, p. 371.

Beck, Thorsten, Demirguc-Kunt Asli and Levine, Ross. 'Law and Finance: Why Does Legal Origin Matter?' *Journal of Comparative Economics*, vol. 31, 2003, p. 653.

Bell, John. *Judiciaries Within Europe: A Comparative Review*. Cambridge: Cambridge University Press, 2006 (*Cambridge Studies in International and Comparative Law*).

Bell, John, Boyron, Sophie and Whittaker, Simon. *Principles of French Law* 2nd ed. Oxford and New York: Oxford University Press, 2008.

Bennett, Roger. *European Business*. London: M & E Pitman 1997.

Benson, Bruce L. 'The Spontaneous Evolution of Commercial Law'. *Southern Economic Journal*, vol. 55, 1989, p. 644.

Berkowitz, Daniel and Clay, Karen. 'American Civil Law Origins: Implications for State Constitutions'. *American Law and Economics Review*, vol. 62, 2005, p. 62.

Berkowitz, Daniel and Clay, Karen. 'The Effect of Judicial Independence on Courts: Evidence from the American States'. *Journal of Legal Studies*, vol. 35, 2006, p. 399.

Berkowitz, Daniel, Pistor, Katharina and Richard, Jean-François. 'Economic Development, Legality, and the Transplant Effect'. *European Economic Review*, vol. 47, 2003, p. 165.

Berman, Harold J. *Law and Revolution*. Cambridge, MA: Harvard University Press, 1983.

Berman, Harold J. *Law and Revolution II: The Impact of the Protestant Reformations on the Western Legal Tradition*. Cambridge, MA and London. Belknap, 2003.

Bermann, George A. and Picard, Etienne. *Introduction to French Law*. Alphen aan den Rijn and Frederick, MD: Kluwer Law International (*Introduction to International Law* series).

Berndt, Markus. *Global Differences in Corporate Governance Systems: Theory and Implications for Reforms*. Wiesbaden: Deutscher Universitäts-Verlag, 2002.

Bernstein, Lisa. 'Merchant Law in a Merchant Court: Rethinking the Code's Search for Immanent Business Norms'. *University of Pennsylvania Law Review*, vol. 144, 1996, p. 1765.

Biddinger, Brian P. 'Limiting the Business Method Patent: A Comparison and Proposed Alignment of European, Japanese and United States Patent Law'. *Fordham Law Review* 2523, vol. 69, 2001, n6.

Bilder, Mary Sarah. *The Transatlantic Constitution* Cambridge, MA: Harvard University Press, 2009.

Blackstone, William. *The Commentaries on the Laws and Constitution of England*. 1796.

Blanchet, Didier. 'Analyses Exploratoires des Indices Proposés par les Rapports *Doing Business* 2005 et 2006 de la Banque Mondiale'. In Programme de Recherches Attractivité Economique du Droit, Working Paper No. AED-2006-03, 2006.

Bocken, Hubert and de Bondt, Walter. *Introduction to Belgian Law*. Bruxelles, The Hague and London: Bruylant; Kluwer Law International 2001.

Bogart, Dan and Richardson, Gary. 'Making Property Productive: Reorganizing Rights to Real and Equitable Estates in Britain, 1660–1830'. *European Review of Economic History*, vol. 13, 2009, p. 3.

Bogart, W. A. '"Guardian of Civil Rights ... Medieval Relic": The Civil Jury in Canada'. *Law and Contemporary Problems*, vol. 62, 1999, p. 305.

Bogusz, Barbara. 'Bringing Land Registration into the Twenty-First Century: The Land Registration Act 2002'. *Modern Law Review*, vol. 65, 2002, p. 556.

Booth, Richard A. 'Insider Trading: There Oughta Be a Law – Or Not'. *Regulation*, Fall 2015. Online: http://object.cato.org/sites/cato.org/files/serials/files/regulation/2015/9/regulation-v38n3-2.pdf (accessed 1 September 2016).

Bostock, Sally-Lloyd and Thomas, Cheryl. 'Decline of the "Little Parliament": Juries and Jury Reform in England and Wales'. *Law and Contemporary Problems*, vol. 62, 1999, p. 7.

Braeutigam, Ronald, Owen, Bruce and Panzar, John. 'An Economic Analysis of Alternative Fee Shifting Systems'. *Law and Contemporary Problems*, vol. 47, 1984, p. 173.

Brenncke, Martin. 'Is "Fair Use"' an Option for UK Legislation?' *Virtschaftsrecht*, Heft 71, November 2007.

Brister, Scott. 'The Decline in Jury Trials: What Would Wal-Mart Do?' *Texas Law Review*, vol. 47, 2005, p. 191.

Buckley, Melody. *Civil Procedure and Practice: An Introduction.* Dublin: Thomson Round Hall, 2004 (*Essential Law Texts*).

Burns, Kylie. 'The Role of the Judiciary: Passive or Active?' *Legaldate*, vol. 18, 2006, no. 2, p. 4.

Cabrelli, David and Siems, Mathias M. 'Convergence, Legal Origins, and Transplants in Comparative Corporate Law: A Case-Based and Quantitative Analysis'. *American Journal of Comparative Law*, vol. 63, 2015, p. 109.

Caenegem, R. C. van. *Judges, Legislators, and Professors: Chapters in European Legal History.* Cambridge and New York: Cambridge University Press 1987 (Goodhart Lectures, 1984–1985).

Calavita, Kitty *Invitations to Law and Society: An Introduction to the Study of Real Law.* Chicago: University of Chicago Press 2010.

Cameron, Neil, Potter, Susan and Young, Warren. 'The New Zealand Jury'. *Law and Contemporary Problems*, vol. 62, 1999, p. 103.

Caramani, Daniele. *Comparative Politics* 2nd ed. Oxford and New York: Oxford University Press 2011.

Carbonara, Emanuela and Parisi, Francesco. 'The Paradox of Legal Harmonization'. *Public Choice*, vol. 132, 2007, p. 367.

Carbonara, Emanuela and Parisi, Francesco. 'Choice of Law and Legal Evolution: Rethinking the Market for Legal Rules'. *Public Choice*, vol. 139, 2009, p. 461.

Carbonnier, Jean. *Droit civil* 1re éd. Paris: Quadrige/Presses universitaires de France 2000.

Cardozo, Benjamin N. *The Nature of the Judicial Process.* New York: Feather Trail Press 2009.

Carothers, Thomas. *Promoting the Rule of Law Abroad: In Search of Knowledge.* Washington: Carnegie Endowment for International Peace 2006.

Cerioni, Luca. *EU Corporate Law and EU Company Tax Law.* Cheltenham: Edward Elgar 2007 (*Corporations, Globalisation and the Law* series).

Chase, Oscar G. 'American "Exceptionalism" and Comparative Procedure'. *American Journal of Comparative Law*, vol. 50, 2002, p. 227.

Chesterman, Michael. 'Criminal Trial Juries in Australia: From Penal Colonies to a Federal Democracy'. *Law and Contemporary Problems*, vol. 62, 1999, p. 69.

Chirico, Filomena and Larouche, Pierre. *Economic Analysis of the DCFR: The Work of the Economic Impact Group within the CoPECL.* Munich: Sellier European Law 2010.

Clark, Bryan. *Scottish Legal System* 2nd ed. Dundee: Dundee University Press 2009 (*Law Essentials*).

Clark, Elias, Lusky, Louis, Murphy, Arthur W., Ascher, Mark L. and McCouch, Grayson M. P. *Gratuitous Transfers: Wills, Intestate Succession, Trusts, Gifts, Future Interests, and Estate and Gift Taxation. Cases and Materials.* St Paul, MN: Thomson West 1999.

Clark, Stuart S. 'Thinking Locally, Suing Globally: The International Frontiers of Mass Tort Litigation in Australia'. *Defense Counsel Journal*, vol. 74, 2007, p. 139.

Clermont, Kevin M. and Eisenberg, Theodore. 'Trial by Jury or Judge: Transcending Empiricism'. *Cornell Law Review*, vol. 77, 1992, p. 1124.

Coleman Folkard, Henry and Starkie, Thomas. *The Law of Slander and Libel* 7th ed. London: Butterworth 1908.

Colombatto, Enrico. *The Elgar Companion to the Economics of Property Rights*. Cheltenham: Edward Elgar 2004.

Congleton, Roger D. and Swedenborg, Birgitta. *Democratic Constitutional Design and Public Policy. Analysis and Evidence*. Cambridge, MA: MIT Press 2006.

Cools, Sofie. 'The Real Difference in Corporate Law Between the United States and Continental Europe: Distribution of Powers'. *Delaware Journal of Corporate Law*, vol. 30, 2005, p. 697.

Cooney, Sean, Gahan, Peter G. and Mitchell, Richard. 'Legal Origins, Labour Law and the Regulation of Employment Relations'. *SSRN Electronic Journal*, vol. 12, 2009.

Cooter, Robert D. 'Structural Adjudication and the New Law Merchant: A Model of Decentralized Law'. *International Review of Law and Economics*, vol. 14, 1994, p. 215.

Cooter, Robert D. 'Decentralized Law for a Complex Economy: The Structural Approach to Adjudicating The New Law Merchant'. *University of Pennsylvania Law Review*, vol. 144, 1996, p. 1643.

Cooter, Robert and Kornhauser, Lewis. 'Can Litigation Improve the Law Without the Help of Judges?' *Journal of Legal Studies*, vol. 9, 1980, p. 139.

Cooter, Robert and Ulen, Thomas. *Law and Economics* 6th ed. New York: Pearson Addison Wesley 2011.

Cotter, Thomas F. 'Fair Use and Copyright Overenforcement'. *Iowa Law Review*, vol. 93, 2008, pp. 1271–1320.

Craig, P. P. and Búrca, G. de. *EU Law: Text, Cases, and Materials* 5th ed. Oxford and New York: Oxford University Press 2011.

Crain, Mark W. and Tollison, Robert D. 'Constitutional Change in an Interest-Group Perspective'. *Journal of Legal Studies*, vol. 8, 1979, p. 165.

Crain, Mark W. and Tollison, Robert D. 'The Executive Branch in the Interest-Group Theory of Government'. *Journal of Legal Studies*, vol. 8, 1979, p. 555.

Cremers, Jan and Wolters, Elwin. *EU and National Company Law: Fixation on Attractiveness* electronic ed. Brussels: ETUI (Report – European Trade Union Institute) 2011.

Crew, Michael A. and Twight, Charlotte. 'On the Efficiency of Law: A Public Choice Perspective'. *Public Choice*, vol. 66, 1990, p. 15.

Crews, Kenneth D. 'The Law of Fair Use and the Illusion of Fair-Use Guidelines'. *Ohio State Law Journal*, vol. 62, 2001.

Cribbet, John E., Johnson, Corwin W., Findley, Roger W. and Smith, Ernest E. *Property Law: Cases and Materials* 8th ed. New York: Foundation Press 2002 (*University Casebook* series).

Cross, Frank B. 'Law and Economic Growth'. *Texas Law Review*, vol. 80, 2002, p.1737.

Cross, Frank B. 'Identifying the Virtues of the Common Law'. *Supreme Court Economic Review*, vol. 15, 2007, p. 21.

Cross, Frank B. 'Tort Law and the American Economy'. *Minnesota Law Review*, vol. 96, 2011, p. 28.

Cross, Frank B. and Donelson, Dain C. 'Creating Quality Courts'. *Journal of Empirical Legal Studies*, vol. 7, 2010, p. 490.

Dalvi, Manoj and Refalo F. James. 'An Economic Analysis of Libel Law'. *Eastern Economic Journal*, vol. 34, 2008, p. 74.

Dam, Kenneth V. 'Legal Institutions, Legal Origins, and Governance'. University of Chicago Law and Economics, Olin Working Paper No. 303, 2006.

Dam, Kenneth W. *The Law-Growth Nexus: The Rule of Law and Economic Development.* Washington: Brookings Institution Press 2006.

Dari-Mattiacci, Guiseppe, Deffains, Bruno and Lovat, Bruno. 'The Dynamics of the Legal System'. *Journal of Economic Behavior and Organization*, vol. 79, 2001, p. 95.

Davies, Martin. 'Time to Change the Federal Forum Nonconveniens Analysis'. *Tullane Law Review*, vol. 77, 2002, p. 209.

Davis, Kevin E. and Kruse, Michael B. 'Taking the Measure of Law: The Case of the *Doing Business* Project'. *Law and Social Inquiry*, vol. 32, 2007, p. 1095.

Dawson, John P. *Oracles of the Law*. Ann Arbor: University of Michigan 1968.

Deakin, S. F., Johnston, Angus Charles and Markesinis, Basil. *Markesinis and Deakin's Tort Law* 5th ed. Oxford and New York: Oxford University Press 2003.

Deakin, Simon, Sarkar, Prabirjit and Singh, Ajit. 'An End to Consensus? The Selective Impact of Corporate Law Reform on Financial Development in ECGI'. Law Working Paper, No.182/2011, 2011.

Descheemaeker, Eric. *The Division of Wrongs: A Historical Comparative Study*. Oxford and New York: Oxford University Press 2009.

Dessemontet, François and Ansay, Tuğrul. *Introduction to Swiss Law* 3rd ed. The Hague and Frederick, MD: Kluwer Law International 2004.

Dezalay, Yves and Garth, Bryant G. *Asian Legal Revivals: Lawyers in the Shadow of Empire*. Chicago: University of Chicago Press 2010 (*Chicago Series in Law and Society*).

Dimov, Daniel. 'Software Patent Law: EU, New Zealand, and the US Compared'. *Management, Compliance and Auditing* 2013. Online at http://resources.infosecinstitute. com/software-patent-law-eu-new-zealand-and-the-us-compared/ (access date).

Dine, Janet, Koutsias, Marios and Blecher, Michael. *Company Law in the New Europe: The EU Acquis, Comparative Methodology and Model Law*. Cheltenham and Northampton, MA: Edward Elgar 2007 (*Corporations, Globalisation, and the Law* series).

Dixit, Avinash. 'Two-Tier Market Institutions'. *Chicago Journal of International Law*, vol. 5, 2004, p. 139.

Djankov, Simeon, Glaeser, Edward, La Porta, Rafael, López-de-Silanes, Florencio and Shleifer, Andrei. 'The New Comparative Economics'. *Journal of Comparative Economics*, vol. 31, 2003, p. 595.

Djankov, Simeon, McLiesh, Caralee and Shleifer, Andrei. 'Private Credit in 129 Countries'. *Journal of Financial Economics*, vol. 12, 2007, no. 2, p. 77.

Dreyfuss, Rochelle C. 'The Federal Circuit: A Case Study in Specialized Courts'. *New York University Law Review*, vol. 64, 1989, p. 1.

Du Marais, Bertrand. 'Les Limites Méthodologiques des Rapports *Doing Business*'. Programme de Recherches Attractivité Economique du Droit, Working Paper No. AED-2006-01, 2006.

Du Marais, Bertrand, Khartchenko-Dorbec, Anna, Blanchet, Didier and Du Bois de Gaudusson, Jean. *Des indicateurs pour mesurer le droit?* Paris: la Documentation française 2006 (*Perspectives sur la justice* series).

Duff, Peter. 'The Scottish Criminal Jury: A Very Peculiar Institution'. *Law and Contemporary Problems*, vol. 62, 1999, p. 173.

Dutta, Manoranjan. *The United States of Europe: European Union and the Euro Revolution*. Bingley: Emerald Group (*Contributions to Economic Analysis* series vol. 292).

Edwards, Linda Holdeman. *Legal Writing and Analysis*. New York: Aspen 2003.

Edwards, Vanessa. *EC Company Law*. New York: Oxford University Press 1999.

Eisenberg, Theodore, Hannaford, Paula L., Heise, Michael, LaFountain, Neil and Ostrom, Brian. 'Juries, Judges, and Punitive Damages: Empirical Analyses Using the Civil Justice Survey of State Courts 1992, 1996, and 2001 Data'. *Journal of Empirical Legal Studies*, vol. 3, 2006, p. 263.

Engelbrekt Bakardijeva, Antonina. 'Toward an Institutional Approach to Comparative Economic Law?' In *New Directions In Comparative Law*, Antonina Engelbrekt Bakardijeva andt Joakim Nergelius eds. Cheltenham: Edward Elgar 2010.

Engert, Andreas and Smith, Gordon D. 'Unpacking Adaptability'. *Brigham Young University Law Review*, vol. 2009, 2009, p. 1533.

Engle, Eric Allen. 'When is Fair Use Fair? A Comparison of E.U. and U.S. Intellectual Property Law'. *The Transnational Lawyer*, vol. 15, 2002.

Enriques, Luca. 'EC Company Law Directives and Regulations: How Trivial Are They?' *University of Pennsylvania Journal of International Economic Law*, vol. 27, 2006, no. 1.

Epstein, Richard A. 'A Theory of Strict Liability'. *Journal of Legal Studies*, vol. 2, 1973, p. 151.

Epstein, Richard A. 'Reflections on the Historical Origins and Economic Structure of the Law Merchant'. *Chicago Journal of International Law*, vol. 5, 2004, p. 1.

Erdos, David 'Aversive Constitutionalism in the Westminster World: The Genesis of the New Zealand Bill of Rights Act'. *International Journal of Constitutional Law*, 2007, no. 5, p. 343.

Erdos, David 'Ideology, Power Orientation and Policy Drag: Explaining the Elite Politics of Britain's Bill of Rights Debate'. *Government and Opposition*, vol. 44, 2009, p. 20.

Erdos, David 'Judicial Culture and the Politicolegal Opportunity Structure: Explaining Bill of Rights Legal Impact in New Zealand'. *Law and Social Inquiry*, 2009, no. 34, p. 95.

Erstling, Jay A., Salmela Amy M. and Woo Justin N. 'Usefulness Varies by Country: The Utility Requirement of Patent Law in the United States, Europe and Canada'. *Cybaris, an Intellectual Property Law Review*, vol. 3, 2012, no. 1.

European Parliament. Overcoming Transatlantic Differences on Intellectual Property. IPR and the TTIP negotiations. Online: www.europarl.europa.eu/RegData/bibliotheque/briefing/2014/140760/LDM_BRI(2014)140760_REV1_EN.pdf, (accessed 27 July 2015).

Ewing, Jack. 'When Taste is a Trade Issue'. *New York Times*, 24 June 2015. Online: http://nyti.ms/1SJoo3q (accessed 11.August 2015).

Fagernäs, Sonja. 'Labour Law, Judicial Efficiency and Informal Employment in India'. ESRC Centre for Business Research, Working Papers 353, 2007.

Fagernäs, Sonja, Sarkar, Prabirjit and Singh, Ajit. 'Legal Origin, Shareholder Protection and the Stock Market: New Challenges from Time Series Analysis'. Centre for Business Research University of Cambridge, Working Paper 343, 2007.

Farber, Daniel A. and Sherry, Suzanna. *Judgment Calls: Principles and Politics in Constitutional Law*. Oxford: Oxford University Press 2009.

Farley, Christine Haight. 'The Protection of Geographical Indications in the Inter-American Convention'. *WIPO Journal*, vol. 6, 2014, p. 68.

Farley, Christine Haight. 'The Protection of Geographical Indications in the Inter-American Convention'. *SSRN Electronic Journal*. DOI: 10.2139/ssrn.2542289.

Faure, Michael and Stephen, Fran. *Essays in the Law and Economics of Regulation in Honour of Anthony Ogus*. Antwerp: Intersentia 2008.

Fauvarque-Cosson, Bénédicte and Kerhuel, Anne-Julie. 'Is Law an Economic Contest? French Reactions to the *Doing Business* World Bank Reports and Economic Analysis of Law'. *American Journal of Comparative Law*, vol. 57, 2009, p. 811.

Federation of European Publishers. FEP Position Paper on a Transposition of Fair Use at EU Level, 2011. Online at: www.djei.ie/en/Consultations/Consultations-files/ Publishing-Ireland-FEP-Paper-on-Fair-Use.pdf (access date).

Feldbrugge, F. J. M. 'Good and Bad Samaritans: A Comparative Survey of Criminal Law Provisions Concerning Failure to Rescue'. *American Journal of Comparative Law*, vol. 14, 1966, p. 630.

Ferrarini, Guido. *Reforming Company and Takeover Law in Europe.* Oxford and New York: Oxford University Press.

Fleming, John G. *The Law of Torts* 8th ed. Sydney: LBC Information Services 1998.

Fon, Vincy and Parisi, Francesco. 'Litigation and the Evolution of Legal Remedies: A Dynamic Model'. *Public Choice*, vol. 116, 2003, p. 419.

Fon, Vincy and Parisi, Francesco. 'Judicial Precedents in Civil Law Systems: A Dynamic Analysis'. *International Review of Law and Economics*, vol. 26, 2006, p. 519.

Fon, Vincy, Parisi, Francesco and Depoorter, Ben. 'Litigation, Judicial Path-Dependence, and Legal Change'. *European Journal of Law and Economics*, vol. 20, 2005, p. 43.

Foote, Daniel H. *Law in Japan: A Turning Point.* Seattle: University of Washington Press 2007 (*Asian Law* series vol. 19).

Forell, Caroline 'Statutes and Torts: Comparing the United States to Australia, Canada, and England'. *Williamette Law Review*, vol. 36, 2000, p. 865.

Foster, Nigel G. and Sule, Satish. *German Legal System and Laws* 3rd ed. Oxford and New York: Oxford University Press 2002.

Frankum, Milner et al. 'United Kingdom' in Andrew B. Ulmer ed. *Media, Advertising and Entertainment Law* 2 vols (London: Multilaw 2010) ch. 36.

Freckelton, Ian. 'Judicial Attitudes Toward Scientific Evidence: The Antipodean Experience'. *University of California Law Review*, vol. 30, 1997.

Friedman, Barry. 'The Politics of Judicial Review'. *Texas Law Review*, vol. 84, 2005, p. 257.

Friedman, David D. *Law's Order: What Economics Has To Do With Law and Why It Matters.* Princeton, NJ: Princeton University Press 2000.

Friedman, Lawrence M. *A History of American Law*. New York: Simon & Schuster 2005.

Froeb, Luke M. and Kobayashi, Bruce H. 'Naive, Biased, Yet Bayesian: Can Juries Interpret Selectively Produced Evidence?' *Journal of Law, Economics and Organization*, vol. 12, 1996, p. 257.

Galanter, Marc. 'The Civil Jury as Regulator of the Litigation Process'. University of Chicago Legal Forum, vol. 1990, 1990, p. 201.

Garner, Bryan A. ed. *Black's Law Dictionary* 10th ed. Eagan, MN: Thomson Reuters 2014.

Garoupa, Nuno. 'Dishonesty and Libel Law: The Economics of the "Chilling" Effect'. *Journal of Institutional and Theoretical Economics*, vol. 155, 1999, p. 284.

Garoupa, Nuno 'The Economics of Political Dishonesty and Defamation'. *International Review of Law and Economics*, vol. 19, 1999, p. 167.

Garoupa, Nuno and Carlos Gómez Ligüerre. 'The Syndrome of the Efficiency of the Common Law'. *Boston University International Law Journal*, vol. 29, 2010, pp. 287–335.

Garoupa, Nuno and Ginsburg, Tom. 'Building Reputation in Constitutional Courts: Party and Judicial Politics'. *Arizona Journal of International and Comparative Law*, vol. 28, 2012, p. 539.

Garoupa, Nuno, Jorgensen, Natalia and Vasquez, Pablo. 'Assessing the Argument for Specialized Courts: Evidence from Family Courts in Spain'. *International Journal of Law, Policy and the Family*, vol. 24, 2010, p. 54.

Garoupa, Nuno and Morriss, Andrew P. 'The Fable of the Codes: The Efficiency of the Common Law, Legal Origins and Codification Movements'. *University of Illinois Law Review*, vol. 2012, 2012, p. 1443.

Garoupa, Nuno and Ogus, Anthony. 'A Strategic Interpretation of Legal Transplants'. *Journal of Legal Studies*, vol. 35, 2006, p. 339.

Garoupa, Nuno, Ogus, Anthony and Sanders, Andrew. 'The Investigation and Prosecution of Regulatory Offences: Is There an Economic Case for Integration?' *Cambridge Law Journal*, vol. 70, 2011, p. 229.

Garoupa, Nuno and Pargendler, Mariana. 'Law and Economics of Legal Families'. *European Journal of Legal Studies*, vol. 7, 2014, pp.33.

Geest, Gerrit de. *Contract Law and Economics* 2nd ed. Cheltenham and Northampton, MA: Edward Elgar 2011 (*Encyclopedia of Law and Economics* vol. 6).

Gennaioli, Nicola and Shleifer, Andrei. 'Overruling and the Instability of Law'. *Journal of Comparative Economics*, vol. 35, 2007, p. 309.

Gennaioli, Nicola and Shleifer, Andrei. 'The Evolution of Common Law'. *Journal of Political Economy*, vol. 115, 2007, p. 43.

Ghestin, Jacques, Huet, Jérôme and Piedelièvre, Stéphane. *Traité de droit civil* 2 éd. Paris: L.G.D.J. 1994.

Giancomo A. M. and Fernandez Patricio A. 'Case Law Versus Statute Law: An Evolutionary Comparison'. *Journal of Legal Studies*, vol. 37, 2008, p. 379.

Gilden, Andrew and Greene, Timothy. 'Fair Use for the Rich and Fabulous?' *The University of Chicago Law Review Dialogue*, vol. 80, 2013.

Gillette, Clayton P. 'The Law Merchant in the Modern Age: Institutional Design and International Usages under the CISG'. *Chicago Journal of International Law*, vol. 5, 2004, p. 157.

Ginsburg, Tom. *Judicial Review in New Democracies. Constitutional Courts in Asian Cases*. Cambridge and New York: Cambridge University Press 2003.

Ginsburg, Tom and Kagan, Robert A. *Institutions and Public Law: Comparative Approaches*. New York: Peter Lang (*Teaching Texts in Law and Politics* series vol. 40).

Glaeser, Edward L. and Shleifer, Andrei. 'Legal Origins'. *Quarterly Journal of Economics*, vol. 117, 2002, p. 1193.

Glaeser, Edward L. and Shleifer, Andrei. 'The Rise of the Regulatory State'. *Journal of Economic Literature*, vol. 41, 2003, p. 401.

Glendon, Mary Ann. *Rights Talk: The Impoverishment of Political Discourse*. New York: The Free Press 1991.

Glenn, Patrick H. *Legal Traditions of the World. Sustainable Diversity in Law* 4th ed. New York: Oxford University Press 2010.

Glenn, Patrick H. 'Are Legal Traditions Incommensurable?' *American Journal of Comparative Law*, vol. 49, 2001, p. 133.

Gold, Andrew S. and Miller, Paul B. *Philosophical Foundations of Fiduciary Law*. Oxford: Oxford University Press 2014 (*Philosophical Foundations of Law* series).

Gold, Michael, Nikolopoulos, Andreas and Kluge, Norbert. *The European Company Statute: A New Approach to Corporate Governance*. Oxford and New York: P. Lang 2009.

Goodman, Carl F. *The Rule of Law in Japan: A Comparative Analysis* 2nd rev. ed. Alphen aan den Rijn and Frederick, MD: Wolters Kluwer Law & Business 2008.

Goodman, John C. 'An Economic Theory of the Evolution of the Common Law'. *Journal of Legal Studies*, vol. 7, 1978, p. 393.

Gorla, Gino and Moccia, Luigi. 'A "Revisiting" of the Comparison between "Continental Law" and "English Law" (16th–19th Century)'. *Journal of Legal History*, vol. 2, 1981, p. 143.

Graham, Stuart J., Hall, Bronwyn, Harhoff, Dietmar and Mowery, David. 'Post-Issue Patent "Quality Control": A Comparative Study of US Patent Re-examinations and European Patent Oppositions'. Cambridge, MA: National Bureau of Economic Research 2002.

Grajzl, Peter and Dimitrova-Grajzl, Valentina. 'The Choice in the Lawmaking Process: Legal Transplants vs. Indigenous Law'. *Review of Law and Economics*, vol. 5, 2009, p. 615.

Grant, Hayden M. and Bodie, Matthew T. 'The Uncorporation and the Unraveling of "Nexus of Contracts" Theory'. *Michigan Law Review*, vol. 109, 2011, no. 6, pp. 1127–1144.

Gravelle, Hugh. 'The Efficiency Implications of Cost-Shifting Rules'. *International Review of Law and Economics*, vol. 13, p. 3.

Greenfield, Kent. *The Failure of Corporate Law: Fundamental Flaws and Progressive Possibilities*. Chicago: University of Chicago Press 2006.

Greif, Avner. 'Institutions and Impersonal Exchange: From Communal to Individual Responsibility'. *Journal of Institutional and Theoretical Economy*, vol. 158, 2002, 168.

Greif, Avner. 'Impersonal Exchange Without Impartial Law: The Community Responsibility System'. *Chicago Journal of International Law*, vol. 5, 2004, p. 109.

Greif, Avner. *Institutions and the Path to the Modern Economy: Lessons from the Medieval Trade*. Cambridge: Cambridge University Press, 2006.

Greif, Avner, Milgrom, Paul and Weingast, Barry R. 'Coordination, Commitment, and Enforcement: The Case of the Merchant Guild'. *Journal of Political Economy*, vol. 102, 1994, p. 745.

Grier, Robin M. 'Colonial Legacies and Economic Growth'. *Public Choice*, vol. 98, 1999, p. 317.

Grosswald Curran, Vivian. 'Symposium on Legal Origins Thesis: "[N]on scholae sed vitae discimus"'. *American Journal of Comparative Law*, vol. 57, 2009, p. 863.

Grundmann, Stefan. 'The Structure of European Company Law: From Crisis to Boom'. *European Business Organization Law Review*, vol. 5, 2004, pp. 601–633.

Grundmann, Stefan and Möslein, Florian. *European Company Law: Organization, Finance and Capital Markets*. Antwerp and Holmes Beach, FL: Intersentia 2007 (*Ius communitatis* series vol. 1).

Grundmann, Stefan and Schauer, Martin. *The Architecture of European Codes and Contract Law*. Alphen aan den Rijn: Kluwer Law International 2006 (*Private Law in European Context* series vol. 8).

Gubin, Rehana. 'Borrowing Privileges: How Does (or Should) Copyright Law define a Derivative Work? Patents, Innovation and Economic Performance'. OECD Conference Proceedings, *Harvard Journal of Law and Technology*, 2015, pp. 9–13.

Gudmestad, Terje. 'Patent Law of United States and the United Kingdom: A Comparison'. *Loyola of Los Angeles International and Comparative Law Review*, vol. 5, 1982.

Gummow, William. 'The Injunction in Aid of Legal Rights: An Australian Perspective'. *Law and Contemporary Problems*, vol. 56, 1993, p. 83.

Hadfield, Gillian K. 'Bias in the Evolution of Legal Rules'. *Georgetown Law Journal*, vol. 80, 1992, p. 583.

Hadfield, Gillian K. 'The Levers of Legal Design: Institutional Determinants of the Quality of Law'. *Journal of Comparative Economics*, vol. 36, 2008, p. 43.

Hadfield, Gillian K. 'The Strategy of Methodology: The Virtues of Being Reductionist for Comparative Law'. *University of Toronto Law Journal*, vol. 59, 2009, p. 223.

Hale, Matthew. *The History of the Common Law of England* 2nd ed. London 1716.

Hall, Browyn H., Thoma, Grid and Torrisi, Salvatore. 'The Market Value of Patents and R&D: Evidence from European Firms'. NBER Working Paper Series, vol. 13426, September 2007.

Haller, Axel. 'Financial Accounting Developments in the European Union: Past Events and Future Prospects'. *European Accounting Review*, vol. 11, 2002, no. 1, pp. 153–190.

Halperin, Jean-Louis. *The French Civil Code* 2nd ed. Avec la collaboration de Basil Markesinis and Jörg Fedtke eds. London: UCL Press 2006.

Hansmann, Henry and Mattei, Ugo. 'The Functions of Trust Law: A Comparative Legal and Economic Analysis'. *New York University Law Review*, vol. 73, 1998, p. 434.

Harding, Andrew. 'Global Doctrine and Local Knowledge: Law in South East Asia'. *International and Comparative Law Quarterly*, vol. 51, 2002, p. 35.

Harnay, Sophie and Marciano, Alain. 'Should I Help my Neighbor? Self-Interest, Altruism and Economic Analyses of Rescue Laws'. *European Journal of Law and Economics*, vol. 28, 2009, p. 103.

Harris, Donald, Campbell, David and Halson, Roger. *Remedies in Contract and Tort*. Cambridge: Cambridge University Press 2002.

Hathaway, Oona A. 'Path Dependence in the Law: The Course and Pattern of Legal Change in a Common Law System'. *Iowa Law Review*, vol. 86, 2001, p. 601.

Hause, John C. 'Indemnity, Settlement, and Litigation, or I'll Be Suing You'. *Journal of Legal Studies*, vol. 18, 1989, p. 157.

Heckman James J., Nelson, Robert L. and Cabatingan, Lee. *Global Perspectives on the Rule of Law*. Oxford: Routledge 2009.

Hersch, Joni and Viscusi, Kip. 'Punitive Damages: How Judges and Juries Perform'. *Journal of Legal Studies*, vol. 33, 2004, p. 1.

Hogue, Arthur R. *Origins of the Common Law*. Bloomington: Indiana University Press 1966.

Holmes, Oliver Wendell. *The Common Law* 1945ᵉ édition. Little, Brown & Co. 1881.

Holmes, Oliver Wendell. *The Common Law*, Introduction by Sheldon M. Novick (New York: Dover 1991).

Hopkins, Paul. *ADR Client Strategies in the UK*. Eagan, MN: Aspatore 2008.

Hopt, Klaus J. and Wymeersch, E. *European Company and Financial Law: Texts and Leading Cases* 4th ed. Oxford and New York: Oxford University Press 2007.

Horan, Jacqueline. 'Perceptions of the Civil Jury System'. *Monash University Law Review*, vol. 31, 2005, p. 120.

Hugenholtz, Bernt P. and Senftleben Martin R. F. 'Fair Use in Europe: In Search of Flexibilities', 14 November 2011. Online at http://ssrn.com/abstract=1959554 (access date).

Hylton, J. Gordon, Callies, David L., Mandelker, Daniel R. and Franzese, Paula A. *Property Law and the Public Interest: Cases and Materials* 3rd ed. Newark, NJ: LexisNexis Matthew Bender 2007.

Hylton, Keith N. 'An Asymmetric-Information Model of Litigation'. *International Review of Law and Economics*, vol. 22, 2002, p. 153.

Hyman, David A. 'Rescue Without Law: An Empirical Perspective on the Duty to Rescue'. *Texas Law Review*, vol. 84, 2006, p. 653.

Jackson, John D., Quinn, Katie and O'Malley, Tom. 'The Jury System in Contemporary Ireland: In the Shadow of a Troubled Past'. *Law and Contemporary Problems*, vol. 62, 1999, p. 203.

Jordan, Cally. 'Cadbury Twenty Years On'. *Faculty Papers & Publications*, 2012, no. 4. Online: http://scholarship.law.georgetown.edu/ctls_papers/4, (accessed 18 November 2015.

Josselin, Jean-Michel and Marciano, Alain. 'The Paradox of Leviathan: How to Develop and Contain the Future European State?' *European Journal of Law and Economics*, vol. 4, 1997, p. 5.

Kadens, Emily. 'Order Within Law, Variety Within Custom: The Character of the Medieval Merchant Law'. *Chicago Journal of International Law*, vol. 5, 2004, p. 39.

Kaplow, Louis. 'Shifting Plaintiffs' Fees Versus Increasing Damage Awards'. *RAND Journal of Economics*, vol. 24, 1993, p. 625.

Keeton, W. P. *Prosser and Keeton on the Law of Torts* 5th ed. St Paul, MN: West 1984 (*Hornbook* series).

Kelsen, Hans 'Judicial Review of Legislation: A Comparative Study of the Austrian and the American Constitution'. *Journal of Politics*, vol. 4, 1942, p. 183.

Kerhuel, Anne-Julie and Cosson-Fauvarque, Bénédicte. 'Is Law an Economic Contest? French Reactions to the *Doing Business* World Rank Reports and Economic Analysis of the Law'. *American Journal of Comparative Law*, vol. 57, 2009, p. 811.

Kessler, Amalia D. *A Revolution in Commerce: The Parisian Merchant Court and the Rise of Commercial Society in Eighteenth Century France.* New Haven, CT: Yale University Press 2007.

Khalil, Manal Z. 'The Applicability of the Fair Use Defense to Commercial Advertising: Eliminating Unfounded Limitations.' *Fordham Law Review*, vol. 61, 1992, no. 3.

Klar, Lewis N. 'The Impact of the U.S. Tort Law in Canada'. *Pepperdine Law Review*, vol. 38, 2011, p. 359.

Klerman, Daniel. 'Jurisdictional Competition and the Evolution of the Common Law'. *University of Chicago Law Review*, vol. 74, 2007, p. 1179.

Klerman, Daniel and Mahoney, Paul G. 'Legal Origin?' *Journal of Comparative Economics*, vol. 35, 2007, p. 278.

Klerman, Daniel, Mahoney, Paul G., Spamann, Holger and Weinstein, Mark. 'Legal Origin and Colonial History'. *Journal of Legal Analysis*, 2011, p. 379.

Koch, Bernard A. and Koziol Helmut. *Tort and Insurance Law Vol. 4: Compensation for Personal Injury in a Comparative Perspective*. Wien and New York: Springer 2003.

Kornhauser, Lewis. 'The Economic Analysis of Law' in *The Stanford Encyclopedia of Philosophy*. Online at http://plato.stanford.edu/archives/sum2015/entries/legal-econanalysis/ (accessed 28 September 2015).

Kötz, Hein. 'The Value of Mixed Legal Systems'. *Tulane Law Review*, vol. 78, 2003, p. 435.

Kraakman, Reinier H. *The Anatomy of Corporate Law: A Comparative and Functional Approach* 2nd ed. Oxford and New York: Oxford University Press 2009.

Krawiec, Kimberly D. 'Fairness, Efficiency, and Insider Trading: Deconstructing the Coin of the Realm on the Information Age'. *Northwestern University Law Review*, vol. 95, 2001, no. 2, p. 443.

Krishnamurthy, Shuba Haaldodderi. 'U.S. Patent Reform Act of 2011 ("America Invents Act"): The Transition from First-to-Invent to First-to-File Principle'. *JIPITEC – Journal of Intellectual Property, Information Technology and E-Commerce Law*, vol. 5, 2014.

Kritzer, Herbert M. 'Lawyer Fees and Lawyer Behavior in Litigation: What Does the Empirical Literature Really Say?' *Texas Law Review*, vol. 80, 2002, p. 1943.

Kublicki, Nicolas Marie. 'An Overview of the French Legal System From an American Perspective'. *Boston University International Law Journal*, vol. 12, 1994, p. 58.

Kur, Annette. 'The EU Trademark Reform Package: (Too) Bold a Step Ahead or Back to Status Quo?' *Marquette Intellectual Property Law Review*, vol. 19, 2015, no. 1, p. 14–38.

Kur, Annette and Dreier, Thomas. *European Intellectual Property Law: Text, Cases and Materials*. Cheltenham: Edward Elgar 2013.

La Porta, Rafael, Lopez-de-Silanes, Florencio, Shleifer, Andrei and Vishny, Robert W. 'Law and Finance'. *Journal of Political Economy*, vol. 46, 1998, no. 2, p. 1113.

La Porta, Rafael, Lopez-de-Silanes, Florencio and Shleifer, Andrei. 'Corporate Ownership Around the World'. *Journal of Finance*, vol. 54, 1999, no. 2.

La Porta, Rafael; Lopez-de-Silanes, Florencio; Shleifer, Andrei; Vishny, Robert. 'Investor Protection and Corporate Governance'. *Journal of Financial Economics*, vol. 58, 2000, nos 1–2, p. 3.

La Porta, Rafael, López-de-Silanes, Florencio, Eleches Pop, Cristian and Shleifer, Andrei. 'Judicial Checks and Balances'. *Journal of Political Economy*, vol. 112, 2004, p. 445.

La Porta, Rafael, Lopez-de-Sillanes, Florencio and Shleifer, Andrei. 'The Economic Consequences of Legal Origins'. *Journal of Economic Literature*, vol. 46, 2008, pp. 285–322.

Landes, William M. and Posner, Richard A. 'The Independent Judiciary in an Interest-Group Perspective'. *Journal of Law and Economics*, vol. 18, 1975, p. 875.

Landes, William M. and Posner, Richard A. 'Salvors, Finders, Good Samaritans, and Other Rescuers: An Economic Study of Law and Altruism'. *Journal of Legal Studies*, vol. 7, 1978, no. 1, p. 83.

Landes, William M. and Posner, Richard A. 'Adjudication as a Private Good'. *Journal of Legal Studies*, vol. 8, 1979, p. 235.

Landes, William M. and Posner, Richard A. *The Economic Structure of Intellectual Property Law*. Cambridge, MA: Harvard University Press 2003.

Lando, Henrik and Caspar, Rose. 'On the Enforcement of Specific Performance in Civil Law Countries'. *International Review of Law and Economics*, vol. 24, p. 473.

Langbein, John H. 'The Contractarian Basis of the Law of Trusts'. *Yale Law Journal*, vol. 105, 1995, p. 625.

Langbein, John H. 'The Secret Life of the Trust: The Trust as an Instrument of Commerce'. *Yale Law Journal*, vol. 107, 1997, p. 165.

Langbein, John H., Lerner, Renée Lettow and Smith, Bruce P. *History of the Common Law: The Development of Anglo-American Legal Institutions*. Austin and New York: Wolters Kluwer Law & Business; Aspen.

Lasser, Mitchel de S.-O.-l'E. *Judicial Deliberations: A Comparative Analysis of Judicial Transparency and Legitimacy*. Oxford: Oxford University Press 2009 (*Oxford Studies in European Law* series).

Lasser, Mitchel de S.-O.-l'E. *Judicial Transformations: The Rights Revolution in the Courts of Europe*. Oxford and New York: Oxford University Press 2009 (*Oxford Studies in European Law* series).

Lee, Thomas R. 'Stare Decisis in Historical Perspective: From the Founding Era to the Rehnquist Court'. *Vanderbilt Law Review*, vol. 52, 1999, p. 647.

Legrand, Pierre. 'European Legal Systems Are Not Converging'. *International and Comparative Law Quarterly*, vol. 45, 1996, p. 52.

Legrand, Pierre. 'Against a European Civil Code'. *Modern Law Review*, vol. 60, 1997, p. 44.

Legrand, Pierre. *Fragments on Law-As-Culture*. Deventer: W.E.J. Tjeenk Willink 1999.

Legrand, Pierre. 'Econocentrism'. *University of Toronto Law Journal*, vol. 59, 2009, p. 215.

Lehavi, Amnon. 'The Property Puzzle'. *Georgetown Law Journal*, vol. 96, 2008, p. 1987.

Lele, Priya P. and Siems, Mathias M. 'Diversity in Shareholder Protection in Common Law Countries'. *Journal of Institutional Comparisons in Journal of Institutional Comparisons*, Spring 2007, p. 1.

Levine, Philippa. *The British Empire: Sunrise to Sunset*. Harlow and New York: Pearson Longman 2007 (*Recovering the Past* series).

Levitsky, Jonathan E. 'The Europeanization of the British Legal Style'. *American Journal of Comparative Law*, vol. 42, 1994, p. 347.

Levmore, Saul. 'Waiting for Rescue: An Essay on the Evolution and Incentive Structure of the Law of Affirmative Obligations'. *Virginia Law Review*, vol. 72, 1986, p. 879.

Levmore, Saul. 'Variety and Uniformity in the Treatment of the Good-Faith Purchaser'. *Journal of Legal Studies*, vol. 16, 1987, p. 43.

Lloyd-Jones, Jonathan. *ADR Client Strategies in the UK: Leading Lawyers on Preparing Clients, Navigating the Negotiation Process, and Overcoming Obstacles*. Boston, MA: Aspatore 2008 (*Inside the Minds* series).

Luppi, Barbara and Parisi, Francesco. 'Litigation and Legal Evolution: Does Procedure Matter?' *Public Choice*, vol. 152, 2012, p. 181.

Lyon, Larry, Toben, Bradley J. B., Underwood, James M., Underwood, William D. and Wren, James. 'Straight from the Horse's Mouth: Judicial Observations of Jury Behavior and the Need for Tort Reform'. *Baylor Law Review*, vol. 59, 2007, p. 419.

Mahoney, Paul. 'The Common Law and Economic Growth: Hayek Might Be Right'. *Journal of Legal Studies*, vol. 30, 2001, no. 2, pp. 503–526.

Main, Brian G. M. and Park, Andrew. 'The Impact of Defendant Offers into Court on Negotiation in the Shadow of the Law: Experimental Evidence'. *International Review of Law and Economics*, vol. 22, 2002, p. 177.

Main, Brian G. M. and Park, Andrew. 'An Experiment with Two-Way Offers into Court: Restoring the Balance in Pre-Trial Negotiation'. *Journal of Economic Studies*, vol. 30, 2003, p. 125.

Martinez, Catalina and Guellec Dominique. 'Overview of Recent Changes and Comparison of Patent Regimes in the United States, Japan and Europe: Patents, Innovation and Economic Performance'. OECD Conference Proceedings, 2007e tome, pp. 127–162.

Masada, Steven T. 'Australia's "Most Extreme Case": A New Alternative for U.S. Medical Malpractice Liability Reform'. *Pacific Rim Law and Policy Journal*, vol. 13, 2004, p. 163.

Mattei, Ugo. 'Three Patterns of Law: Taxonomy and Change in the World's Legal Systems'. *American Journal of Comparative Law*, vol. 5, 1997, no. 45.

Mattei, Ugo. *Comparative Law and Economics*. Ann Arbor: University of Michigan Press 1997.

Mattei, Ugo, Schlesinger, Rudolf B., Ruskola, Teemu and Gidi, Antonio. *Schlesinger's Comparative Law: Cases, Text, Materials* 7th ed. New York: Foundation Press; Thomson Reuters (*University Casebook* series).

Mattiacci Dari, Giuseppe, Garoupa, Nuno and Gómez Pomar, Fernando. 'State Liability'. *European Review of Private Law*, vol. 18, 2010, p. 773.

Mautner, Menachem. *Law and the Culture of Israel*. Oxford and New York: Oxford University Press 2011.

McCahery, Joseph, Moerland, Piet, Raaijmakers, Theo and Luc Renneboog. *Corporate Governance Regimes: Convergence and Diversity*. Oxford and New York: Oxford University Press 2002.

McChesney Fred S. and Shughart, William F. *The Causes and Consequences of Antitrust* 2nd ed. Chicago: University of Chicago Press 1995.

McChesney, Fred S. 'Rent Extraction and Rent Creation in the Economic Theory of Regulation'. *Journal of Legal Studies*, vol. 16, 1987, p. 101.

McCormack, John L. 'Torrens and Recording: Land Title Assurance in the Computer Age'. *William Mitchel Law Review*, vol. 18, 1992, p. 61.

McLean, Sheila. *Compensation For Damage: An International Perspective*. Aldershot and Brookfield VT: Dartmouth 1993.

Ménard, Claude and Du Marais, Bertrand. 'Can We Rank Legal Systems According to Their Economic Efficiency?' *Washington University Journal of Law and Policy*, vol. 26, 2008, p. 55.

Menger, Pierre-Michel and Ginsburgh, Victor. *Essays in the Economics of the Arts: Selected Essays*. New York: Elsevier 1996 (*Contributions to Economics Analysis* series vol. 237).

Merrill, Thomas W. 'Does Public Choice Theory Justify Judicial Activism After All?' *Harvard Journal of Law and Public Policy*, vol. 21, 1997, p. 219.

Merrill, Thomas W. 'Institutional Choice and Political Faith'. *Law and Social Inquiry*, vol. 22, 1997, p. 959.

Merryman, John Henry. 'The French Deviation'. *American Journal of Comparative Law*, vol. 44, 1996, p. 109.

Meunier, Sophie and McNamara, Kathleen R. *Making History: European Integration and Institutional Change at Fifty*. New York: Oxford University Press 2007.

Miceli, Thomas J. 'Legal Change: Selective Litigation, Judicial Bias, and Precedent'. *Journal of Legal Studies*, vol. 38, 2009, p. 157.

Miceli, Thomas J. and Sirmans, C. F. 'An Economic Theory of Adverse Possession'. *International Review of Law and Economics*, vol. 15, 1995, p. 161.

Michaels, Ralf. 'The True Lex Mercatoria: Law Beyond the State'. *Indiana Journal of Global Legal Studies*, vol. 14, 2007, p. 447.

Michaels, Ralf. 'Comparative Law by Numbers? Legal Origins Thesis, *Doing Business* Reports, and the Silence of Comparative Law'. *American Journal of Comparative Law*, vol. 57, 2009, p. 765.

Milhaupt, Curtis J. 'Beyond Legal Origin: Rethinking Law's Relationship to the Economy – Implications for Policy'. *American Journal of Comparative Law*, vol. 57, 2009, p. 831.

Miller, Ruth A. 'The Ottoman and Islamic Substratum of Turkey's Swiss Civil Code'. *Journal of Islamic Studies*, vol. 11, 2000, p. 335.

Montgomery, Sarah. 'What is the Social Impact of the World Bank's Support to Regulatory Reform? Don't Ask the Bank'. 20 November 2014. Online at: www.brettonwoodsproject.

org/2014/11/social-impact-banks-support-regulatory-reform-dont-ask-bank/ (accessed 10/10/2016).

Morriss, Andrew P. 'Codification and Right Answers'. *Chicago-Kent Law Review*, vol. 74, 1999, no. 2, p. 355.

Mulheron, Rachael. *The Class Action in Common Law Legal Systems*. Oxford: Hart 2004.

Münchener Kommentar zum Bürgerlichen Gesetzbuch, Band 5, Auflage 4. München: Beck 2004.

Myerson, Roger B. 'Justice, Institutions and Multiple Equilibria'. *Chicago Journal of International Law*, vol. 5, 2004, p. 91.

Neal, Larry. *The Economics of Europe and the European Union*. Cambridge, New York: Cambridge University Press 2007.

Neumann, Richard K. *Legal Reasoning and Legal Writing: Structure, Strategy, and Style* 5th ed. New York: Aspen 2005.

Niblett, Anthony. 'Do Judges Cherry Pick Precedents to Justify Extra-Legal Decisions? A Statistical Examination'. *Maryland Law Review*, 2010, no. 70, p. 234.

Niblett, Anthony. 'Case-By-Case Adjudication and the Path of the Law'. *Journal of Legal Studies*, vol. 42, 2013, p. 303.

Niblett, Anthony, Posner, Richard A. and Shleifer, Andrei. 'The Evolution of a Legal Rule'. *Journal of Legal Studies*, vol. 39, 2010, p. 325.

Nussim, Jacob and Tabbach, Avraham D. 'Controlling Avoidance: Ex Ante Regulation Versus Ex Post Punishment'. *Review of Law and Economics*, vol. 4, 2008, p. 45.

Nyantung Berry, Laura. 'Insider Trading Laws and Stock Markets Around the World: An Empirical Contribution to the Theoretical Law and Economics Debate'. *Journal of Corporate Law*, vol. 32, 2007, no. 2, p. 237.

O'Connell, Jeffrey and Partlett, David. 'An America's Cup for Tort Reform? Australia and America Compared'. *University of Toronto Law Journal*, vol. 21, 1988, p. 443.

O'Connor, Erin O'Hara and Ribstein, Larry E. *The Law Market*. Oxford and New York: Oxford University Press 2009.

Oda, Hiroshi. *Japanese Law* 3rd ed. Oxford and New York: Oxford University Press 2009.

Ogus, A. I. 'Competition Between National Legal Systems: A Contribution of Economic Analysis to Comparative Law'. *International and Comparative Law Quarterly*, vol. 48, 1999, p. 405.

Ogus, Anthony. 'The Economic Basis of Legal Culture: Networks and Monopolization'. *Oxford Journal of Legal Studies*, vol. 22, 2002, p. 419.

Ogus, Anthony. 'What Legal Scholars Can Learn from Law and Economics'. *Chicago-Kent Law Review*, vol. 79, p. 383.

Ogus, A. I. *Costs and Cautionary Tales: Economic Insights for the Law*. Oxford and Portland, OR: Hart 2006.

Ogus, Anthony and Faure, Michael. *Économie du droit. Le cas français*. Paris: Éditions Panthéon-Assas 2002: L.G.D.J. Diffuseur (Droit comparé).

O'Hara, Erin and Ribstein, Larry E. 'From Politics to Efficiency in Choice of Law'. *University of Chicago Law Review*, vol. 67, 2000, p. 1151.

Ohnesorge, John. 'Legal Origins and the Tasks of Corporate Law in Economic Development: A Preliminary Exploration'. *Brigham Young Law Review*, vol. 2009, 2009, no. 6, p. 1619.

Olson, Christina. 'A Practical Guide to the Fair Use Doctrine in American Copyright Law: Briefing Book Signal/Noise 2k5 – Creative Revolution?' *Harvard Journal of Law and Technology* 2005, pp. 2–9.

Ong, David M. 'The Impact of Environmental Law on Corporate Governance: International and Comparative Perspectives'. *European Journal of International Law*, vol. 12, 2001, no. 4.

Oppenheimer, Andrew ed. *The Relationship Between European Community Law and National Law: The Cases*. Cambridge: Cambridge University Press 1994–2003.

Örücü, E. ed. *Mixed Legal Systems at New Frontiers*. London: Wildy, Simmonds & Hill 2010 (*JCL Studies in Comparative Law* vol. 2).

Örücü, Esin. 'What is a Mixed Legal System: Exclusion or Expansion'. *Electronic Journal of Comparative Law*, vol. 12, 2008, p. 1.

Örücü, Esin, Attwooll, Elspeth and Coyle Sean. *Studies in Legal Systems: Mixed and Mixing*. The Hague: Kluwer Law International 1996.

Palmer, Vernon V. *Mixed Jurisdictions Worldwide: The Third Legal Family*. Cambridge and New York: Cambridge University Press 2001.

Palmer, Vernon V. 'Two Rival Theories of Mixed Legal Systems'. In *Mixed Legal Systems at New Frontiers*, Esin Örücü ed. London: Wildy, Simmonds & Hill 2010.

Palmer, Geoffrey. *Compensation for Incapacity: A Study on Law and Social Change in New Zealand and Australia*. Wellington: Oxford University Press 1979.

Pargendler, Mariana. 'Politics in the Origins: The Making of Corporate Law in Nineteenth-Century Brazil'. *American Journal of Comparative Law*, vol. 60, 2012, no. 3, p. 805.

Pargendler, Mariana. 'The Rise and Decline of Legal Families'. *American Journal of Comparative Law*, vol. 60, 2012, no. 4, p. 1043.

Parisi, Francesco and Fon, Vincy. *The Economics of Lawmaking*. Oxford and New York: Oxford University Press 2009.

Patentanwälte Reinhard Skuhra Weise and Partner. Information for Intellectual Property Users Summer 2002.

Patents, Innovation and Economic Performance. OECD Conference Proceedings 2004.

Peel, Edwin and Treitel, G. H. *The Law of Contract* 12th ed. London: Sweet & Maxwell 2007.

Peerenboom, R. P. *China's Long March Toward Rule of Law*. Cambridge and New York: Cambridge University Press.

Phillips, Emma. 'The War on Civil Law? The Common Law as a Proxy for the Global Ambition of Law and Economics'. *Wisconsin International Law Journal*, vol. 24, 2010, p. 915.

Piotrowska, Joanna and Vanborren, Werner. The Corporate Income Tax Rate–Revenue Paradox: Evidence in the EU. Luxembourg: EUR-OP (taxation papers, working paper, 12).

Pistor, Katharina, Keinan, Yoram, Kleinheisterkamp, Jan and West, Mark. 'Innovation in Corporate Law'. *Journal of Comparative Economics*, vol. 31, 2003, p. 676.

Pistor, Katharina, Keinan, Yoram, Kleinheisterkamp, Jan and West, Mark D. 'The Evolution of Corporate Law: A Cross-Country Comparison'. *University of Pennsylvania Journal of International Law*, vol. 23, 2002, no. 4, pp. 791–871.

Polinsky, Mitchell A. and Rubinfeld, Daniel L. 'Optimal Awards and Penalties When the Probability of Prevailing Varies Among Plaintiffs'. *RAND Journal of Economics*, vol. 27, 1996, p. 269.

Polinsky, Mitchell A.; Rubinfeld, Daniel L. 'Does the English Rule Discourage Low-Probability-of-Prevailing Plaintiffs?' *Journal of Legal Studies*, vol. 27, 1998, p. 519.

Ponte, Lucille M. 'Reassessing the Australian Adversarial System: An Overview of Issues in Court Reform and Federal ADR Practice in the Land Down Under'. *Syracuse Journal of International Law and Commerce*, vol. 27, 2000, p. 335.

Posner Richard A. 'Intellectual Property: The Law and Economics Approach'. *Journal of Economic Perspectives*, vol. 19, Spring 2005, pp. 57–73.

Posner, Richard A. 'Utilitarianism, Economics, and Legal Theory'. *Journal of Legal Studies*, vol. 8, 1979, p. 103.

Posner, Richard A. 'Will the Federal Courts of Appeals Survive Until 1984? An Essay on Delegation and Specialization of the Judicial Function'. *Southern California Law Review*, vol. 56, 1983, p. 761.

Posner, Richard A. *Law and Legal Theory in England and America*. Oxford and New York: Clarendon Press; Oxford University Press (*Clarendon Law* series).

Posner, Richard A. *Economic Analysis of Law* 8th ed. New York: Aspen 2011 (*Aspen Casebook* series).

Priest, George L. 'The Common Law Process and the Selection of Efficient Rules'. *Journal of Legal Studies*, vol. 6, p. 65.

Pritchard, A. C. and Zywicki, Todd J. 'Finding the Constitution: An Economic Analysis of Tradition's Role in Constitutional Interpretation'. *North Carolina Law Review*, vol. 77, 1999, p. 409.

Prosser, William Lloyd and Plant, Marcus L. *Selected Topics on the Law of Torts: Five Lectures Delivered at the University of Michigan February 2, 3, 4, 5 and 6, 1953*. Ann Arbor: University of Michigan Law School 1953.

Puri, Poonam. 'Legal Origins, Investor Protection, and Canada'. CLPE Research Paper No. 3, 2010.

Ramello, Giovanni Battista. 'What's in a Sign? Trademark Law and Economic Theory'. POLIC Working Paper, vol. 73, 2006.

Ratcliffe, James M. *The Good Samaritan and the Law*. Gloucester, MA: Peter Smith 1981.

Reflection Group on the Future of EU Company Law. European Commission Internal Market and Services 2011.

Reimann, Mathias. 'Towards a European Civil Code: Why Continental Jurists Should Consult their Transatlantic Colleagues'. *Tulane Law Review*, vol. 73, 1999, p. 1337.

Reinganum, Jennifer F. and Wilde Louis L. 'Settlement, Litigation, and the Allocation of Litigation Costs'. *RAND Journal of Economics*, vol. 17, 1986, p. 557.

Reinsch, Paul Samuel. 'English Common Law in the Early American Colonies'. Bulletin of the University of Wisconsin 1899.

Reitz, John. 'Legal Origins, Comparative Law, and Political Economy'. *American Journal of Comparative Law*, vol. 57, 2009, p. 847.

Reitz, John. 'Toward a Study of the Ecology of Judicial Activism'. *Toronto University Law Review*, vol. 59, 2009, p. 185.

Revesz, Richard L. 'Specialized Courts and the Administrative Lawmaking System'. *University of Pennsylvania Law Review*, vol. 138, 1989, p. 1111.

Reyes, Francisco and Vermeulen, Erik P. M. 'Company Law, Lawyers and "Legal" Innovation: Common Law Versus Civil Law'. Legal Research Bulletin, Graduate School of Law, Kyushu University, vol. 2, 2012.

Robinson, William A. *Justice in Grey: A History of the Judicial System of the Confederate State of America*. Cambridge, MA: Harvard University Press 1941.

Roe J., Mark and Siegel, Jordan I. 'Finance and Politics: A Review Essay Based on Kenneth Dam's Analysis of Legal Traditions in the Law-Growth Nexus'. *Journal of Economic Literature*, vol. 47, 2009, p. 781.

Roe, Mark J. 'Chaos and Evolution in Law and Economics'. *Harvard Law Review*, vol. 109, 1996, p. 641.

Roe, Mark J. 'Legal Origins, Politics, and Modern Stockmarkets'. *Harvard Law Review*, vol. 120, 2006, p. 460.

Roe, Mark J. 'Juries and the Political Economy of Legal Origin'. *Journal of Comparative Economics*, vol. 35, 2007, p. 294.

Rosen, Mark D. 'Do Codification and Private International Law Leave Room for a New Law Merchant?' *Chicago Journal of International Law*, vol. 5, 2004, p. 83.

Rosenthal, Howard and Voeten, Eric. 'Measuring Legal Systems'. *Journal of Comparative Economics*, vol. 35, 2007, p. 711.

Roth, Günter H. and Kindler, Peter. *The Spirit of Corporate Law: Core Principles of Corporate Law in Continental Europe*. Oxford: Hart 2013.

Rubin, Paul H. 'Why is the Common Law Efficient?' *Journal of Legal Studies*, vol. 6, 1977, p. 51.

Rubin, Paul H. 'Common Law and Statute Law'. *Journal of Legal Studies*, vol. 11, 1982, p. 205.

Rubin, Paul H. *Business Firms and the Common Law: The Evolution of Efficient Rules*. New York: Praeger 1983.

Rubin, Paul H. 'Micro and Macro Legal Efficiency: Supply and Demand'. *Supreme Court Economic Review*, vol. 13, 2005, p. 19.

Ruoff, Theodore B.F. *An Englishman Looks at the Torrens System* Sydney: Law Book Company of Australasia 1957.

Schauer, Frederick. *Thinking Like a Lawyer: A New Introduction to Legal Reasoning*. Cambridge, MA: Harvard University Press 2009.

Schlanger, Margo 'What We Know and What We Should Know about American Trial Trends'. *Journal of Dispute Resolution*, vol. 2006, 2006, p. 35.

Schlechtriem, Peter. 'The Borderland of Tort and Contract: Opening a New Frontier?' *Cornell International Law Journal*, vol. 21, 1988, p. 467.

Schuck, Peter H. 'Tort Reform, Kiwi-Style'. *Yale Law and Policy Reform*, vol. 27, 2008, p. 187.

Schwartz, Alan and Scott, Robert E. 'Rethinking the Laws of Good Faith Purchase'. *Columbia Law Review*, vol. 111, 2011, p. 1332.

Seabury, Seth A., Pace, Nicholas M. and Reville, Robert T. 'Forty Years of Civil Jury Verdicts'. *Journal of Empirical Legal Studies*, vol. 1, 2004, p. 1.

Shapira, Amos and DeWitt-Arar, Keren C. *Introduction to the Law of Israel*. The Hague and Boston: Kluwer Law International 1995.

Shapiro, Robert J. and Mathur, Aparna. The Economic Implications of Patent Reform. The Deficiencies and Costs of Proposals Regarding the Apportionment of Damages, Post-Grant Opposition, and Inequitable Conduct in SONECON, February 2008. Online at: www.bio.org/sites/default/files/Patent_Reform_Study.pdf (accessed 13 August 2015).

Shavell, Steven. 'Suit, Settlement, and Trial: A Theoretical Analysis Under Alternative Methods for the Allocation of Legal Costs'. *Journal of Legal Studies*, vol. 11, 1982, p. 55.

Shavell, Steven. 'A Model of the Optimal Use of Liability and Safety Regulation'. *RAND Journal of Economics*, vol. 15, 1984, p. 271.

Siems, Mathias M. 'Numerical Comparative Law: Do We Need Statistical Evidence in Law in Order to Reduce Complexity?' *Cardozo Journal of International and Comparative Law*, vol. 13, 2005, p. 521.

Siems, Mathias M. 'Legal Origins: Reconciling Law and Finance and Comparative Law'. *McGill Law Journal*, vol. 52, 2007, no. 1, p. 57.

Siems, Mathias M. 'Legal Originality'. *Oxford Journal of Legal Studies*, vol. 28, 2008, p. 147.

Siems, Mathias M. and Deakin, Simon. 'Comparative Law and Finance: Past, Present, and Future Research'. *Journal of Institutional and Theoretical Economics*, vol. 166, 2010, p. 120.

Singer, Joseph William. *Property Law: Rules, Policies, and Practices* 3rd ed. New York: Aspen Law & Business 2002.

Sitkoff, Robert. 'The Economic Structure of Fiduciary Law'. *Boston University Law Review*, vol. 91, 2011, p. 1039.

Smith, Stephen A. 'Concurrent Liability and Unjust Enrichment: The Fundamental Breach Requirement'. *Law Quarterly Review*, vol. 115, 1999, p. 245.

Smits, Jan. 'A European Private Law as Mixed Legal System'. *Maastricht Journal of European and Comparative Law*, vol. 5, 1998, p. 328.

Smits, Jan. *The Contribution of Mixed Legal Systems to European Private Law*. Antwerp: Intersentia 2001.

Snyder, Edward A. and Hughes, James W. 'The English Rule for Allocating Legal Costs: Evidence Confronts Theory'. *Journal of Economics and Organization*, vol. 6, 1990, p. 345.

Spamann, Holger. 'Large-Sample, Quantitative Research Designs for Comparative Law?' *American Journal of Comparative Law*, vol. 57, 2009, p. 797.

Spamann, Holger. 'Contemporary Legal Transplants, Legal Families and the Diffusion of (Corporate) Law'. *Brigham Young University Law Review*, vol. 2009, 2010, p. 1813.

Spamann, Holger. 'Legal Origin, Civil Procedure, and the Quality of Contract Enforcement'. *Journal of Institutional and Theoretical Economy*, vol. 166, 2010, p. 146.

Spamann, Holger. 'The "Antidirector Rights Index" Revisited'. *Review of Financial Studies*, vol. 23, 2010, p. 467.

Stearns, Maxwell L. and Zywicki, Todd J. *Public Choice Concepts and Applications in Law* St Paul, MN: West 2009 (*American Casebook* series).

Steinberg, Marc I. 'Insider Trading – A Comparative Perspective', 2002. Online at: www. imf.org/external/np/leg/sem/2002/cdmfl/eng/steinb.pdf (access date).

Steiner, Eva. *French Legal Method*. Oxford: Oxford University Press 2002

Stith, Richard. 'Securing the Rule of Law Through Interpretive Pluralism: An Argument From Comparative Law'. *Hastings Constitutional Law Quarterly*, vol. 35, 2008, p. 401.

Stone Sweet, Alec. *Governing with Judges: Constitutional Politics in Europe*. Oxford and New York: Oxford University Press 2000.

Straus, Joseph. *The Present State of the Patent System in the European Union: As Compared With the Situation in the United States of America and Japan*. Luxembourg: Office for Official Publications of the European Communities 1997 (EUR, 17014 EN).

Sunstein, Cass, Hastie, Reid R., Payne, John W., Schkade, David A. and Viscu, Kip W. *Punitive Damages: How Juries Decide*. Chicago: University of Chicago Press 2002.

Swiss Federal Institute of Intellectual Property. *The Effects of Protecting Geographical Indications: Ways and Means of their Evaluation*. Bern (Publikation 7).

Terrebonne, Peter R. 'A Strictly Evolutionary Model of Common Law'. *Journal of Legal Studies*, vol. 10, 1981, p. 397.

The EU Commission Communication from the Commission to the European Parliament, The Council, The European Economic and Social Committee and the Committee of the Region. Better Regulation for Better Results: An EU Agenda. COM (2015) 215 final.

The EU Commission Communication from the Commission to the European Parliament, the Council, The European Economic and Social Committee and the Committee of the

Regions. Action Plan: European Company Law and Corporate Governance – a Modern Legal Framework for More Engaged Shareholders and Sustainable Companies. COM (2012) 740 final.

Tullock, Gordon. *The Selected Works of Gordon Tullock: The Organization of Inquiry, Volume 3*, Charles K. Rowley ed. Liberty Fund 2005.

Tullock, Gordon. 'Rent-Seeking and the Law'. In *The Selected Works of Gordon Tullock: The Organization of Inquiry, Volume 3*, Charles K. Rowley ed. Liberty Fund 2005, p. 186.

Tilbury, Michael and Luntz, Harold. 'Punitive Damages in Australian Law'. *Loyola of Los Angeles International and Comparative Law Journal*, 1995, no. 17, p. 769.

Tobin, Rosemary and Schoeman, Elsabe. 'The New Zealand Accident Compensation Scheme: The Statutory Bar and the Conflict of Laws'. *American Journal of Comparative Law*, vol. 53, 2005, p. 493.

Toran, Janice. 'Settlement, Sanctions, and Attorney Fees: Comparing English Payment into Court and Proposed Rule 68'. *American University Law Review*, vol. 35, 2007, p. 301.

Trakman, Leon E. 'From the Medieval Law Merchant to E-Merchant Law'. *University of Toronto Law Journal*, vol. 53, 2003, p. 265.

Tritton, Guy and Davis, Richard. *Intellectual Property in Europe* 3rd ed. London: Sweet & Maxwell 2008.

Tullock, Gordon. *The Case Against the Common Law*. Durham, NC: Carolina Academic Press 1997

Tunc, André éd. *International Encyclopedia of Comparative Law*. Tübingen: Mohr, 1976.

Tunc, André. *La Responsabilité Civile*. Paris: Économica 1989.

Ulen, Thomas S. *The View from Abroad: Tort Law and Liability Insurance in the United States*, Gerhard Wagner ed. Wein and New York: Springer 2005, pp. 207–238.

US Commercial Service at the US Mission to the European Union. United States Mission to the European Union's Toolkit on Intellectual Property Rights 2010.

Valcke, Catherine. 'The French Response to the World Bank's *Doing Business* Reports'. *University of Toronto Law Review*, vol. 60, 2010, p. 197.

Valcke, Catherine. 'On Comparing French and English Contract Law: Insights from Social Contract Theory'. *Journal of Comparative Law*, vol. 3, 2009, p. 69.

Ventoruzzo, Marco. 'Comparing Insider Trading in the United States and in the European Union: History and Recent Developments'. ECGI Law Working Paper Series, vol. 257, 2014.

Vidmar, Neil. 'The Performance of the American Civil Jury: An Empirical Perspective'. *Arizona Law Review*, vol. 40, 1998, p. 849.

Vidmar, Neil. 'Foreword'. *Law and Contemporary Problems*, vol. 62, 1999, p. 1.

Vidmar, Neil. *World Jury Systems*. Oxford and New York: Oxford University Press 2000 (*Oxford Socio-Legal Studies*).

Vidmar, Neil and Hans, Valerie P. *American Juries*. New York: Prometheus 2007.

Vitols, Sigurd and Kluge, Norbert eds. *The Sustainable Company: A New Approach to Corporate Governance*. Brussels: ETUI aisbl 2011.

Volckart, Oliver and Mangels, Antje. 'Are the Roots of the Modern Lex Mercatoria Really Medieval?' *Southern Economic Journal*, vol. 65, 1999, p. 427.

Vossestein, G. J. *Modernization of European Company Law and Corporate Governance: Some Considerations on its Legal Limits*. Austin, Alphen aan den Rijn and Frederick, MD: Wolters Kluwer Law & Business; Kluwer Law International 2010 (*European Company Law* series vol. 6).

Wacks, Raymond. *The New Legal Order in Hong Kong.* Hong Kong: Hong Kong University Press 1999.

Walpin, Gerald. 'America's Failing Civil Justice System: Can We Learn from Other Countries?' *New York Law School Law Review*, vol. 41, 1997, p. 647.

Wangenheim, Georg von. 'The Evolution of Judge-Made Law'. *International Review of Law and Economics*, vol. 13, 1993, p. 381.

Wasserstein Fassberg, Celia. 'Lex Mercatoria: Hoist with its Own Petard?' *Chicago Journal of International Law*, vol. 5, 2004, p. 67.

Weinrib, Ernest J. 'The Case for a Duty to Rescue'. *Yale Law Journal*, vol. 90, 1980, p. 247.

Weir, David and Schapiro, Mark. *Circle of Poison: Pesticides and People in a Hungry World.* San Francisco CA: Institute for Food and Development Policy 1981.

Weir, Tony. *Economic Torts.* Oxford and New York: Clarendon Press; Oxford University Press 1997 (*Clarendon Law Lectures*).

West, Mark. 'Legal Determinants of World Cup Success'. University of Michigan John M. Olin Center for Law and Economics, 2002, n° Discussion Paper No. 009. Online at: www.law.umich.edu/CENTERSANDPROGRAMS/OLIN/abstracts/discussionpapers/2002/west02-009.pdf, consulted 18.11.2015.

Westbrook, Tory. The Proper Standard of Protection to be Afforded to Geographical Indications. A Discussion of the International Debate Surrounding GIs. Online at: www.academia.edu/8975605/The-proper-standard-of-protection-to-be-afforded-to-geographical-indications-tory-westbrook (accessed 10 August 2015).

White, G. Edward. *Tort Law in America. An Intellectual History* expanded ed. Oxford and New York: Oxford University Press 2003.

White, Robin M. and Willock, Ian Douglas. *The Scottish Legal System* 4th ed. Haywards Heath UK: Tottel 2007.

Whytock, Christopher A. 'Legal Origins, Functionalism, and the Future of Comparative Law '. *Birgham Young University Law Review*, vol. 2009, 2009, no. 6.

Wise, E. M. 'The Doctrine of Stare Decisis'. *Wayne Law Review*, vol. 21, 1975, p. 1043.

Wissler, Roselle, Saks, Michael J. and Hart, Allen J. 'Decisionmaking about General Damages: A Comparison of Jurors, Judges, and Lawyers'. *Michigan Law Review*, vol. 98, 1999, p. 751.

Wittman, Donald. 'Prior Regulation Versus Post Liability: The Choice Between Input and Output Monitoring'. *Journal of Legal Studies*, vol. 6, 1977, p. 193.

Wittman, Donald A. *Economic Foundations of Law and Organization.* Cambridge and New York: Cambridge University Press 2006.

Woolf, Harry. *Access to Justice.* New York: Oxford University Press 1996.

Xu, Guangdong. 'The Role of Law in Economic Growth: A Literature Review'. *Journal of Economic Surveys*, vol. 25, 2011, p. 833.

Youngs, Raymond. *English, French and German Comparative Law.* London and New York: Routledge-Cavendish 2007.

Zimmermann, Reinhard and Reimann, Mathias. *The Oxford Handbook of Comparative Law.* Oxford: Oxford University Press 2006.

Zywicki, Todd. 'The Rise and Fall of Efficiency in the Common Law: A Supply-Side Analysis'. *Northwestern University Law Review*, vol. 97, 2003, p. 1551.

Zywicki, Todd. 'Spontaneous Order and the Common Law: Gordon Tullock's Critique'. *Public Choice*, vol. 135, 2008, p. 35.

Index

aboriginal law 91, 93
Accident Compensation Corporation 40
accountability 16, 79–80, 82, 122, 157
Act of Union 94
adaptability channel 25–6, 146
administrative law 7, 77, 79–82, 93, 95
adquisitio a non domino 61
adverse possession 33
adverse selection 79
Africa 34, 91, 105
agency costs 155
aid agencies 150
America Invents Act (AIA) 125–9, 131
American Law Institute 100
American Revolution 30
American Tort Reform Association 40
Anspruchkonkurrenz 66
anti-director index 147
Arthur J.S. Hall & Co. v. Simons 42
asymmetric information 43, 60, 66,
    121–2
attorneys 82, 134
Australia 6, 32–6, 39, 41–5, 106
Austria 84

bail-outs 153
banking 5, 11–12, 60, 106, 145, 150, 157
bankruptcy 4, 153
barristers 42
Belgium 148
benchmarks 8, 12, 64
Berne Convention 135, 137
bias 5, 15–16, 18, 26, 35; in common law
    37–8, 40; in corporate law 147–8, 151,
    153, 158; governance 79–80; in private
    law 59
Black's Law Dictionary 30
Blackstone, W. 14–15
bona fide purchase 61–3

Botswana 12
bottom-up law 18, 59
Brazil 145
Britain 17, 31, 33, 81, 90, 93–4, 131, 147,
    149
British Empire 90
bureaucracy 79
business methods 129–30
bystanders 68

California 31, 123
Canada 6, 32–6, 39, 41–5, 106, 145
capital flows 11
capital markets 145–6, 148, 150, 158–9,
    162
capture 7, 17–18, 33, 78–82, 84
Cardozo, Justice 14
case law 16, 18, 25, 30, 32, 41–2, 44, 59,
    65–6; and common law 44; intellectual
    property 117, 128; and mixed law 97;
    and private law 59, 65–6; value
    maximization/orientation 153
Central Europe 84
chambers of commerce 82
cherry-picked doctrines 5–6, 9, 32, 45, 61,
    158, 162
Chiarella v. US 159
Chile 11
China 92, 106, 146
civil code/s 16, 18, 32, 63, 65–6, 100,
    104–5
civil juries 39–40, 43–4
civil law 3–8, 11–12, 16–18, 43, 59, 62,
    65, 67–8, 82–4; comparisons 22, 24–7;
    contrasts 77–89; and corporate law
    144–69; cost rules 42–3; evolution 31,
    34, 39; insider trading 158, 161;
    intellectual property 115–43; and mixed
    law 90–9; and private law 59–76; trusts

99–107; value maximization/orientation 158

climate change 157

Code du commerce 82

codification 25, 31, 90, 96–7, 99–100; codes of conduct 147, 150; corporate law 146; insider trading 159; intellectual property 128, 132, 136; movement 14

coding errors 147–50

colonialism 7, 22, 30–1, 36, 90–1, 93–5

commercial law 18, 44, 60, 77, 80, 82–3, 95

common law 3–9, 11–12, 59, 65, 83; comparisons 22, 24–7; contrasts 77–89; and corporate law 144–69; definitions 30; efficiency 14–21, 34–9; evolution 30–56; insider trading 158, 160; intellectual property 115–43; meaning 30–56; and mixed law 90–9; and private law 59–76; trusts 99–107; value maximization/orientation 153–4, 157

communism 84

Community Trademarks 118, 120

comparative advantage 123

comparative law 18, 22–9, 91–2, 95, 144, 147–8, 150, 158–62

compensation 33, 39–40, 42, 44, 64–6, 131, 155

confidentiality 130, 159

Conseil d'État 77, 80

constitutional law 26, 77, 79–80, 83–4, 93, 117, 125

constructive trusts 100

contingency fees 43

contract law 5–7, 11, 25, 31–2, 35, 61, 64–7, 92, 95–6

Convention on the Law Applicable to Trusts and on their Recognition 105–7

copyright 116–17, 132–7

Copyright Acts 133–6

Copyright, Designs and Patent Act (CDPA) 135

Corporate Governance Principles 146–7

corporate law 8, 113, 144–69

corruption 12, 16, 42

cost rules 42–3

cost-benefit analysis 77, 81, 84, 134

Cour d'appeal 82

Court of Appeals for the Federal Circuit (CAFC) 129

court workloads 77–8

Court/s of Appeal 44, 129

criminal law 11, 43–4, 63, 68, 94–5

Cyprus 92, 105–6

damages 7, 39–41, 44, 60, 65–7, 128, 160

databases 132, 146

Davies v. Mann 39

de facto/jure judicial independence 16, 95

Defamation Acts 41, 44

defamation law 39, 41–2, 44

Delaware 148, 156

demand 17, 34

Denmark 119

Department for Courts 44

designs 116, 135

Doing Business 5, 8, 11–12, 60, 150–1

D'Orta-Ekenaike v. Victoria Legal Aid 42

dual patrimony theory 103–4

dualism 91, 93

duty to rescue 68

Eastern Europe 84

ecclesiastical courts 17, 30

econometrics 26, 90

economic growth 3, 6–9, 11–12, 16, 25–7; comparisons 22, 24–5; corporate law 144, 152; evolution 33; governance 77, 81, 83; insider trading 159; mixed law 90, 96, 98–9; private law 59, 61, 64

economics 3, 8, 26, 33, 36; common law 39, 41; corporate law 144; financial crises 145, 147, 149–50, 153–4, 157–8; insider trading 158; intellectual property 116; private law 60; value maximization/orientation 153–4

economists 3–7, 9, 15, 26, 33, 61, 82–3, 96, 124, 145

efficiency 4–6, 8, 66, 95–6, 98–9; common law 14–21, 34–9; comparisons 22, 24–6; copyright 132–7; corporate law 150–3; danger 11–13; definitions 3; evolution 30–56; insider trading 158–62; intellectual property 115, 117–24, 128–31; patents 124–7; private law 59–76; trusts 99, 102–3, 105; value maximization/orientation 153–8

Electronic Commerce Regulations 41

employer-employee inventions 130–1

England 6–7, 16, 22, 30–2, 34–40; common law 44–5; corporate law 145–8; English rule 42–3; governance 81; intellectual property 129; mixed law 5, 93, 97, 99; private law 59, 62–6, 68

English language 7, 93, 95, 97, 149

environmental costs 154
equity courts 17, 30, 34, 95
Europe 17, 36, 84, 90–1, 93, 117–18, 122–3, 125, 132, 147, 150, 156
European Court of Justice 117, 161
European Patent Convention (EPC) 125–8
European Patent Office (EPO) 126–8
European Union (EU) 92, 94–5, 113, 115–16, 146; copyright 132–7; corporate law 144–69; insider trading 158–62; intellectual property 117–24; patents 124–31; value maximization/ orientation 153–8
Exchange Act 159–60
executive branch 7, 25, 31, 78, 80, 82
express trusts 100, 106

Fair Use 7, 117, 132–7
false imprisonment 43–4
family law 31, 94
federal law 34, 43, 98, 117–19, 129
Federal Rules of Civil Procedure 43
fiduciary duties 104, 159
financial crises 145, 147, 149–50, 153–4, 157–8
financial markets 3, 12, 22, 24, 102, 106, 148, 150, 153
financiers 154
first-to-file/invent principles 128–9
Foodstuff Regulation 121
formalisms 16
Fortune 500 156
France 3–9, 12, 14, 16, 18; *bona fide* purchase 61; common law 24–6; comparisons 22; corporate law 145–6, 148, 155; governance 77, 80, 82–4; intellectual property 122–3, 129; mixed law 90, 93, 95, 100, 106; private law 59–64, 66–7
fraud 43–4, 62–3, 159
free market 153, 155
free riders 121–3, 130
functional equivalents 147–9

gatekeepers 154–5
generalizations 9, 32, 60, 102
geographic indications (GIs) 120–4
Germany 5, 22, 24–5, 64–6, 84, 90, 92, 94, 146, 149, 158
global warming 157
globalization 59, 102, 119, 127, 144, 151, 153, 155
Good Samaritan Rule 67–8

governance 7, 61, 77–89, 144, 146, 151, 153–7
gross domestic product (GDP) 11–12, 25, 115–16
guild courts 17, 82
Gutnick v. Down Jones & Co. 41

Hague Conference on Private International Law 105
Hayek, F. 59
Henderson v. Merrett Syndicates Ltd. 65
High Court/s 42, 44
Hill v. Church of Scientology 41
historians 36, 82
Holmes, Justice 14
Hong Kong 92
hybrid systems 7, 59, 91–2, 102–3, 105–7, 129

ideology 34, 148
imperialism 90
implicit markets 4
incorporation 153, 156
indicators 22, 61, 146, 149
Industrial Revolution 132
inequality 157
Inequitable Conduct Doctrine 129
Information Society Directive (ISD) 137
initial conditions 15–16, 35, 38
innovation 115–16, 124–6, 128–30, 146–7, 157
insider trading 158–62
insurance 26, 33, 64
intellectual property 7–8, 113, 115–43
Inter-American Convention 123
internal affairs doctrine 156
international community 12, 147, 150
International Monetary Fund (IMF) 150
International Trademark Association 119
inventions 116, 119, 124, 127–31
investors 128, 144, 147, 150, 154, 157–60, 162
Ireland 6, 32–4, 36, 39, 41, 43, 45, 92, 95
Israel 12, 34, 94–5
Italy 65, 93, 106

Jamaica 12
Japan 90, 92, 94
John v. MGN Ltd. 44
judge-made law 6, 14, 16–18, 25, 32–4, 41, 60, 65, 117, 126
judicial independence 4, 11, 16
judicial reviews 83

jurisdictions 90–112, 156

Kelsen, H. 83–4
Korea 4, 92, 94

labour 4, 40, 157
laissez-faire 153, 156
land registration/titling 33, 64
Lanham Act 118, 121
Latin America 84
Latvia 12
Law on Contracts 65
lawyers 31, 42–3, 94, 97, 102
legal origins theory 3–10; coding errors
    147–50; comparative law 18, 22–9;
    comparisons 22, 25–6; copyright 132,
    135, 137; corporate law 144; dangers
    11–13; evolution 14–16, 30–56, 67, 95;
    inherent flaws 144–50; insider trading
    158, 161–2; institutes 57, 151–62;
    intellectual property 116–17, 126–7,
    129, 131; mixed law 95–6, 98–9;
    modern dilemmas 113; persisting
    influence 150–1; private law 63; value
    maximization/orientation 155–8
legislation 12, 15, 17–18, 22, 25; common
    law 30, 33, 41, 44; governance 78–9,
    83–4; intellectual property 115–17,
    119, 122, 125, 129–30, 136; mixed law
    91, 94–5; nexus-of-contracts 152;
    private law 59; value maximization/
    orientation 153, 155, 157–9, 161
Lehmann Brothers 157
lex mercatoria 82
Leximetric approach 144–5
libel 41, 43–4
licenses 80, 128, 131–2
limited liability 154, 157–8
Lithuania 12
loans 12, 33, 64
local determinants 6–7, 30, 32, 36, 39, 43,
    60–1, 97, 145
Louisiana 31–2, 34, 104
Luxembourg 106

magistrates 79
Malaysia 4
malicious prosecution 43–4
Malta 92–3, 104, 106
Market Abuse Regulation 161
market failure 96, 121, 134, 153
Massachusetts 31
mathematical models 6, 34, 37–8
Meiji Restoration 94

merchants 63, 82
Middle Ages 82
military 90, 95
misappropriation theory 159
mixed law 90–112, 115
modern dilemmas 113
Monaco 106
moral hazard 155
moral rights 132, 135
movable property 33, 61–3
multiple equilibria 36, 38–9, 43
mutual consent 66–7

negative legislator model 83–4
nemo dat rule 61–2
neo-liberalism 154
net social value 134
Netherlands 31, 84, 93, 95, 106, 136
New York State 31
New York Stock Exchange 150
New York Times v. Sullivan 41
New Zealand 6, 32–4, 36, 40–1, 43–4,
    130
nexus-of-contracts theory 152
non-cumul principle 64–7
North Carolina 31
Northern Ireland 45
Norway 4

*Oceanic Sun Line Special Shipping Co. v.
    Fay* 41
Office for Harmonization of Internal
    Market (OHIM) 119
opportunity costs 17
Organization for Economic Co-operation
    and Development (OECD) 146–7
Ottoman Empire 90, 93–4
ownership 61–2, 101–4, 118, 128, 131,
    144, 148, 152, 154–5, 157–8, 160

Palestine 94
parity-of-information theory 160
Patent Reform Acts 125
patent trolls 128
patents 7, 116–17, 124–31
Patents Acts 128, 130–1
path dependence 15, 35–6, 96, 99
Pennsylvania 31
pluralism 91–3, 97
Poland 11
political economy 78
politics 31, 34, 37, 40, 42; corporate law
    145–8, 155–6; governance 77, 82–4;
    intellectual property 120, 136; mixed

law 93–5, 98–9; political channel 25–6, 146
pollution 157
Posner, R.A. 4, 14–18, 32, 34–5, 38, 116, 126
possession theory 160
precedent 15, 17, 34–5, 37–8, 94, 96
preferences 98–9
private law 7, 18, 59–77, 91–9, 105
procedural rules 4, 39, 79, 81, 93, 95
professional responsibility 39, 42
profits 121, 124, 130, 145, 155–6, 158, 160
property law 5–6, 11, 25, 31–3, 35, 59, 61–4, 80, 95–6, 115–43
protected designation of origin (PDO) 121–2, 124
protected geographical indication (PGI) 122, 124
provenance 120
psychology 154
Public Company Accounting Oversight Board (PCAOB) 147
public employment 81
public goods 81, 97, 121
public interest 41, 134, 153
public law 7, 91–9
Puerto Rico 95, 104
Puritans 31

quasi contracts 67, 95, 100
Quebec 34, 99, 105, 145

random shocks 15, 35
real estate 33, 63–4
recording systems 64
registration systems 33, 64
rent-seeking 16–17, 33, 59–60, 97
Republic of Ireland 45
responsabilité contractuelle 67
resulting trusts 100
reverse causation 148, 151
Rondel v. Worsley 42
royal courts 17, 30
royalties 131
Rylands v. Fletcher 39

Saif Ali v. Sydney Smith Mitchell & Co. 42
Sarbanes-Oxley Act 150
Scandinavia 5, 22, 84
Scotland 33, 94–5, 99, 103
Scottish Law Commission 103–4
SEC v. Dorozhko 159

SEC v. Texas Gulf Sulphur 159
Security Exchange Commission (SEC) 147, 150, 159–60
shareholders 3, 24–5, 121, 145–9, 151–8
shop right doctrine 131
short-termism 154–5
slander 41, 43
slavery 31
social costs 154
software 125, 129–30
solicitors 42
South Africa 34, 105
South Carolina 31
South Korea 4
sovereignties 7, 93–5, 98
Spain 4, 31, 64, 84, 93, 95, 119
special-interest groups 37
specialization of courts 77–89, 129
stakeholder orientation 153–8
stakeholder value orientation 153–8
state intervention 7, 11–12, 22, 24–5, 31, 59–60, 79–82, 122
Statute of Monopolies 129
statutory law 6, 14–18, 25, 27, 30–4, 44, 59, 146
stock markets 25, 149–50, 154, 158
structured mixed systems 91
substantive law 6, 31–2, 61, 77, 79, 93, 146
supply 17, 34
Supreme Court/s 34, 41, 43–5, 159
sustainability 156–7
Switzerland 106

Taiwan 84, 92, 94
taxonomy of countries 144–7
technology 115, 119, 124–5, 128–9, 133, 135, 149
territoriality 116–17
Thailand 90
theft 62
Tonga 12
top-down law 18, 59
Torrens system 33
tort law 5–6, 16, 18, 31, 35, 39–42, 44, 60–1, 64–7, 80, 95–6
trade 8, 11, 62, 82, 94, 116, 120–1, 127, 135–6
trade associations 121
Trade Related Aspects of Intellectual Property Rights (TRIPS) 120, 127, 135–6
trade-offs 60, 64, 81
trademarks 7, 116–20, 123–4

transaction costs 4, 15, 67–8, 96–8, 116, 120, 124, 134
transparency 147, 157, 159
Tribunaux de commerce 82
triple crisis 157
trusts 99–107

'Understanding Regulation' 12
Uniform Commercial Code (UCC) 62–3
unionization 81
United Kingdom (UK) 24–5, 32–3, 39, 41–4, 92; copyright 135–6; corporate law 145, 150; House of Lords 39, 42; intellectual property 127–8, 130–1; mixed law 95, 106; Privy Council 31; value maximization/orientation 154
United States Patent and Trademark Office (USPTO) 126–7, 130
United States (US) 3–4, 6–7, 14, 16–17, 24–5; American rule 43; common law 30–8, 40–5; Congress 117, 125, 134, 160; copyright 132–7; corporate law 144–69; First Amendment 41; geographic indications 120–4; governance 81, 84; House of Representatives 134; insider trading 158–62; intellectual property 115–20; mixed law 92–4, 99; modern dilemmas 113; patents 124–31; private law 64–6, 68; Southern States 90, 95–6, 98; trusts 106; value maximization/orientation 153–8
unstructured mixed systems 91
utilitarianism 132, 153–5

value maximization/orientation 153–8
vested interests 37, 78–80, 84, 161
Virginia 31

Wales 6, 32, 34, 43–4
Ward v. James 44
Williams Act 159
willingness to pay 3, 155
Woodhouse Report 40
Woolf reforms 43
workers 40, 81, 152, 155
World Bank 5, 11–12, 60, 150
World Economic Forum 12
World War II (WWII) 94
wrongful arrest 44

Zambia 11

 Taylor & Francis eBooks

Helping you to choose the right eBooks for your Library

Add Routledge titles to your library's digital collection today. Taylor and Francis ebooks contains over 50,000 titles in the Humanities, Social Sciences, Behavioural Sciences, Built Environment and Law.

Choose from a range of subject packages or create your own!

Benefits for you
- » Free MARC records
- » COUNTER-compliant usage statistics
- » Flexible purchase and pricing options
- » All titles DRM-free.

Benefits for your user
- » Off-site, anytime access via Athens or referring URL
- » Print or copy pages or chapters
- » Full content search
- » Bookmark, highlight and annotate text
- » Access to thousands of pages of quality research at the click of a button.

 REQUEST YOUR **FREE** INSTITUTIONAL TRIAL TODAY | **Free Trials Available** We offer free trials to qualifying academic, corporate and government customers.

eCollections – Choose from over 30 subject eCollections, including:

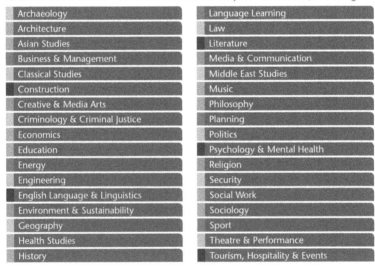

Archaeology	Language Learning
Architecture	Law
Asian Studies	Literature
Business & Management	Media & Communication
Classical Studies	Middle East Studies
Construction	Music
Creative & Media Arts	Philosophy
Criminology & Criminal Justice	Planning
Economics	Politics
Education	Psychology & Mental Health
Energy	Religion
Engineering	Security
English Language & Linguistics	Social Work
Environment & Sustainability	Sociology
Geography	Sport
Health Studies	Theatre & Performance
History	Tourism, Hospitality & Events

For more information, pricing enquiries or to order a free trial, please contact your local sales team:
www.tandfebooks.com/page/sales

 Routledge
Taylor & Francis Group | The home of Routledge books | **www.tandfebooks.com**

For Product Safety Concerns and Information please contact our EU
representative GPSR@taylorandfrancis.com
Taylor & Francis Verlag GmbH, Kaufingerstraße 24, 80331 München, Germany

www.ingramcontent.com/pod-product-compliance
Ingram Content Group UK Ltd.
Pitfield, Milton Keynes, MK11 3LW, UK
UKHW020954180425
457613UK00019B/681